Degrees of Success

Degrees of Success

Pam Mendelsohn

Peterson's Guides
Princeton, New Jersey

Copyright © 1989 by Pam Mendelsohn

All rights reserved. No part of this book may be reproduced, stored in a retrieval system, or transmitted, in any form or by any means—electronic, mechanical, photocopying, recording, or otherwise—except for citations of data for scholarly or reference purposes with full acknowledgment of title, edition, and publisher and written notification to Peterson's Guides prior to such use.

Library of Congress Cataloging-in-Publication Data

Mendelsohn, Pam, 1944–
   Degrees of success.

   1. Women—Education (Higher)—United States—Case studies.
2. Women college graduates—United States—Case studies. 3. Success—United States—Case studies. I. Title.
LC1756.M337   1989   378'.008042   88-34484
ISBN 0-87866-717-2

Composition and design by Peterson's Guides

Cover illustration by Carol Norby

Printed in the United States of America

10 9 8 7 6 5 4 3 2 1

In memory of my father, William Mendelsohn, M.D., who truly believed that learning is a lifelong process.

CONTENTS

Preface ix
Acknowledgments xiii
Introduction 1

Running the Obstacle Course
1 Against All Odds 13
2 Taking It Slow 27
3 Confronting Family Resistance 41
4 Never Too Old 55

Going After the Job You Really Want
5 Approaching College with Clear-cut Goals 71
6 Setting and Clarifying Goals 83
7 Ensuring Job Security and Advancement 97
8 Closed Doors, Revolving Doors 105

There's More to a College Degree Than Finding a Job
9 Seeking Personal Development 121
10 College as a Family Affair 135

continued

Changes/Transitions

11	Dropouts, Stop-Outs, and Drop-Ins	155
12	Back to School for Another Degree	173
13	Ripening Goals	185
14	Special Family Circumstances	199

Epilogue	217
Appendix: Suggestions for Success	221

PREFACE

In the spring of 1976, I was 31 years old and facing several major crossroads—none paved with yellow bricks. After six months of "taking stock," I chose the path labeled "single parent, graduate student."

That September, my 2-year-old daughter, Rebekah, and I were both enrolled at Humboldt State University, just 7 miles from our home in Eureka, California. I was in a master's degree program in psychology, and Rebekah was a student at the wonderful campus preschool.

I had many questions, apprehensions, and concerns during the admissions process and those first few weeks of school. Anxiety reigned. Some of my worst fears had the habit of making cameo appearances at three o'clock in the morning!

I was very concerned about putting my child into her first daycare situation. My study habits had been in storage for ten years. On top of everything else, I was trying to figure out how I was going to juggle school, Rebekah, and some sort of paid employment.

I decided to turn to a book for advice. "What have you got in the way of books that address the special needs of older students?" I asked the local bookstore owner. I was flabbergasted when he replied that the book I needed was yet to be written.

I met other reentry student/parents at the campus toddler center and preschool. We quickly established an informal support network, and I was fascinated by the group—how well everyone was doing academically, despite the many hurdles we were all jumping. The busier we were, the more energy we seemed to manufacture.

As I wended my way through those first few months on campus, I realized that what reentry students craved was an omniscient best friend. This ideal friend would be a totally reliable resource with all the answers concerning academia, careers, financial aid, and child care. She would know how to add a student role to our already busy lives in the smoothest possible way. And she would provide endless amounts of moral support.

The summer following my first year in the program—armed with the self-confidence that so many reentry students report—I drafted a proposal for a resource and support book for women returning to school and sent it to E. P. Dutton. Realizing that the influx of mature women onto college campuses was not a fad but a topic whose time had come, they gave me a contract.

During my second (final) year in graduate school, I was juggling Rebekah, classes, a master's thesis, internships at the campus career development center and family counseling center, a new relationship that has now lasted over a decade, and a book contract.

Fatigue was my constant companion, but I remember that year as exhilarating and filled with personal growth. And somehow there was plenty of time left over for Rebekah. "Sleep tight," I would say to her. "Work tight," she would reply.

My goal for that first book, *Happier by Degrees*, was to create the best friend every reentry woman student deserves. Toward that end, I sent off 100 letters to friends and heads of reentry programs, asking if they would be willing to conduct in-depth, taped interviews with adult women students, using a questionnaire I had designed. The letters yielded forty-four interviewers.

The first interviews were conducted in early 1978. I received a total of ninety-four completed questionnaires and taped interviews that averaged 45 minutes to 1 hour in length. As people responded to the questions, their stories unfolded. Each account involved apprehensions, successes, risks, and—above all—change.

Some of the women simply spoke into a tape recorder, responding to the questionnaire without an interviewer present. I had also designed questionnaires for husbands, companions, and children. Many of the interviewers arranged to speak with family members. I transcribed every tape, culling the very best advice from each.

Mine was not a scientific study. It was informal and used snowball sampling techniques. *Happier by Degrees* is a how-to book that provides concrete information, advice, and support from over 160 people who have been through the process of a return to school.

One chapter of *Happier by Degrees* is devoted to presenting the stories of fourteen women who went back to school. After the book was published in 1980, reviews and letters from readers indicated great enthusiasm for that chapter in particular.

When they were first interviewed, most of the women were either still in school or only recently graduated. It was inevitable that I would begin to wonder: What happened to them? How were they feeling about their lives? Was going back to school worth it?

In 1985, Ten Speed Press agreed to publish an updated edition of *Happier by Degrees*. The revised edition came out in 1986. Updating the book prompted me to recontact some of the women who had first been interviewed in 1978.

I assumed these women had changed their lives in significant ways. But I was completely unprepared for the extent of change and for the overall well-being and joie de vivre that permeated their correspondence with me.

Thus began my encounter with what came to be known among my friends as "Pam's amazing stories." For example, Tracy, when last

Preface

heard from, had been a community college student whose major work experience had been as a chambermaid, bartender, and waitress. The year 1985 found her just graduating from law school with a position as a corporate lawyer waiting in the wings.

Carla, the only one among her many siblings to graduate from high school, had completed college and realized a lifelong ambition: to be an elementary school teacher in her rural Arkansas community. Her husband, a disabled veteran who never had the opportunity to complete high school, was with her every step of the way.

Laura, who chose sociology as her major because the courses fit into her child-care schedule, had become the long-range planner for her town. Diana stepped back into academia at the age of 59. In 1984, at age 70, she received a master's degree in human development and set up a private counseling practice.

Vivian, the mother of fifteen children, had graduated from college alongside child number eight. Debbie, too skittish to learn how to drive a car until she was nearly 30, had landed a position as a counselor in the social work program from which she graduated. As a sideline, she had also actualized her wildest fantasy: to become a professional torch singer.

Not all of those interviewed were doing what they had expected to be doing. For example, Florence, teaching credential in hand, was happily at home with her two preschoolers. April, who had received an associate degree in electrical engineering, adored her work as a masseuse.

Marilyn, at age 51, armed with a bachelor's degree in English, had gotten her first job: chief liaison between two enormous oil fields. Job requirements: driving a one-ton truck, operating a shortwave radio, figuring out which burner tips to order for the dehydrators. Unlikely job for an English major? You bet.

My appetite was whetted. I wanted to hear all the stories, and in as much detail as possible. In December of 1986, Peterson's provided the vehicle—a book contract and a big vote of confidence for this book, *Degrees of Success.*

Have you ever tried to track down old friends after no news for nearly a decade? Imagine trying to locate ninety-four women, most of whom you've never met. People had changed last names, first names, where they lived, whom they lived with, their jobs, and more. Each day I was greeted by piles of "Addressee unknown/Return to sender" envelopes.

In the end, ninety of the ninety-four women were located. (You other four: if you are reading this book, please get in touch with me!) Of the ninety, seven decided not to be involved with the new book. In most cases, this was a passive decision: interviewer and interviewee did not manage to get together or deadlines were missed. I had hoped for an 80 percent return, so I was delighted to have 88 percent of the original group contribute to *Degrees of Success.* Because we had natural restraints on the size of the book, seventy-three of the stories were finally chosen as the most detailed and representative.

Former interviewers were asked to do new interviews, whenever

Degrees of Success

possible. Some interviewees had friends ask them the questions instead. Others did self-interviews. Once again, the length of interview ranged from 45 minutes to 1 hour.

Some participants were enthusiastic about attaching their names and other identifying information to their stories. Others wanted complete anonymity. In order to provide consistency and to protect the privacy of all family members, I have used fictitious names throughout the book. Whenever specific cities, states, and schools are cited, however, they are factual.

Degrees of Success is filled with stories about expectations met and unmet, relationships strengthened and broken, and the far-reaching transformations that result from personal growth and development.

I hope you enjoy getting to know these remarkable women and that some of their odysseys show what opportunities are available to you.

The final refrain from an old Shaker hymn states so simply what one might hope for in a world where *change* is ever present:

> . . . to turn, turn,
> 'twill be our delight
> 'til by turning, turning
> we come 'round right.

ACKNOWLEDGMENTS

This book represents an incredible commitment of time and energy on the part of many people.

I am indebted to all of the interviewers, particularly Dr. Margaret McKoane, Meredith Michaels, Sondra Finegold, Rima McKinzey, Roberta Rothman, Carolyn Wells, Barbara Cousineau, Paula Poag, Randye Farmer, and Irene Rich. I especially wish to thank Charlotte Goode, an interviewer whose ability to track down people in the unlikeliest of places went far beyond the call of duty and friendship. Likewise, my appreciation goes to Doris Riefling, who transcribed many of the interviews.

The following people offered me a great deal of moral support during the process of writing this book: Jane Hill, Marjorie Levy, Dr. Adele Clarke, Mary Elizabeth Burgess, Miriam Horowitz, Blanche Palmquist, Peter Burgess, Lynne Levine, and Mary McCarty Sullivan.

I am also grateful to the University of Michigan's Center for Continuing Education of Women, a true pioneer in the field of reentry education. It is very exciting to have access, through its publications, to the extensive research in which the center is involved. The U.S. Department of Education's Office of Educational Research and Improvement, particularly Clemma Carrington, has also been very helpful.

Casey Hegener, Peterson's editor in chief, generously contributed her expertise and enthusiasm. Dick Bohlander, a former editor at Peterson's, served as the book's midwife for nearly two years. I am grateful to both of them.

Writing a book about the changes that occur as we wend our way through various developmental stages has made the *constants* in my own life even more precious. My family—Rebekah Burgess and Peter Palmquist—has been with me every step of the way. Their optimism, encouragement, and patience are treasured.

Peter has critiqued the manuscript, photocopied the pages, and made countless trips to the post office. Most important, he has nurtured the author. Rebekah has been a great source of inspiration to me; her excitement about learning is contagious. At age 13, she was not only supportive of my job as a writer, but she also became actively involved by offering to read the chapters in manuscript form. Her perceptive comments and suggestions were a truly special fringe benefit.

Finally, I would like to thank the eighty-three women and their assorted family members who were interviewed for *Degrees of Success*. They have become old friends of mine since our initial contact in 1978. The bonds—established through tapes, correspondence, and telephone calls—are cherished. Those interactions and now the sharing of the stories are my biggest rewards from writing this book.

INTRODUCTION

Twenty years ago, if you were a woman over 30 on a college campus, people automatically assumed that you were faculty, staff, or somebody's mother.

Today, people 35 and older constitute the fastest-growing student population in higher education—and two out of every three of these students are women. In fact, women aged 25 and over accounted for 44 percent of the total growth in the number of people enrolled in college from 1972 to 1982. By the year 2000, according to the College Board's Office of Adult Learning Services, there will be more students over the age of 25 than under.

Pursuing an education after a significant break from the academic world has become a major avenue for personal and professional development. However, most adults approach the college scene with an incredibly complex set of responsibilities. The role of student gets added into a juggling act that often includes already demanding commitments as parent, spouse, and worker.

Is it possible to take on academia when your life is already in full swing? Furthermore, is it worth it? The answer to those two questions, in most cases, is a resounding yes.

Degrees of Success presents the stories of women from all walks of life who have one thing in common: they went back to school during their adult years. They have dealt with very real issues and problems along the way: divorce, widowhood, relocation, financial hardship, elderly parents, teenagers' departure from home, family resistance to change, the obligation to balance study with the needs of young children, head-on confrontation with their own aging process, uncertainty about career direction, and, not least, lack of confidence.

Women of all ages are included in this study, with birth years ranging from 1914 to 1955. Their median age at the point when they returned to school was 35. Seven participants assumed student roles after they turned 48, while seven identified themselves as reentry students even though they were under 24 when they enrolled. The group includes representatives of twenty-two states plus Canada, with one woman keeping in touch from the Middle East, where she is teaching.

Today, this is a highly educated group. There are five lawyers, one physician, one woman with a Ph.D., forty-one women with master's degrees, twenty-nine with bachelor's degrees, two who are registered nurses, two with associate degrees, and two who have done several years toward a bachelor's degree.

POSITIVE PERSONAL CHANGES

With very few exceptions, the women interviewed for *Degrees of Success* can be described as self-confident, happy, energetic, healthy, and productive, and as leading fulfilling lives—both personally and professionally.

A resounding 91 percent said their self-confidence increased *as a direct result* of going back to school. Ninety-seven percent said that school had been worth it in terms of their personal growth and development.

Terry, an artist whose story is told in Chapter 9, recalls the kind of self-doubt she experienced just before returning to school: "I remember when my psyche lived like a pale shoot under a rock, which was my sense of my own limitations; it blocked out the sun. Those limitations were of my own making and were in my power to remove."

Debbie, featured in Chapter 13, is the director of a fund-raising federation of fourteen social action and service organizations. She commented about the effect of her student role on her life: "My entire life changed. I felt like a different person. I regained the self-confidence to do new things. I instituted a lot of personal changes, such as giving up an eighteen-year smoking habit. I quit biting my nails.... Before I went back to school, I just got up and grumbled my way through the day—without goals, without anything. I didn't acknowledge that I had any choices...."

Degrees of Success includes women whose success may run counter to any preconceived notions of the concept: seven dropped out of school and seven others have never worked in their intended field. Yet, self-confidence and personal development permeate the stories. These pluses can be a result of the *process* itself—going to college—not just because a degree or career goal is attained.

Donna, in Chapter 8, for example, made it through architecture school but works now as operators manager for a business owned by her parents. Her return to school served an important purpose nevertheless: "It gave me license to be creative," Donna stated. "Prior to school I did a lot of dabbling. Now I know more about the creative process. I can take an intellectual concept and translate it into reality."

Donna, recently divorced when she began architecture school, is happily remarried. With Wesley and her two children, she has achieved one of her long-range goals: to work as a team on creative projects. The entire family has become involved with costume competitions, winning national awards for their mini–theatrical productions complete with music and voice-overs.

What about dropping out? Of the seven women who did, none claims that school was a waste of time. In fact, all of them continue to take courses for the sheer pleasure of learning.

Dorothy (Chapter 11), for example, pulled out of a Ph.D. program in classics just at the point when she would have begun to work on her thesis. Her interests had changed, and she wanted to spend more time with her young son. Today she combines free-lance translating with work as a farm and nursery assistant.

One does not sense any regrets in Dorothy about having logged so many hours in graduate school. She is currently studying Spanish and Hebrew and said recently: "My higher education is, as always, an unending source of pleasure for me in terms of books, television, movies, conversations, travel, and friendships. But it did not lead to work in which I felt happy and fulfilled. I feel I succeeded because I value my education and love my work."

The women interviewed for *Degrees of Success* reported other very positive changes: nearly three quarters of them said that they learned to manage their time better, and 80 percent indicated they had become more assertive.

An improved self-image is almost a guaranteed outcome of a return to school. Personal growth and an increase in self-confidence, with very few exceptions, are simply part of the reentry package.

HOW FAMILY RELATIONSHIPS FARE

Forty-eight percent of the women whose stories are told in this book experienced a change in their marital status right before returning to school, during their college days, or afterward. Some shifted from marriage to divorce, others from divorce to remarriage. Four are now widowed, and two have married for the first time. Of the 52 percent who had no change in their marital status, thirty-seven are still married, four are still divorced, and two have never married.

In general, the good marriages got even better, and the tenuous relationships disintegrated. In almost every case, the marriages ending in divorce were already very strained by the time the woman went back to school.

Connie and Russell (Chapter 14) are an example of a couple who feel that their relationship improved because of her return to school. While she was in nursing school, she commented: "He's much more interested in me as *me* now, not just as his wife." He enthused: "It's fantastic! She's excited and energetic."

Before Ruth (Chapter 4) returned to school at the age of 54, she described herself as "useless, tense, anxious, desperate, and depressed." Her husband, Joe, completely backed her desire for an education. He stated, "She has fulfilled a lifelong ambition. Ruth has always been extremely capable, but she never believed it. Now she no longer feels any difference in intellect at social gatherings. She speaks out, is much more assertive—a pleasure to be with."

Susan, in Chapter 2, describes what many husbands fear the

most: "When I started taking classes, I was dissatisfied with my marriage, although I hadn't pinpointed it at the time. I was unhappy with myself and life in general. Then, it was as if doors opened for me, and I could see that there was something beyond the life I was living."

The marriage ended. "I think my marriage would have ended anyway," she explained, "but maybe not as soon as it did. When I went back to school, it saved my life. My spirit was dying. But it also turned my life upside down. It was an excellent decision. I am finally on my way to a place where I can shine."

Large and small families are represented in *Degrees of Success*. Seven women did not have any children; twenty-two women had four or more. One woman had fifteen children in sixteen years. Over half of the women in the sample had either two or three children.

Exactly half the mothers in this sample said their relationships with their children actually improved because of their return to school. Forty percent claimed that their academic role had no effect whatsoever on the mother-child relationship. The remaining 10 percent described those relationships as being in a state of flux during their academic years.

Helen (Chapter 3) and her 23-year-old daughter, Lynn, received their associate degrees at the same time. Lynn complained bitterly at age 14 when Helen first went back to school: she felt her mother ignored her and demanded that she do more than her share of the housework. Nine years later, however, Lynn commented: "She understands my generation better. She's grown, and she's closer to me because she's been in school with kids my age. Our relationship has gotten better since she returned to school. Mom should continue to a four-year college. She's really smart, and I'm really proud of her. She has so much to teach everybody, and there's so much to learn out there for everyone."

Several "second generation" reentry stories are featured: women who return to school tend to produce children who *also* return to school. Marissa (Chapter 14) and her mother, Ruth, are such a case. Mother and daughter both received degrees in social work.

Marissa explains that her mother served as her role model: "My mother tackled her fears rather than being paralyzed by them. Through watching her and interacting with her, I felt as if some limits were lifted off me as well. If my mother could go to college, then I could do things that were scary for me."

FINDING A JOB OR CAREER

Certainly a critical question to address is whether or not it was worth it to go back to school in terms of finding a job or career. Seventy-eight percent of the sample said that it was.

Many of the women approached their education with clear-cut goals. An equal number hadn't a clue what they wanted to do for a career. Several made dramatic switches in career goals once they became involved with school. Others, several years into the career they had targeted, had already identified new career goals.

Is it worth it to get a degree in terms of one's earning power? If you put any faith in statistics, the evidence is clear: the more education you have, the more money you are capable of earning.

The U.S. Census Bureau published a study in 1987 called *What's It Worth?* which looked at the relationship between educational background and economic status as of spring 1984. College graduates were earning $900 more a month on the average than those who held high school diplomas. The average monthly income for the people with college degrees was $1,910. High school graduates earned $1,010—47 percent less.

The survey broke the monthly salaries into categories by degree earned: $3,265 for those with doctorates, $2,288 for master's degrees, $1,841 for bachelor's degrees, and $1,346 for associate degrees. Those with professional degrees had the highest monthly income average of all: $3,871.

College graduates are also less likely to be found in the ranks of the unemployed. According to the Bureau of Labor Statistics, in the prime working-age group, ages 24 to 54, the unemployment rate for people with four or more years of college was 2.3 percent in 1987. Among those who had stopped their education after high school, almost three times as many were unemployed.

OVERALL WELL-BEING

What happens to the quality of life when a woman adds more and more roles to her juggling act? Does a life-style that includes the roles of paid worker and/or student in addition to mother, daughter, and spouse necessarily translate into infinitely more stress?

Rosalind Barnett and Grace Baruch point out in their paper "Toward Economic Independence: Women's Involvement in Multiple Roles" (from *Women's Lives: New Theory, Research and Policy*, edited by Dorothy McGuigan, Center for Continuing Education of Women, University of Michigan) that the well-being of women is actually *facilitated* by the development of the capacity for economic independence and occupational competence. They also found that when women hold multiple roles, including that of paid worker, the effects are often very positive.

"Our failure to prepare women for occupational competence," they stated, "results in a developmental disability that eventually culminates for many women in difficulty coping with the circumstances of their lives, leaving them vulnerable to and at high risk for poverty, psychiatric symptomatology and diminishing well-being."

True, women who combine working with an active family life often feel pulled apart. However, Barnett and Baruch state that non-employed mothers experience this kind of stress *more* strongly and *more* frequently than working mothers.

"As a person takes on roles, she often contracts or simplifies others," they explained. "Married, employed women, even those with several children, rarely experience their paid work as purely additive. Indeed the role of paid worker seems far less manageable to those out of it than to those in it. . . . Having outside commitments may permit homemakers to set limits on the otherwise endless demands made upon them at home."

If you enjoy your work, it stimulates you. Many of the women in Barnett and Baruch's survey reported improved relationships with children and spouses. "Paid work often turns out to be a major source of self-esteem and good feelings."

The good feelings and self-esteem help to establish priorities that are in keeping with personal development. Women who reported the *most* well-being were married mothers in high-prestige jobs, according to *Lifeprints: New Patterns of Love and Work for Today's Women*, an excellent book by Barnett, Baruch, and Caryl Rivers.

"How could I possibly be feeling this good when I have so much to do?" The conclusions of Paula Pietromonaco, Jean Manis, and Katharine Forhardt-Lane ("Psychological Consequences of Multiple Social Roles," Center for Continuing Education of Women Research Report, University of Michigan, 1984) confirm what Baruch, Barnett, and Rivers have to say about the relationship between multiple roles and well-being.

Pietromonaco et al. surveyed 500 working women whose number of roles ranged from one to five: working; working and partner; working, partner, and parent; working, partner, parent, volunteer or student; or all of the above. Ninety-five percent of these women were college graduates, and many held master's degrees, graduate professional degrees, or Ph.D.'s.

Higher self-esteem and greater job satisfaction were associated with holding *more* roles. Further, women who held three, four, or five roles reported no more stress than those who were involved in just one or two roles. *All* the working women reported that their lives were fairly stressful. However, women with three or more roles indicated slightly more sources of enjoyment in their lives.

Given the various role combinations described above, which set of circumstances weighed in with the most self-esteem? Women who worked, had a partner and one or more children, were students, and engaged in at least one volunteer activity evidenced the most positive feelings about themselves!

The traditional view that juggling multiple roles inevitably leads to psychological distress is called into serious question. In fact, Pietromonaco et al. cite research concluding that women with multiple roles experience less psychological distress, greater life satisfaction, and fewer physical ailments.

Helen Markus, in "Work, Women, and Well-Being: A Life Course Perspective" (*Women's Lives: New Theory, Research and Policy*), draws fascinating conclusions about the relationship between self-esteem and paid employment, based on a survey of over 1,000 women, most of whom have at least a bachelor's degree. High self-esteem belongs even to those who *think* they have a career or are *planning* one—whether or not they are actually employed. Women who enjoy their work, she states, have high self-esteem, regardless of career commitment. These women are much more apt to describe themselves as attractive, socially acceptable, independent, and resourceful than women who do not enjoy their work.

This sort of positive attitude permeates most of the interviews with the women in *Degrees of Success* during their reentry days. Like the women described in Markus's study, many were planning to have a career once they graduated from school. Others took great pleasure in the "work" itself—the whole process of being a student. Accepting a new challenge and having a goal to reach for, rather than taking energy *away* from one's already busy life, can bring renewal.

Most reentry women mention that being busy with school helped them to become much clearer about their priorities. When there is *less* time, it is often easier to discover what is really important. "I'm busier but I get a lot more done," is a frequent comment. It is easier to be efficient and organized when you *have* to be.

Having multiple roles can act as a healthy buffer against strained circumstances in some aspect of your life, according to Pietromonaco et al. Returning women students certainly report, again and again, vivid examples of the ways in which their student role positively affects all aspects of their lives.

Relationships with children improve in so many cases, for example, because the quality of the time spent together is so much better. "I'm too busy to smother them" is a common refrain.

Similarly, a return to school can help to stabilize a marriage. In Shirley's case (Chapter 3), there was a strong desire to prove to herself that she could stand on her own if she ever wanted to. Gathering marketable skills in college gave her the assurance that she needed. Knowing that she could be autonomous was more important than actually setting off on her own. She believes her marriage improved because she achieved the potential for self-sufficiency.

Carla (Chapter 10) at age 50 had no marketable skills, and her husband was in very poor health. It was Carla's husband who convinced her that a college education would lead to self-confidence and a satisfying job. By the time he died in 1981, Carla had developed the capacity for economic independence and was working as a special education teacher.

FORTIFYING ONESELF FOR CHANGE

With a median birth year of 1940, the women featured in *Degrees of Success* are confronting or have dealt with a wide variety of transitions: children leaving home, divorce, the care of elderly parents, the aging process, retirement of a spouse, the death of loved ones, relocation. Both the process of education and the end result can help prepare for such life transitions.

In Maureen's case (Chapter 5), she described her career as an "anchor" when her husband died suddenly at age 39. "No matter how shocked I was by grief, I was very grateful to have that job to go to."

A teacher of English as a second language, she was able to arrange her schedule so that she could be there when her two children came home after school. Now that they are away at college, Maureen has accepted a job that actualizes her dream: she is teaching in China.

Tamara, featured in Chapter 1, recently left a secure position after twelve years as a college counselor in order to move closer to the man she intended to marry. Because of her degree, she was able to find work immediately. The relationship didn't work out, but Tamara was fortified: "My education and self-esteem gave me the strength to live through this heartbreak. . . . I was able to pick up the pieces and put my life back together."

In so many cases, the experiences gathered during the student years provided invaluable tools that could be used over and over again to confront life's transitions and changes. Rachel discusses this point in Chapter 9: "I was able to achieve something that I really wanted. Therefore, when I'm up against something new, I can say, 'Well, I did it once, and I'm going to be able to do it again.' You create a tremendous amount of confidence in your ability to go out and meet a new challenge."

Judith Bardwick questions the assumption of a connection between aging and mental deterioration in her paper "The Seasons of a Woman's Life (*Women's Lives: New Theory, Research and Policy*). She states, "The mental deterioration which has customarily been attributed to aging is, instead, a response to an invariant world of no challenge or stimulation. When your world is too repetitive and simple, then you lose the feeling that you are coping with change. Those least able to risk something new are probably aging housewives who are psychologically dependent and not significantly involved in anything."

HEALTHY AND ACTIVE

Are women being encouraged to leave their sheltered lives in order to enter a working world that will lead to stress and subsequent ill health? To the contrary.

Recent research indicates that working women are a physically healthy group. "Contrary to popular belief," reported Lois Verbrugge and Jennifer Madans (*Milbank Memorial Fund Quarterly:* Health and Science, 1985) "having the triple roles of job, spouse, and mother is linked with the best physical health profile for American women. . . ." They continued, "The prospects for women's future health are optimistic. As more women become employed and have long careers, more will enjoy the financial, educational, social, and emotional benefits that employment offers. Though there are added pressures for women with multiple roles, the net impact on health seems to be positive."

Are working women, like their male working colleagues, having more heart attacks? The Framingham Heart Study found no increased coronary risks among most working women, with one exception: women in clerical jobs, who have relatively little control over the content and pace of their working day.

Introduction

For the most part, the women featured in *Degrees of Success* take good care of themselves. Reports of an increase in energy and stamina are common. For example, Norma (Chapter 13), now a clinic administrator, commented during her student days on how her academic role was changing her life: "I'm not just happy. I'm high, full of joy. Even when something isn't going right, I feel something good will come out of it. Before I made the decision to go back to school, I was often tired, depressed, annoyed at minor problems, and just generally feeling very dull."

In Chapter 4, Gloria, aged 64, lists bike riding, cross-country skiing, and tennis among her favorite activities. Lee, also in Chapter 4, recently celebrated her seventieth birthday as a Peace Corps worker in the Marshall Islands. She commented: "I don't ever want to stop working. I'm not kidding. I'd like to work until I'm at least 85 or 90."

The women featured in *Degrees of Success* are, generally speaking, very active and healthy. In fact, there are only four instances in which illness or personal physical disability was mentioned. It's interesting that two of these women—Daphne and Cindy (both in Chapter 11)—are among the seven who dropped out of school.

The third, Brenda (in Chapter 14), was incapacitated by severe back problems for several years as a result of the work she adored: weaving. Consequently, she has had to focus less on weaving and more on other art forms. In addition, she has had to make time to learn how to take care of her back.

The fourth is Jill, featured in Chapter 3. She sprinted through the years 1977 to 1985, getting undergraduate and law degrees, remarrying, and carrying on a 75-hour-a-week legal practice. Then a spinal disk rupture in 1987 forced her to cut her workweek to 30 hours, make her beautiful 100-acre farm her headquarters, and completely reevaluate her harried life-style.

During her four-month confinement, fortified by the knowledge that she is someone who can deal with change effectively, she decided to alter the balance between her personal and professional life. She has opted for far less time on the job and much more time with her husband, their children, and their grandchildren.

Jill, at age 52, shares a sentiment frequently voiced by women who choose education as a route to personal and/or professional development: "I intend to age with a lot of grace and style."

RUNNING THE OBSTACLE COURSE

CHAPTER 1
AGAINST ALL ODDS

It's hard to imagine investing time and money in an education when you're working as hard as you can and just scraping by. Likewise, when every job interview results in a dead end, the stirring of a career goal can begin to feel like a frivolous pipe dream.

Degrees of Success involves many people who, against all odds, have achieved far more than they ever dreamed possible. This chapter focuses on the stories of women who approached a college campus with tremendous family responsibilities and no money. How were they able to switch gears, get the degree, and find a fulfilling career?

"There's no way I could possibly afford a college education." When you have no financial resources, this statement certainly seems to be a reasonable conclusion. Yet, Tracy, Tamara, Cathy, and Cheryl were all on welfare while they were in school. And all were single parents for most of their student days.

These women found ways to get through school with minimal out-of-pocket expense. They attended inexpensive or tuition-free community colleges. Tamara enrolled in a federally funded academic program that prepared Native Americans for careers in teaching. Tracy was awarded a full scholarship.

Cathy and Cheryl chose inexpensive state universities. Cheryl shared her house with another single-parent reentry student. This brought in some extra money, and the two women could offer each other moral support in addition to child care. Cheryl's work-study position evolved into the founding of a nonprofit child services agency with an annual budget of $1.5-million!

Tamara became a community college counselor who, as part of her job, provided students with information about financial aid. She advises reentry students to be persistent and resourceful: "There's all kinds of money out there. You just have to figure out how to connect with it. Make the financial aid counselors work for you. They are being paid to help you, so use them!"

None of these women had gathered a great deal of inspiration or confidence during their high school years. Tracy (now an attorney) and Cathy (an educational administrator) were both told by guidance counselors that they were not college material. Three of the women were the first in their families—parents, siblings, aunts, uncles, and cousins—to get a college degree.

These women were not afraid to start over in several important domains of their lives. They dramatically changed their family configurations. Each remarried; each had another child. Cathy, Cheryl, and Tracy had their second child at least nine years after their first. Tamara's seventh was born six years after her sixth. As part of their educational process, all of these women completely reevaluated their future working years.

Anyone on welfare may find it hard to imagine transformation, several years later, into a lawyer, college counselor, administrator, or psychologist. The transformation is not sudden, but it certainly can and does occur.

Low-paying jobs without career potential can serve as the major motivating factor for pushing on. The four women in this chapter had worked as chambermaids, waitresses, secretaries, and store clerks. Although their career goals were not clear when they first went back to school, these women were sure that they wanted to be able to provide well for their children.

When financial security is the primary motivating factor, it pays to pick a field of study that will provide marketable skills in a wide variety of settings. Tamara's counseling expertise, for example, was easily transferred from a rural college setting to the mental health department of a major metropolis. As a lawyer, Tracy can work anywhere. Cheryl developed strong administrative skills that she quickly transferred from a nonprofit agency setting to her own travel management business. Cathy used her master's degree in psychology as a stepping-stone in the field of education.

Obviously, being poor during one's student days is an enormous hardship. However, the women featured here did not let this deter them from obtaining an education and the skills that would lead to the financial security they wanted.

FROM WELFARE MOM TO CORPORATE LAWYER

In 1976, Tracy and her second husband were enrolled at a community college in New England. Tracy's son, Jonathan, was in second grade. The family lived on approximately $4,000 a year. Nine years later, Tracy was graduated from law school and was immediately hired as a corporate lawyer. She now earns $45,000 a year.

Tracy's educational journey is quite a saga. In high school, she had spent as little time as possible on her schoolwork. Even though she had a B average, she lacked confidence in her intellectual ability. After graduating in 1967 she spent the next nine years working at low-paying jobs such as waitressing, bartending, picking apples, and being a chambermaid.

"I was sick of that kind of work," she asserts. "I knew I had more potential. I felt unfulfilled. And I was sick of having no money. I knew I had to get a degree. I was already concerned about providing for my son's education. It was going to take money to give him the things I wanted to give him. I wanted to go back to school. I guess I got a rush of courage."

Tracy's husband had started at the community college the year before, and Tracy had agreed to provide most of the income. However, she soon decided that she was going to register for school too. She had collected Aid to Families with Dependent Children (AFDC) for several years before she went back to school and used this resource throughout her undergraduate days.

Tracy was only 27 when she added a student role to her life—young by reentry standards. But, because it had been nine years since she had been inside a classroom, she was apprehensive about how she would perform academically. "The biggest adjustment," she said, "was getting my brain in working order again. I hadn't done heavy reading, memorizing, or studying for a long, long time. It took some doing because I wasn't used to it."

Tracy quickly found that she could do very well—all it took was studying and juggling time. "When I first started school, I spent all of my time on schoolwork. I was obsessed with getting good grades, doing well, and proving myself. I had fallen so far back in high school, I was disgusted with myself. I wanted to do it right this time."

In her nervousness, she says, "I began to neglect Jonathan, to shrug him off sometimes, to tell him I had schoolwork to do. If I had some spare time, I'd make up some schoolwork to do."

This situation resolved itself when Tracy's college grades started coming in—all A's. She began to relax a little about tests and papers; family and school began to balance. In fact, by her sophomore year, Tracy felt that her relationship with both her husband and son had improved because she was happier.

In 1978, she had said of her relationship with her husband, "We have very little money and spare time, but when we get together, we have a lot more to offer each other. Our relationship has grown."

Tracy's mother and sister offered a great deal of encouragement. In fact, her sister was back in school, too. Tracy's in-laws lived right next door and helped care for Jonathan.

Becoming a lawyer was the furthest thing from Tracy's mind when she had to choose a major. In fact, when she went back to school, she didn't have a specific career goal.

"I chose what looked like the easiest program in the catalog. It didn't require the SAT or a specific high school average. It was called the Human Services Program. But it didn't give the appropriate background for going on to a B.A. degree." As soon as she realized how limiting the Human Services Program was, she switched to a liberal arts major.

By the middle of her second year at the community college, Tracy was interested in sociology and thought she might like to do research in that field. She graduated with an associate degree in 1978 and was salutatorian of her class. Her second son, Adam, was born just one month later.

Tracy took only one class the next year, but her husband continued as a full-time student majoring in communication disorders. Tracy spent her time enjoying Adam, applying to various colleges and universities, and taking a calculus course.

While applying to four-year schools, she aimed for the top and was accepted at a prestigious women's college, which has a supportive reentry program. She was given a full scholarship.

Even though Tracy got A's at the community college, she was apprehensive about her ability to succeed at a more competitive school. Reflecting on her success at the community college level, she commented, "I figured if I could do it, anyone could do it; or the course must be easier this year; or maybe the professor felt sorry for me," she said.

By the end of her junior year, she began to feel more confident. Even so, she was unsure of how well she could do in the "real world." There are not, after all, many help-wanted ads for people with a bachelor's degree in sociology. She felt she needed another degree. She was interested in law and was sure it would lead to a well-paying job.

Tracy graduated in 1982, cum laude and Phi Beta Kappa, and was accepted into law school. She had reached a crossroads. Her husband was against the next step in her education. Tracy thinks that he sensed her advanced education would be their demise. He had just dropped out of a master's degree program and told his wife that he had pursued college only to please her.

"He used to say that he would do whatever was necessary to keep the family together and make me happy," Tracy said. "But he was never happy in school, and he never worked in his field. He went back to moving furniture."

Because their goals and values diverged, they separated shortly after Tracy began law school. "I was a single parent taking a full load of courses at the law school and working 15 to 20 hours a week. I wouldn't recommend it to anybody."

The AFDC rug was pulled out from under her at this critical point. "I reapplied for welfare and food stamps, and the agency decided I was ineligible because of my student loans and student status. My student loan put me over the poverty line. Being a graduate student was considered a privilege, not a necessity."

While she was in law school, her relationship with her son Jonathan had its ups and downs over such issues as how much baby-sitting he was expected to do. Tracy had been leaving Adam with Jonathan at night while she went to the library, but when this upset Jonathan, Tracy studied more at home. Adam attended quite a few law school classes and even got an honorary A in one course—for cooperation and fine behavior!

"Both of my children were extremely proud of me when I graduated from law school," said Tracy. While in school she had involved them in her dreams and goals. The family's pride in their collective success helped erase the memory of the day-to-day frustrations. Tracy believes it is important for mothers who might be undertaking such an arduous schedule to sit down and talk to their children about what school will mean in the long run—for all of them.

Tracy found a position as a corporate lawyer before she graduated. She loves her work. Financial problems still burden her, however, since she borrowed so much money for law school. It will be eight more years before her student loans are paid.

Within the next few years, Tracy hopes to purchase a home, travel, and have time for a meaningful relationship. For the moment, she wants to keep her corporate job but branch into other legal work within the company. She considers starting her own firm but fears the expense. "I don't want to be poor again!" she says with conviction.

NATIVE AMERICAN MOTHER OF SEVEN FINDS CAREER IN COUNSELING

When Tamara graduated from a community college in 1955, she married and was sure she would live happily ever after. Fourteen years later, 34 years old, divorced, and with six children, she went back to school. This meant giving up her job, moving away from a familiar setting, and going on welfare.

Living happily ever after had turned out to be a fantasy for Tamara very soon after she was married. Her dream of combining family responsibilities with her keen interest in fine arts hadn't materialized. Her ex-husband was not able to support their family financially, and Tamara scrambled for money in the small town where she grew up.

By 1968, she was working as a teacher's aide, a job she found particularly frustrating. She felt that if she were the teacher, she would do things differently. As an assistant, she had no power. Then she heard about a new federal program that funded the college education of Native Americans who wanted to become teachers. One hundred fifty-five people applied, and Tamara landed one of the eighteen slots.

Moving to the university setting meant leaving the town in which she had grown up. She was very worried about how her children would adapt to the new area. "My youngest was only 3 then, and I put a lot of energy into finding the right person to look after her," Tamara said. "My other children were in school, and it was hard for them to leave their friends."

Tamara returned to school for very specific reasons. She wanted a career that she could be sure would provide enough income to support her family. She was proud of her Native American heritage and wanted to contribute to her community as a teacher and as an educational resource person.

Imagine the challenges of combining the single parenting of six children with studying. "There were many, many times when I would be in my bedroom studying, and the kids would leave my meals by the door," Tamara recalled.

When Tamara graduated in 1972, she was offered the position of Native American counselor at a nearby community college. In this capacity, she had a good salary and the opportunity to serve other Native Americans.

She became involved in all aspects of increasing educational opportunities for Native Americans at the community college. She counseled students on their academic programs, careers, financial aid, goals, and personal problems. She also participated in community outreach. When she wasn't counseling she was teaching—Native American studies and classes in study skills, guidance, peer advising, and career development for the general student population. Reentry students naturally gravitated toward her classes and office.

Tamara had come a long way since being a teacher's aide. Her job at the community college gave her, for the first time in her working life, the power to mold her career. While she was working there, she said, "I'm in a strong position to help Native Americans with their adjustment to college and teach them the value of education. I enjoy the autonomy, a superb atmosphere, and a good working relationship with the administrators."

Tamara was as busy in her personal life as she was in her professional life. Shortly after she graduated, she remarried—this time to a very traditional Native American. Her seventh child was born in 1972.

However, once again, Tamara had married a man who was not a provider of material things. She became the sole supporter for her family of nine. At the time, she claimed she was comfortable being the breadwinner.

Tamara began to wonder if a master's degree might someday be required for her job. She also knew that with the extra degree she'd earn more money for the job she was already doing. In 1976, she once again returned to school. "I wanted that master's degree," she said, "so no one could say I didn't have one. I didn't want to be hassled by a licensing bureau, a credentials office, or anyone at any institution I might ever work for."

Tamara combined her studies with her obligations as mother, wife, and full-time counselor. Surprisingly, she felt she had more personal freedom as a master's candidate than she had back at the community college over twenty years earlier when she was single.

"Back then, it was work and school—that was it," she said. "I wasn't able to do anything else. I carried 19 or 20 units and worked nights as a waitress. I missed a lot of things. I was nominated for football queen, but I couldn't attend those things. If I had taken time off, I would have lost my job. Now I have more money and more free time."

Spending so much time away from her children was the hardest thing about pursuing the master's degree. She commented recently, "It was hard not being there to help them with their homework or to sit down and talk about their friends. Sometimes I could feel them slipping away."

On the other hand, Tamara thinks that her children greatly benefited from having a student mother as a role model. She said, "My youngsters saw me as an example. They value education. They have waited to start their families later in life. They have insight and ability to plan for the future, and they are more consistent about their goals. They don't seem complacent or stuck. My sons share household and child-rearing tasks. They don't say things like 'I can't do dishes, that's for girls' or 'You can't chop kindling, that's for men.'"

Tamara's second marriage dissolved in 1980. Her newfound confidence gave her the "courage to end a bad situation."

She took her time—six years—getting through school, graduating in 1982 with a master's degree in counseling psychology and a pupil personnel services credential. Her thesis was a guidebook for educators and counselors working with Native American high school students.

In her spare time, Tamara codeveloped a presentation of songs and dances by thirty representatives of four tribes at a statewide conference for music educators. She also served on many boards of directors that were involved with Native American and human rights issues.

After working at the community college for twelve years, Tamara left in 1984 to move closer to a man she intended to marry. She quickly found a job as a mental health counselor for referred offenders. She was challenged by a different setting and thrilled about the new commitment in her personal life.

However, the relationship did not turn out as planned. "We parted as friends," she said, but her disappointment was enormous. "I was hoping Alan would be somebody I could finally settle down with, relax with. My education and self-esteem gave me the strength to live through this heartbreak. . . . I was able to pick up the pieces and put my life back together."

At age 50, with only one child still at home, Tamara began to focus less on earning money and more on the quality of her life. "My goal now," she says, "is to relax more and take only enjoyable work."

Her new goals mirror one of her original goals: to be a resource to her own people. In 1986, she returned to her hometown and her tribe. "I love this area," she said. "I love the environment. This is the home of my mother and grandfather. It's where I want to be."

Tamara was able to find work as a county mental health counselor. For the tribal council, she is a volunteer counselor for Indians who have substance abuse problems or who require services under the Indian Child Welfare Act. She also serves on many tribal council committees.

Because her interest in substance abuse counseling has grown, she would like to become certified in that field. She is also taking art classes, learning the healing properties of local plants, and reading as much as possible. Working part-time feels right. Tamara is back home with plenty to occupy her, both professionally and personally.

She believes that her education gave her two of the ingredients she needed to lead a meaningful life: self-esteem and earning power.

HURDLING ONE CAREER GOAL AFTER ANOTHER: FROM WELFARE TO $33,000 A YEAR

In 1966 Cathy was a secretary at a university and could attend school tuition-free. She took night classes, got good grades, and began to formulate some career goals. However, she got married shortly after this, supported her husband (who was in school), and reduced her study load to only one or two classes a semester.

In 1972, when her son, Joshua, was 2, she and her husband separated. Cathy quickly concluded that she had to pursue her degree more actively in order to get a decent job.

As Cathy explained, "Being the head of a household and responsible for a child, I felt a very strong need to be self-supporting. I wanted to have a job, a career, and financial security. I had been a secretary, and I knew I couldn't support us on that kind of salary." Two women she worked with who had successful careers encouraged her to go on welfare in order to pursue her degree. Cathy gave it a try.

Her major concern was child care. While she was earning her associate degree, she was able to find two single mothers who took children into their homes. Once Joshua turned 3, he qualified for state-subsidized, on-campus child care at the community college.

Later, when Cathy transferred to a university, she again was able to enroll Joshua in a campus child-care center. It was expensive, but she managed her budget carefully in order to secure this for her son.

Cathy had always been interested in psychology and chose it as her major. Once she got used to being a student, she did very well academically. Good grades and the respect of professors and students nurtured her self-assurance. "I realized I was doing OK, and that motivated me to continue with school," she said recently.

After eleven years, Cathy got her bachelor's degree in 1977. She immediately set her sights on a master's degree in psychology and a career as a school psychologist. She and Joshua moved from one end of California to the other.

The challenge of finding money and child care became more acute. Joshua turned 6; by law, Cathy had to register with the welfare department as being eligible for work. "I felt like I was fighting time," she explained. At any point the welfare department could insist that she accept posted positions, no matter how menial. That would have meant the end of school, since none of her program's classes were offered at night.

Cathy's comments on welfare are familiar to anyone who has traveled the route of an impoverished student. "Getting by on the bare essentials is a challenge. Eating out occasionally became a real treat. Entertaining at home at minimal cost was interesting. Not being able to buy clothes except at thrift stores became depressing. But thinking about the degree and a decent-paying job was energizing."

Locating an after-school child-care program was quite difficult, Cathy noted. "I got my son into the town's only day-care center for school-age children. It was just amazing that the elementary schools didn't offer any after-school care for the children of working and student parents."

Cathy graduated in 1979 with her master's degree in psychology and a straight-A average. Her next hurdle was an internship as a school psychologist. She had a specific location in mind, and she wanted to be well paid. Naturally, she was not alone in locating the ideal internship. The competition was fierce but Cathy was chosen. Her salary as an intern was $10,000 a year, a windfall for 1979. "It was a wonderful feeling to get off the welfare rolls," Cathy said.

Credentials in hand, she moved back to the East Coast and the hometown she had left nearly fifteen years earlier. She married a childhood neighbor. Initially, Cathy's husband supported her drive to find a job as soon as possible. However, three months after they married Cathy was pregnant with her second son and she suddenly met resistance to her plans.

"In arguments I would say that I didn't get a master's degree and do an internship to stay at home. I said I was going back to work; that had been a given when we married. I had worked so hard for this; I just wasn't going to allow anyone to stand in my way."

The couple compromised. Cathy went back to work part-time when her son was four months old, working up to full-time employment when he was nine months old. She reached her goal and was hired as a school psychologist. After working in this capacity for four years, she decided that she wanted an administrative position.

In 1983, Cathy went back to school, this time for an administrative credential. Being a student was a lot easier this time. The campus was close to home, and classes met two or three nights a week. Her husband cared for the two children during the evenings she had classes.

How did her husband feel about Cathy's return to school? "At first he didn't appreciate having additional responsibilities placed on him. He wanted to come home at night and find his wife there," Cathy said. "He had to cook dinner and put the kids to bed when I had classes.

"It turned out to be a positive experience. Having Daddy cook and eat dinner with the children gave them special time together. In the long run, I hope they see him as a good role model. Dads cook and clean house, too."

The marriage changed. "As a result of my going back to school, our marriage is no longer a traditional one. Our roles shift back and forth constantly, even on a daily basis. Our expectations have become more reasonable. Priorities have changed. The pressures from role expectations have greatly diminished. But it didn't happen overnight, and there were arguments and animosity."

Cathy received her administration certification in 1985. She now coordinates a center for handicapped children and earns $33,000 for the academic year.

Cathy takes a great deal of pleasure in her accomplishment. "I enjoyed every moment of my schooling. I love my job. I love working, and I know I couldn't stand to stay at home. I am a happier person as a result, and this is reflected in my family life. If I didn't have something to do with my life, I would be bored and miserable. In terms of the financial contribution to the family, if I weren't working, we wouldn't have the life-style we do. It's not extravagant, but two incomes allow a very comfortable life."

There is a certain isolation, however, in the land of success. With two incomes, Cathy and her husband can afford a home in an affluent neighborhood where very few mothers work.

Because she lives 5 minutes from her childhood hometown, Cathy has resumed old friendships as well. But those friends assume that the only reason Cathy works is because of the income her job generates. "Some of my friends don't understand that I have a career because I want to do something in addition to being a mother and wife. They are very nice people, but I'm not interested in hearing about their tennis games, and they aren't interested in hearing about my job.

"As far as the men go, I'm in education, and that field is a farce to begin with in their minds. They always refer to me as a teacher instead of a school psychologist. They cannot get beyond the stereotype—all women in education are teachers. Other people don't know the difference between a school psychologist and a clinical psychologist and assume that I analyze them, which they find threatening. Even though I get these messages from some of the people I socialize with, I get support from the people I work with."

Because her work with handicapped children is so intense, Cathy has realized she must leave her job behind at night and on the weekends. "I've separated my career from my personal life. My job is nonstop, and I need breaks from it."

Having achieved her long-term goal of financial security, Cathy has been able to focus on how to put her particular blend of interests and skills to the best use. She sees her current job as a steppingstone to an administrative position in the field of education.

She said, "I hope to become an assistant principal or principal, preferably in a program for handicapped children. A second choice would be a job as director of special education in a local school district. I want to start climbing the educational administration ladder."

WELFARE MOM SPEARHEADS $10-MILLION STATEWIDE MOVEMENT FOR PREVENTION OF CHILD ABUSE

When Cheryl was asked why she dropped out of college, she said she just couldn't deal with the institutional bureaucracy. "I couldn't even deal with the procedures for dropping the classes, so I flunked out," she said.

Since then, Cheryl has learned to harness bureaucracy in ways that make it work for the causes she believes in. She founded a nonprofit child services agency and organized a statewide movement in child abuse prevention that obtained over $50-million through state legislation for programming.

Cheryl dropped in and out of three colleges before she and her husband moved and settled at a state university in a rural setting. By the time Cheryl received her bachelor's degree in psychology (1973), she was divorced and had a one-and-a-half-year-old daughter. She did not want to work full-time because she didn't want to put Ashleigh in child care 8 hours a day.

Cheryl decided to get a master's degree in education, with an emphasis in family counseling. Luckily, a university out of the area created a pilot program in which classes would be offered near Cheryl in the evenings and on weekends.

"The program seemed like a good idea," Cheryl said at the time. "It was a relatively simple degree to get. I wanted part-time involvement because of Ashleigh. I knew I could complete my education and keep our home life stable. It seemed like a logical step."

Cheryl's ex-husband had dropped out of school and was unemployed. Once Cheryl committed herself to getting a degree, she went on welfare. Being on AFDC helped her formulate her career goal. "I felt that through AFDC society was contributing to my education, and that I would repay this someday through my contribution to society. I decided to commit five years to repaying that debt."

Desperation served as a catalyst in the formation of Cheryl's career. During the last year of her undergraduate studies, all the parents whose children were at the campus child-care center were asked to volunteer some time at the center. Cheryl refused because Ashleigh was having problems separating from her. Cheryl felt that these problems would only get worse if she spent time at the center. "Also, I was too impatient to work with young children. I couldn't stand it," she noted. "I would have lasted 15 minutes as a day-care worker."

She knew she would have to contribute in some way, however. "I felt so guilty about not working on the floor with the rest of the parents that I dreamed up a job for myself—I would try to work out problems between the family and the center, or the staff and the staff, or whatever. The university funded the position as a work-study job."

The center was going through tremendous turmoil. After losing three directors in three months, it again needed a new director. No one would step forward—except Cheryl. "I got the job by drawing the short straw," she explained. "No one else would do it." Thus while Cheryl earned her master's degree, she also directed the university's child-care center. She earned a good salary and was able to make her workday flexible enough to include plenty of time with Ashleigh—after hours.

Cheryl enjoyed the work. "I found intellectual challenge in unraveling the center's problems," she said. "It was like a big jigsaw puzzle. I had to put the puzzle together, even though some of the pieces were missing. I was unknotting the problems. My goals were administratively oriented, for example, pay the staff and get buildings. I wasn't interested in figuring out programming. I hired competent staff to do that."

Cheryl also discovered she was a wizard at writing grant proposals. Toward the end of her master's degree program, she received a $400,000 state grant she proposed to put toward expansion of the center's services.

The university was not able to undertake such an expansion at that point, however, so Cheryl decided to form a nonprofit organization that would be able to receive some of the grant money.

With $100,000 of the state funding, Cheryl opened a nonprofit agency with a staff of two to provide a range of family services, such as day care, resources for child-care providers, referrals for children's services, and advocacy for increased and improved services throughout the county.

A year later, the staff had expanded to five, and the budget began growing. After a year and a half, the budget was close to $1-million, the staff had grown to thirty, and Cheryl was appointed by the governor to a special advisory committee on improving child-care services throughout the state. By the time Cheryl left the area, the agency had a staff of fifty-five and an annual budget of $1.5-million.

In just a few short years, Cheryl had created a position for herself as executive director of a productive and prosperous agency. She had also remarried, moved to a metropolitan area, and was expecting a second child. And she was just warming up.

While still director of the agency, Cheryl had created several pilot projects for child abuse prevention, the first of their kind in the state. These initial projects led to a statewide movement focusing on child abuse prevention, with Cheryl at the helm. She eventually wrote two state bills that were critical to the funding of child abuse prevention programs. One provided $10-million annually and stipulated that the funding be available to every county in the state.

"It was like realizing a dream. Most of the counties had never seen funds like that for child abuse prevention programs," she explained. In fact, other states have followed this example—the impact is nationwide.

Juggling her personal and professional life, Cheryl had the bill and the baby within months of each other—the baby was born in April, and the bill was signed in September.

Cheryl and her husband, Mark, wanted to spend as much time as possible with their new baby, Rebecca. Cheryl felt her needs had changed. "I felt I had reached the peak in my field. I had done the lobbying, done the bill, and set up the fund for the kids. And I had had a baby. It felt like it was time to stay home for a while, take a rest, and think of other things."

Mark, a lawyer, created a victim restitution practice in which he represents child abuse victims, and Cheryl manages his practice.

Cheryl also wanted to start a business of her own. She considered real estate sales and stock brokering, but she ultimately decided on travel management. Through an extended learning program at a nearby university, she picked up the courses that she needed. Classes met on Saturdays; child care was not a problem because Mark and Ashleigh were at home.

These days Cheryl spends her time working at home as a travel manager and the manager of Mark's business. She continues to be involved with children's services, writing grant proposals, evaluating child abuse prevention programs, and doing management consulting.

Cheryl's plans include working on projects that provide flexibility, creativity, and a good income, but she continually reassesses her direction and goals. Because her life moved so quickly for so long, she finds time for reflection very precious.

Cheryl said of her method of identifying goals, "You need to think about what you want to look back on at the end of your life. Set your goals from that perspective. I used to tell my staff: Imagine you're looking at yourself at the end of all this. See what kinds of pathways you want to create. Then go back, and start doing those things you need to do in order to create those pathways."

CHAPTER 2
TAKING IT SLOW

Adults who attend college on a part-time basis are usually combining their student role with many other activities and responsibilities, especially parenthood, a job, or both. This chapter features women who have each taken more than a decade to earn the academic degree they desired.

A common bond among the five women in this chapter is that it feels as if their education has taken an eternity. They are not alone, however. Nearly half of all people working toward a college degree today are attending part-time, and the number continues to grow. At the graduate level, well over half of all students are part-timers; for women the figure is 60 percent.

Part-time studies can be the path of least resistance in terms of maintaining a stable family life. Judith's and Julia's husbands are high school graduates. Both showed signs of feeling threatened at the widening gap between their education and their wives'—the longer route was perhaps easier to cope with for them.

Among these part-time students, Susan is the only one whose marriage has ended in the past ten years, but the other women have experienced tense moments as well. When Christine started college, her long-term relationship ended. And Elaine felt that her husband, Doug, did not take her student role seriously because it was taking so long to get her degree.

There are advantages to attending school part-time. Most important, life doesn't go on hold. Elaine and her husband, for instance, have relocated and had three children during the eleven years she has been in school. Julia has been a pioneer in the field of working with nonverbal, nonvocal children. Christine has established a solid psychotherapy practice and a committed relationship. All have seen tremendous growth and change during their student days—personally, academically, and professionally.

To avoid feeling discouraged, part-time students often set short-term goals and rewards for themselves. Christine, for example, wants to do lots of traveling once she has completed her doctorate. But rather than postpone all travel plans, she and her companion, Michael, take short trips whenever a spare minute presents itself.

There are good reasons for prolonging one's academic stint, and there are definite rewards to be found along the way.

ELEVEN YEARS AS AN UNDERGRADUATE

Elaine went back to school at age 26 in 1976. She and her husband, Doug, had served in the navy, so they were both able to finance full-time schooling through veterans' benefits. They had no children.

Doug got his degree from a technical school in 1978 and landed a position as a service planner with a computer corporation. Elaine took eleven years to get her bachelor's degree. During that time, they moved from one state to another because of Doug's job, Elaine had many jobs, and they had three children.

Elaine, whose schedule always accommodated family needs first and educational demands second, felt as though she had been in school forever. She took one or two courses each semester, and none during relocations, pregnancy, or financial difficulties.

In retrospect, Elaine said, "If I had to do it over again, I probably would have gone a lot faster. I would have taken out a loan, forgotten about work, gone full-time, and finished in a couple of years."

This situation is common. The family needed two incomes to live in comfort. When Elaine took low-paying jobs for which she qualified, the time commitment prevented her from getting her degree sooner and also kept her tied to less rewarding jobs, both financially and intellectually. Seeing this, Elaine persisted in her degree program. She had had her fill of jobs without stimulation. She didn't want to be a receptionist or a cashier ever again.

Each time she went back to school, she reminded herself of why she was there. "We are poor right now," she commented at one point. "I have no business being in school; I should be making money for the family. But my degree will be worth our financial sacrifices. Not being able to pay the bills for a couple of years will be worth it."

When Elaine and Doug were both in school—and childless—their life-style was relatively uncomplicated. "The two of us were going to school together and studying together," Elaine said.

Three children and a working husband made a dramatic difference in the couple's life-style. "Doug wants to be supportive; he tries to be supportive," Elaine said. "But sometimes we argue about his not being supportive. I may have to study all day, and this means he has to take care of the three kids, including a 3-month-old. It's difficult for him. It's hard for him to come home from work as I'm running out the door. He's got to change diapers and cook supper."

Elaine also believed that often her student role was not taken seriously by family and friends because of her part-time program. Even Doug, she said, interrupted her studies more than necessary. "When you're studying, people don't think of it as your job. You wouldn't call somebody at their job to ask what's for dinner!"

Over the years, Elaine's motivation for continuing her studies was her desire for fulfilling employment. "If I didn't have a goal, it would be senseless to go back to school. You have to be thinking about something—a job, a career, something." She felt strongly that regional or environmental planning in her own region would provide the ideal job. Today, she is happily serving as the junior planner of her town.

Elaine did well in school, achieving a 3.6 grade point average. "I was afraid I was going to fail. I had no confidence. I would study constantly and have no time for anything else. I was so nervous I practically memorized books. I was constantly afraid I was going to flunk out. My first course was a summer course. I hadn't had a test in six or seven years. I studied and studied for that first test. I studied for a week straight, 3 hours a night. I took the test, came home, and was practically in tears. I said to my husband: 'I've failed. I've flunked this test.' I was so upset."

The next day she got her test back. "I got a 97, the highest mark in the class! The instructor was praising me up and down, saying what a good paper it was. I couldn't believe it. I thought it had to be somebody else's paper or that he hadn't seen all the mistakes I made. Even when I don't think I've done very well, I end up with an A nine times out of ten."

Elaine credits school with giving her more confidence in herself. "Having confidence changes your life, your relationships with others, your feelings about yourself. I used to worry about what other people thought, and now it doesn't matter as much. If you feel good about yourself, that's what counts."

Elaine pinpoints a specific college experience that helped her develop confidence. One of the first classes she took was a speech course, which she dreaded. "I felt I would never be able to say anything in front of an audience," Elaine recalled. "I turned out to be good at it! I guess I had hoped that going back to school would give me more confidence, but when it did, I was surprised."

JUGGLING A PH.D., A COMMITTED RELATIONSHIP, AND A JOB

Christine's life-style runs counter to the typical image of Ph.D. candidates: alone in their ivory towers, immersed in theory, books their only companions.

Having studied eleven years beyond her bachelor's degree, Christine, age 38, expects to receive her Ph.D. in counseling psychology soon. In the meantime, her life is not on hold.

Professionally, she is already in full swing. She earns $36,000 a year in a psychotherapy practice she started in 1980. Her personal life is also thriving. She and her companion, Michael, set up housekeeping in 1986, just after her dissertation topic was approved.

It was while Christine was in Malaysia with the Peace Corps that she formulated her original academic and career goals: to pursue a master's degree and become a counselor. She enjoyed working with people and believed that the additional degree would increase her earning power. She wanted the potential of being completely self-supporting.

Christine had gone into the Peace Corps because that was what a former companion wanted to do. The couple agreed that Christine would go to school upon their return.

However, when they got back to the States, Christine's reentry plans were upset: she was put on the waiting list at the university she had applied to, and she discovered she had hepatitis.

After a few months, Christine's determination to go to school returned. She made several trips to the university, a 4-hour drive from where she lived—"to hustle the department," as she says.

"I was looking for ways to get in the next year," she explained. "I found a loophole and discovered that I could go into a different department and start taking classes. I would be able to transfer into the program I wanted after a semester."

During her first term back in school, Christine left early Wednesday morning, drove the 4 hours to school, took classes from 1 to 10 p.m., spent the night with her mother (adding another hour to her commute), took another class Thursday morning, and drove home.

Of the amazingly rigorous schedule, Christine says, "It gave me personal space. I was alone. I had time to think, sing, and enjoy the beauty of that highway as it changed from winter to spring."

The physical distance between school and home also helped Christine gain perspective on her personal life. She realized she had to choose between school and her rural life-style; she opted for school. Her goal was absolutely clear, and she was sure school would get her there.

Her relationship ended and Christine decided to relocate in order to put an end to her commute. "It was not an easy decision," she commented at the time. "I had to give up living in a fantastic house in the woods with a sauna. And I had to leave some good friends." She also had to move far from her younger sister, to whom she is very close.

Her studies demanded tremendous effort, but she was willing to apply herself because she enjoyed the program. She felt she had more energy because she was focused and certain about what she was doing.

One major hurdle was learning how to study again. "I was so rusty I had to read over and over before I could comprehend a chapter. I also couldn't write." Fortunately, Christine was able to view her problem as mechanical rather than intellectual. She found the university's learning center and read up on how to improve her reading speed and comprehension. She got some tutoring on the fundamentals of writing. She graduated with a straight-A average.

In 1976, when Christine began her master's program in counseling psychology, she had no plans to get a Ph.D. Her original goal was to counsel reentry students in a college setting, but as she got more involved, she decided to focus on family and individual counseling.

One of her friends in the program decided to pursue a doctorate. "I figured if she could do it, I could do it," Christine said. "I took the GRE and thought, 'I'll just apply, and, if I get in, I'll think about it.'"

She applied to the Ph.D. in counseling program and was accepted. However, with her master's degree in hand she was eager to begin her career as a psychotherapist. Should she get her Ph.D. and then start her practice? Get her practice going, then get a Ph.D.? She chose to do both at the same time, even though it meant adding several more years to her Ph.D. program.

After two years of full-time classes and two additional years of conducting research and writing three major papers, she prepared for her orals. "It was frightening. It was terrifying. There were going to be six professors grilling me, telling me whether or not I could advance in the doctoral program," she said.

Personal counseling helped her deal with her fears. Through programs offered at the university's counseling center, Christine was able to learn relaxation exercises, stress reduction techniques, and visualization. She spent a year in the counseling center's support group for Ph.D. students. Encouragement from fellow students, her friends, and family was also critical. Then came a gigantic snag.

"After the orals, I spent a year writing my dissertation proposal. I had wanted to conduct a study of eating disorders through a creative and nontraditional research approach. My dissertation committee was highly intrigued, and they approved the proposal. However, another committee set up by the university to oversee proposals rejected it on the grounds that it was not experimental research.

"I then spent an entire year defending my proposal to this committee. I made four revisions, wrote rebuttals to the attacks on my proposal, and finally had to stand up and orally defend it to this committee. I won. It was quite a victory."

About this time Christine and her companion, Michael, decided to live together. Christine says that Michael is supportive of both her student role and her need for individuality. Working on her dissertation requires many of her evenings and weekends, but Michael also has work to do in the evenings. Christine believes that clearly delineated times for work and study help them both.

Christine made a conscious decision not to let her education take over her entire life. "I decided to have friends, to start my business, to live with somebody, to travel, and to do things for myself such as daily exercise, weekly manicures, and shopping for nice clothes. Basically, I decided to lead a balanced life," she said.

Finding the balance is extremely difficult. Christine describes what it takes: "Sometimes I feel that nobody could know how much it hurts to struggle to stay on top of this 'balanced life' I've created. Sometimes it feels like ten lives packed into one, and I have total responsibility for each one. The irresponsible part of me or the part of me that just wants to let go, get wild, and not care about another human soul feels locked away."

She says that to maintain the balance is work. "I hardly stop. Even the meditating or quiet time has to be scheduled in. I can let myself relax completely but only for the allotted time. I'm aware of burnout, so I exercise and take care of myself. Even that becomes 'what I have to do.' Sometimes I wonder whether I would do it again."

Christine says she never questions whether or not she'll finish because she's too determined. "But truthfully," she notes, "the Ph.D. process takes tremendous stamina and requires personal compromises that can be very painful. It hurts to turn down four out of five invitations. It hurts not to be involved in the daily lives of my niece and nephew. It hurts not to be able to give more to the man I live with. I feel so selfish sometimes."

Even though Christine has already developed a good psychotherapy practice, she expects the Ph.D. and her expertise in eating disorders to qualify her as a consultant and program developer. In addition to her dissertation and psychotherapy practice, she has started a weight management program at a local medical center.

In retrospect, Christine can see ways she might have minimized the length of time it is taking to get her degree. For example, she wonders if she might not have been able to focus some of her reports so that they could have been used as chapters in her dissertation. She thinks better on-campus guidance could help students move through Ph.D. programs more swiftly.

Christine and Michael now own their own home. Christine has found an effective method for speeding up work on her dissertation: "I'm taking one week off every four weeks. I go away to a quiet country setting with my computer, and, without the distractions, I concentrate on writing." When she's finished, she intends to continue her psychotherapy practice, do some consulting, and write.

EVEN SPORADIC STUDIES CAN MEAN MAJOR LIFE-STYLE ADJUSTMENTS

Judith is 63 and has been enrolled in courses for academic credit since 1974. She is still two classes away from receiving her bachelor's degree with a major in interdisciplinary studies from the City University of New York.

Judith enjoys the life-style she and her husband, Richard, a retired businessman, have created. They spend six months a year in Florida, away from the harsh weather of the Northeast. While south, Judith does research—for academic credit—for several of her professors. When the couple returns home, Judith usually takes one or two courses during the summer semester.

When Judith went back to school, she and her husband had to make some major adjustments. They had been married for thirty years. Judith had not worked outside their home since the children were born. Her husband provided financial security for the family, and she was responsible for raising the three children. By deciding to take college classes, she upset the delicate balance of her family life.

While Judith was in the decision-making process, Richard appeared to be all for it. "But once I started," Judith recalled, "it was obvious there was a problem. Whatever I had to do for school was fine, as long as I did it when my husband wasn't home. He was very proud that I was going, but he didn't want it to interfere with our time together." Because of Richard's feelings, Judith never took classes at night and she did all her reading between 4 and 7 a.m.

Richard, who is seven years older than Judith, was only a few years away from retirement when Judith started to take classes. Judith knew she would eventually have to plan her studies around the travels and vacations of retirement.

She also had to be sensitive to the fact that she was going beyond Richard's education level, even though she did not have a degree in mind when she started taking college classes.

"It's a threat to a man," she said. "Richard happens to be very intelligent, so he expanded a great deal through his work. He didn't feel the lack of education the way I did. Now, he's proud when I finish the crossword puzzle before he does, but he'd rather finish it before I do once in a while. I was very dependent on him before. We still lead a very traditional kind of marriage, but I'm much more independent in my thinking. I was subservient before."

Several years into her studies, a crisis arose. "I had an exam coming up. Richard was ready to go to Florida for a couple of weeks. I went with him, missed my classes, but did all my studying down there. He resented it. We both blew up."

Fortunately, a longtime friend of Richard's figured out what was going on. As Judith explains it, "David spoke to him and made him see how important it was for me to do what I was doing. Richard changed." He became willing to sit down and discuss vacations so that Judith could continue school.

Richard was used to having his wife "at his beck and call," as Judith puts it, but the couple was able to adapt. As Richard became more sensitive to Judith's needs, Judith, in turn, became more accommodating of Richard's needs. "When he became less resentful, I started to try to understand his point of view. It was a meeting of the minds."

The couple's three children are all college graduates, and Richard has become much more comfortable with Judith's desire to pursue a degree. Resentment has turned into pride.

"I invited my history professor over one day because I had done a research project for him, and he came to pick it up. I invited him for lunch, with his wife and baby. He and Richard had never met. He told Richard, 'You know, your wife is the second-best student I have ever had.' My ears perked up, of course, but Richard beamed."

When Judith returned to school, back in 1974, she did not have a career objective. In fact, she wasn't particularly interested in pursuing a degree program. She went to college simply to learn as much as she could. "I went to school in order to enhance my well-being, my self-awareness," she explained. "I always trusted my instincts, but I had nothing to back up my opinions."

When she was in high school thirty-five years earlier, she had worked hard to get good grades and assumed college would be too difficult for her. Besides, although her parents emphasized education for her brothers, they did not think it was as important for women.

Judith was very apprehensive about how she would do academically. Now, just a few units short of graduating, she has a 3.87 grade point average. Several years ago, Judith said, "I'm on a par with anyone else in the class. Learning is very easy if you set your mind to it. College has given me the background I've needed. I had always felt instinctively that I had some good reactions. I was never ashamed of my gut feelings, but I never knew." The confidence Judith feels in the classroom has also affected her life outside the classroom. "Now that I have the basics—history, literature, mathematics, even physics—I'm much more sure of myself. I venture into things without fear. I'm much more confident in every situation."

Judith believes there is a fine line between projecting confidence and being overbearing. She finds she is sometimes more harsh with people than she used to be. "When that happens, I really don't like myself, but I say, 'The hell with everybody else; this is what I feel, and this is what I want to say.'"

Judith discovered early in her academic career that she loved doing research. In 1983, much to her amazement, her history professor called her after grading a project she had done for him. Would she be interested in helping him with his research? She identifies the day that telephone call came as one of the greatest days of her life. "He made me feel like somebody special—in a way that no one had ever made me feel before," she explained.

Soon the sociology department wanted her to do research for them. Sometimes she receives academic credit in exchange for her efforts; other times she does the research as a favor. The situation is ideal because she can work on these projects in Florida as well as at home. She is not interested in finding a steady job, yet she was flattered when the governor's office contacted her recently about doing research for them on a steady basis.

Judith sees herself as a perpetual student, with or without a degree. She and Richard plan to make Florida their permanent home in the next few years. When they do, she would like to try her hand at volunteer work, and she hopes to continue the research projects indefinitely.

PART-TIME STUDIES: A LIFEBOAT IN A SEA OF CHANGE

In 1977, at age 33, Susan entered a community college. She had no career goals and was not interested in getting a degree. Her children were 7, 8, and 10 at the time.

Ten years later, Susan had a bachelor's degree in home economics, magna cum laude, from a major university. It had taken her six years to get her A.A. degree, and four years to earn her B.A.

College was Susan's mainstay, a cherished constant during years of tremendous personal growth and the breakup of her marriage. "If

I had not gone to school when I did, I don't know what would have happened to me," she said. "I was headed for a nervous breakdown. I was in a terribly unstable emotional state, and going to college was one way I tried to do something about that."

According to Susan, pursuit of education did not cause her marriage to fail. However, she believes the changes that resulted from being in college accelerated its end. As she discovered new things about herself, the couple became more and more incompatible.

"I think my marriage would have ended anyway, but maybe not as soon as it did. Going to college helped me to become more assertive, and that in turn created unhappiness between my ex-husband and me."

George had resisted Susan's return to school from the start. Out of deference to his attitude, she once decided not to take a 3-unit course in art appreciation because it cost $66. "Right after Christmas I did not feel I could ask my husband to pay for it. Instead, I took a 1-unit course. The cost was minimal and my husband was happy."

Susan says of those early years, "When I started taking classes, I was dissatisfied with my marriage, although I hadn't pinpointed it at the time. I was unhappy with myself and life in general. Then, it was as if doors opened for me, and I could see that there was something beyond the life I was living."

She took one course the first semester and three the next. Being a part-time student meant she could savor each class to the fullest. After her second semester, she said, "I am much happier with myself, my husband, and my children. I do not become depressed, dejected, or despairing the way I used to when I was running around doing things of little consequence to fill time. I feel vibrant and alive."

She had grown up believing she was not intelligent. "I was terrified that people would find out. When I got married, George perpetuated this. But then, I allowed him to treat me that way. Going back to school and getting A's in almost every class made me realize I could hold my own with anybody."

Susan was a conscientious student and willing to devote as much time as it took to studying for exams and writing papers. She was contending with dyslexia in addition to rusty study habits. "When I was writing papers, George used to get furious with me because I would stay up all night. He couldn't understand why it took me so long to write papers for school."

Although many reentry students regret having to go to school part-time, Susan's ideal course load per semester was about 9 credits (two or three courses). She was happy to protract her student days. She commented recently, "I wanted to savor being in school. You lose the essence of it by rushing through. You need time to digest, to incorporate what you're learning."

After Susan had been in school four years, she and George started seeing a mediator about separating. The mediator urged Susan to decide where school was taking her. Was she going to prepare for employment? Susan was managing a store on a part-time basis, but she did not want to continue this indefinitely. The following year, after she and George separated and filed for divorce, she focused on school as a means to an end. Her alimony would end early in 1987.

"I had to push so much into the last two years," Susan explained, particularly since she changed her major and needed to complete more requirements. Her new major in home economics education also provided her with a career goal—to teach family relationships, independent living, and child development at the high school level.

"The last couple of years have been very frustrating. I don't like taking 15 or 18 credits per semester. It's horrible. You can't enjoy anything," she notes wryly.

When Susan started at the community college, she took classes only while her three children were in school. "I don't think the children noticed any real changes except that I was probably more animated because I was stimulated." However, she admits she was cranky when she was writing papers.

Jane, who turned 10 shortly after Susan became a student, said at the time, "She seems happier. It's fun to listen to her talk about her tests and her teachers and her homework." James, who was 8, agreed, "It's funny that she comes home and talks about homework and tests when I'm coming home and talking about homework and tests." However, Jane also believed she noticed tension between her parents.

Susan feels that the insight and understanding she gleaned from such courses as adolescent psychology helped her establish a strong rapport with the children during the traumatic years of adjustment after the divorce. She says that her relationship with the children—after much hard work, pain, and frustration—is now excellent.

Susan was going to school, working, coping with a divorce, and trying to provide stability for her children. She felt pressured to get done with school as quickly as possible even though it was her refuge from harsh realities.

"School buffered me against the trauma. I'm not saying that school wasn't traumatic, but it gave me an outside focus. When I was at school, I wasn't involved with emotional upheaval. It was time out. I was with people who didn't know George, so I didn't have to explain anything."

By 1986, Susan was ready to leave school. She encountered a roadblock: she had not passed the chemistry requirement during the fall semester. She had to take one more class in spring 1987 to graduate.

"What had been my liberator in 1977—school—became my prison in 1987! It was no longer stimulating or interesting. At the same time, I was terrified of finishing school, of having to leave its safety and security, of going out into the world, of finding a job, of earning money. As angry, upset, and frustrated as I was at having to repeat chemistry, it gave me an excuse not to face my fear of going into the world. School is a wonderful intellectual liberator, but it can also be very seductive because it is so structured. It becomes as familiar and as comforting as a pair of old slippers. I think it is important to remember school is not the real world, just one of the stepping-stones to getting there."

Susan passed chemistry, and now is substitute teaching while she looks for a permanent teaching position.

Susan summarizes her odyssey this way: "When I went back to school, it saved my life. My spirit was dying. But it also turned my life upside down. Nevertheless, I do not regret for one minute going back to school. It was an excellent decision. I am finally on my way to a place where I can shine!"

A SLOW PACE CAN REVEAL OPPORTUNITIES

Five of Julia's six children were still at home when she resumed her studies, and two of them had disabilities that required a great deal of attention. Furthermore, Julia's husband, Tom, did not fully understand her need to continue her education and was often unemployed.

Julia began college in 1972 at the age of 43. She wanted to learn how to work with her special-needs son, who was in kindergarten. She also wanted financial independence.

"I needed more skills," she explained. She wanted to find work that would be personally and professionally rewarding. She wanted to "make a difference."

She enrolled at a community college near her home. Although she was interested in learning disabilities, she switched to a language disability program when a grant became available in that field. During the nine years she attended the community college part-time, she also worked in the public school system as a paraprofessional, helping children who had learning disabilities, speech articulation problems, and hearing impairments.

Julia graduated from the community college in 1981 and was hired at once as a communication assistant working with hearing-impaired children in her town's public school system. She soon realized that promotions would require a bachelor's degree.

The following year, she quit her job and went to a four-year state college, full-time. She received her bachelor's degree in communication disorders in only a year and a half.

Meanwhile, her state had changed the requirements in her field. Previously, communication disorders work in the public school system required a bachelor's degree. By the time Julia got her bachelor's, the state required a master's degree, passing a national exam, and a 300-hour unpaid practicum. Undaunted, she immediately started graduate school.

The next few years were an ordeal. The 3-hour commute kept her away from her family. Two of the children became very ill. Her husband, a carpenter, lost his job. Julia took a leave of absence from her graduate program in 1985—9 units short of graduation—and became the provider.

First, she interviewed at a pediatric nursing care facility near her home but was convinced she would never be able to work there. "It was frightening to see so many severely disabled children. Besides, they needed a speech pathologist who was certified or licensed, and I was not."

The facility called her back and asked her to come in just to meet a few of the children. "All of them were nonverbal. So here I was—having almost completed my master's in speech, language, and hearing disability—without more than half a lecture on nonvocal, nonverbal children.

"They said, 'Try it,' so I did, and I've been there ever since." Her salary there is four times what she was making after earning her associate degree. Equally important, she loves her job and believes that she is, in fact, "making a difference."

In 1987, the state department of education changed requirements again. They began licensing speech pathologists who could pass a state exam and had work experience in the field. Clearing those hurdles would eliminate the master's degree requirement.

Julia studied for the exam every waking hour. Taking the exam without the master's degree was a big risk: she didn't have the academic background in theory and research. But her wealth of work experience paid off. She passed.

"Passing that exam was more important to me than graduating from college," she said. Becoming board licensed meant a salary increase and less concern about the master's degree, although the degree would give her another salary increase. She is now more marketable in a field with a shortage of experts.

In reflecting on the ways in which her studies have affected her life, Julia says, "I'm totally changed. I'm not the same woman I was fifteen or twenty years ago. I think my husband would have been more satisfied if I had just been perfectly content to be the person I was before I went back to school."

Although Tom, a high school graduate, did not want Julia to go to college, she persisted. "I think my husband perceived himself as competing with me. I'd say to him, 'I don't know anything about what you do. Why do you feel that you have to know everything about what I do?'"

Julia believes that part of Tom's difficulty in adjusting to her educational and career goals has to do with their generation's expectations of women. According to Julia, Tom likes being a carpenter but doesn't find the same kind of satisfaction in his work as Julia finds in hers. "He would love to retire tomorrow," she said, whereas she could work indefinitely. She wants to take classes for the rest of her life. It's difficult, Julia believes, for Tom to understand how she feels.

Julia and Tom started doing quite a bit of camping once their older children were in college. Through camping, they have found a whole new group of friends. Some of these friends have more education than Tom, and he's often defensive about his lack of a college degree. Julia explains, "I tell him they really don't care. They just want to have a good time. I say, 'You're an expert at what you do, and they're experts at what they do. What's the difference if they have a little more education than you do?'"

Four of Julia's and Tom's children graduated from college the same year that Julia earned her bachelor's degree. "We had a great time celebrating that term," Julia said. They identify with her goals and sympathize with her aspirations.

Continuing education is now a pattern in the family. One daughter earned a master's degree, a daughter-in-law is enrolled in a master's program, and another daughter-in-law hopes to take computer classes. Julia's sons share the housework with their families.

Julia's mother, now in her 80s, is also a role model. When she retired at 65, she enrolled for a bachelor's degree and graduated, cum laude, at 70—the oldest person in her class.

Julia, now nearly 60, believes she has a wide array of job options. She is satisfied by her work with nonverbal, nonvocal children and has become interested in people who have lost their ability to speak due to stroke or severe head injuries.

Although Julia has detoured from her original goal of working with hearing-impaired children in a school setting, she is right on target with her ultimate desire—to find work that would "make a difference" and that would be rewarding personally, professionally, and financially.

CHAPTER 3
CONFRONTING FAMILY RESISTANCE

Most adults face mixed reactions from family members when they decide to further their education. Resistance can range from minor insensitivity to total disruption, whether intentional or not.

Taking on an academic role shifts the balance of family life, particularly in families with a well-established routine. As one woman put it, some student-parent-wives try to "sneak back, hoping that no one will notice." However, if college is a significant part of the student's life, it is bound to have an impact on her family as well.

Jill called her college experience her "ticket to freedom." She had endured tremendous strains at home for many years but could see no way "out" until she started college. College precipitated dramatic changes in her self-esteem and gave her the tools for building financial independence.

In her late 30s, Lydia felt tremendous pressure to prepare herself for a career. Part of her motivation stemmed from her deteriorating marriage. But her husband complained that the very earnestness and determination with which she approached school made her totally inaccessible.

Spouses are not alone in resisting change. Some children view their mother's academic commitment as time stolen from them. Others suddenly feel they are competing with mom for good grades.

Resistance can take many forms. Helen's husband, Jim, applauded her decision to pursue a college education and agreed to finance it. But he was impatient when she delayed identifying a major and a career goal. Helen was adamant about not rushing the decision. She also wanted to finance her own education and felt it necessary to get a job to do so. Getting a community college degree has taken her ten years. She has called her own shots, remained married, and identified a career goal.

Sometimes a period of conflict is essential for a relationship to grow. Many student-wives describe a deep malaise that ultimately catapults them onto a college campus. Shirley, for example, said her marriage came as close as it ever has to disintegrating while she was in school. She said at first her husband, Justin, felt threatened by her strong interests outside the family. But shortly after they settled into their new routine, their relationship improved. Shirley no longer felt taken for granted, and the couple learned to communicate more effectively.

Louise had been a traditional homemaker for fifteen years. Her husband, Clarence, and their five children thought it was fine for her to be a coed, but they expected nothing to change at home. Louise explains that she and Clarence successfully argued it out, a tactic many student-wives recommend as a healthier alternative to letting disagreements simmer.

Many women returning to school have already put their husbands through school. After what seems like a lifetime, it's finally their turn to add a student role. The women who have approached their husbands with a "you owe it to me" attitude have not fared well. No one likes to be presented with an emotional debit sheet.

Lydia's ex-husband believes their marital tension could have been alleviated if Lydia had placed distinct time limits on her school-related activities and painting. He recommends scheduling specific time with the family and creating rewards for all family members at the end of a hard stretch.

Misunderstandings may occur daily in any marriage. A recent survey (Stafford and Duncan) indicated married couples average only 15 minutes per day talking to each other. More communication than this is critical to coordinate and balance family life and academic commitment successfully.

TICKET TO FREEDOM

In 1954, when Jill was 19, she dropped out of nursing school to recover from an illness. She went to work at a store owned by her boyfriend, Ralph's, father. Shortly thereafter she married Ralph, and several years later they took over the store. By 1967 they had six children.

Jill's marriage had emotional and other problems from the start. A high school dropout, Ralph told Jill he thought education was a waste for women. Believing that there was no way she could become more educated herself, Jill focused on her children, making sure they valued education.

Because she was active with the schools her children attended, Jill decided to run for the town school board. Serving on the board turned out to be the catalyst for enormous change in her life.

While chairperson in 1976, she discovered a misappropriation of federal funds in her school district. She was shocked when the state department of education did nothing about it.

"I requested an audit from the Department of Education in Washington. When the auditors came, I realized that I knew as much about this kind of funding as they did. Yet they were making $50,000 to $75,000 a year, and I was just a housewife with a high school education."

Before it was all over, both the town and state were called to task. Jill's school board was horrified by exposure of the local administration and its misuse of funds. They tried to remove Jill from office. Mud was slung, and front-page newspaper stories were written.

When the dust cleared, Jill emerged victorious. She was reelected by a landslide. "I realized that I had a brain and knew how to use it. But I didn't have the educational credentials."

In 1977 Jill enrolled as a full-time student at a prestigious private college near her home. With her background and experiences, Jill says, the college was concerned about how she would fit in and how she would perform academically.

Jill proceeded to pack four years of school into three, graduated summa cum laude and Phi Beta Kappa, received a coveted prize from the English department, and delivered a graduation speech. The hard part was coping with family responsibilities and a rapidly deteriorating marriage.

"In order to try to keep the marriage stable," Jill explained, "I would go to bed at night when my husband did. Once he was asleep, I would get up and study half the night. I learned to get along on 3 or 4 hours' sleep."

Jill says she tried to be everything to everybody, and that just increased her compulsion to be perfect. "I was always available when the children needed me. I went to basketball games and took part in special projects. I still baked so there would be snacks waiting after school. I thought it was very selfish to go back to school. The things I needed to do for myself—studying and so forth—I did after everyone went to bed and after everyone else's needs, real or perceived, were met."

Jill's three oldest daughters were in college too. The financial strain was enormous. Tuition for the four of them exceeded the family's annual income. Fortunately, they all qualified for scholarships, grants, or Guaranteed Student Loans.

Initially Jill's children were relieved when she decided to go to college. Seeing her name attacked in the press had upset them. Perhaps going to college would divert her from such activities. Relief quickly turned to alarm, however, when she decided to go to school full-time.

"The older girls—the ones in college—didn't see how I was going to handle it," Jill recalled. "They thought I was crazy. I had gone through a period when I was tired all the time, and now it would just get worse."

One daughter commented at the time: "At first, I felt cheated. It takes all the glory away from us being in college. This is my time. When we come home, she's supposed to say, 'How were your finals?' But we say that to her, or she says, 'Guess what I got on my final!' She's really proud of what she does, and we're really proud of her."

Ann, when she was a sophomore in high school, said, "She gets better grades than I do. I sometimes wonder where I got my brains. I don't do half as well. We've grown closer though. I talk to her more about my problems than I used to."

During her freshman year, Jill's husband said, "She's a superwoman. She's able to do the grocery shopping, do the books and the selling at the store, take care of the kids, and do the housework. If I had thought it was going to affect her negatively, I probably wouldn't have allowed her to go."

Jill and her two oldest daughters all graduated the same year on three successive weekends. Ralph and Jill had separated several months earlier. "I became an independent person. I started to like myself," Jill said.

"I had felt absolutely trapped in my marriage," she notes. "I suddenly realized I didn't have to be anymore. Prior to that time, I felt I might escape only if he died. I was Catholic; divorce was out of the question. The church later found grounds to annul my marriage of twenty-five years. I escaped from a situation that I honestly think would have destroyed me."

When Jill returned to school, her primary motivation had not been eventual employment. She simply sought the education she had always wanted. But slowly she realized that the degree, and the self-confidence it brought, were what she calls a "ticket to freedom."

The marriage was legally dissolved during Jill's first year of law school. While trying to collect her marital settlement, she worked 35 hours a week as a law clerk and attended school full-time. "There wasn't much time left for sleep," she commented.

Jill believes that Ralph and his family think that her return to school caused the marriage to end. She says he has tried to convince the children of this.

"My children are ambivalent about my having gone back to school," said Jill. "They're proud of me in one way; in another way, I don't think they are. They rarely tell anybody that I'm an attorney."

Jill survived law school. At age 48 she searched for a position with a law firm but was confronted by age discrimination: "Very often I was one of the last two candidates for a position, but I was not chosen. It would have been inconsistent with their hiring practices. As a beginning associate I was the age of most senior partners, who were actually beginning to think about retiring."

Eventually Jill was hired as an assistant attorney general for her state. Later, at age 50, she joined a private law practice, combining her work as a trial lawyer with a position as a special assistant attorney general.

In 1985 she married Parker, a widower with several grown children. He is a financial analyst and former educator. Jill and Parker respect and admire each other, both personally and professionally.

In 1987 Jill suffered a fragmented spinal disk rupture, which forced her to take a four-month leave from her law practice. She cut her 75-hour workweek to 30 hours and made her beautiful 100-acre farm her headquarters.

"That period allowed me to step back and look at the situation,"

Jill said. "Here I was, just a little over a year into a wonderful new marriage. Between us, we have ten children, five of whom are married. I have two grandchildren. Yet I was constantly stressed by my job. I was trying to be the perfect wife, mother, mistress, hostess, stepmother, grandmother, trial lawyer, everything. I spend a great deal of time with my clients; I'm determined not to be like some other lawyers. I take a number of cases on a pro bono basis to help women out of difficult situations, and I had been doing that off-hours."

Jill warns of the dangers of trying to be a superwoman. "When you project an image of superwoman, people expect you to be one. Once this monster is created, it's difficult to go back to being normal. It's normal to get discouraged, tired, and depressed. It's normal to need support and nurturing."

After a period of assessment, Jill says, "I decided that what was most important to me at this point in my life was to spend the remainder of it in a happy, productive, and healthy state. I wanted to look for a job that would allow me to devote time and attention to my marriage, my husband, my children, and this wonderful farm."

Jill and Parker decided to become partners in a new professional venture. They came to this idea independently and are thrilled to be able to join forces professionally.

Jill wants a balanced life. "I intend to age with a lot of grace and style. Part of being able to do this means setting goals for how I live my life."

In reflecting on the role that her education has played in changing her life, she commented: "It was tough going—financially and emotionally, but I'll never regret doing it. Going back to school got me where I want to be."

GETTING PAST THE INITIAL RESISTANCE

During her junior year at New York University in 1950, Shirley was trying to find time for a full-time job, a bachelor's degree program at night, and time with her fiancé. Instead, she dropped out of school and got married. Shirley worked and Justin went to law school.

Twenty-two years later, when Shirley decided to become a college student at age 42, she had the usual responsibilities that accompany being a wife and the mother of four children. However, child care was not a problem because the children, aged 9 through 15, were in school.

Shirley expected her family to support her decision. Education had always been a high priority. Justin and the children said her decision to go back to school was fine with them. However, like many other reentry students, Shirley quickly realized the difference between what her family said and what they thought.

"My husband was openly supportive," Shirley explained, "but in some respects, I felt sabotaged. He'd say, 'Let's go away for three or four days.' Terrific! When would you like to go? 'Oh, the end of the week.' I can't, I have school. 'Oh, you can skip a class.' It was like dangling a carrot in front of a donkey. I would love to go! Who wouldn't like four days in 'El Dorado' as opposed to sitting in a stuffy classroom? It was insidious."

Shirley's and Justin's marriage had been traditional. She helped put him through law school by working as an airline receptionist. Once the children came along, she combined full-time parenting with volunteer work for Recording for the Blind and as a braillist.

When the children started school, Shirley worked part-time for a travel agency but arranged her hours around her children's schedules. Living in a suburb of New York City meant lots of car pooling and coordinating the children's after-school activities. Justin's work required travel; Shirley felt doubly responsible for the children.

Shirley said, "I loved being home with my children, but stagnation is almost unavoidable without enormous self-discipline and very specific talents. I felt I had stopped growing."

Shirley decided to take a few classes. Five years later she had earned a master's degree in social work from Adelphi University. Her commitment to an academic program and her plans for a career shifted her focus away from the family. Shirley believes that Justin felt threatened by her desire to chart her own path. Justin commented: "Maybe neglected or inconvenienced but not threatened."

Shirley was quick to add, however, that if school had not triggered a period of strain on the relationship, it would have happened at some other time with a different set of circumstances. "Most marriages go through trials and tribulations based on one thing or another. It may have been the perfect time for a mid-life crisis, but it never reached the crisis stage."

She continued, "We went through a very bad time while I was in school. I think my new assertiveness was the trigger. I don't think Justin felt neglected, but I think he felt threatened by my ability to function outside the sphere we had created together. We came as close to dissolving our household and relationship as we have ever come. But we waited for the tide to turn.

"Now," she says, "our relationship is better. While we both have learned that I am an individual, we don't want to break what connects us. Maybe our relationship benefited because there was less reason to take me for granted. I think that's what I needed at the time. And it has carried over."

Shirley's need to demonstrate her autonomy has lessened over the years. Establishing and maintaining perspectives and interests beyond the family was critical to her own growth and her relationship with Justin. "Once Justin realized I wasn't going to 'burn the bra,' he settled down.

"Before I went back to school," she commented, "I wouldn't say much about things that bothered me. I simply would not see them. Now, I can say, 'Hey, I'm upset when you do that or say that.' Nobody gets wiped out. Conflicts come up that wouldn't have before. As a result, there are no more hidden agendas."

Reflecting back upon Shirley's school years, Justin said, "If I had it to do over again, I would be more helpful. I don't think I was. I pursued my career without regard to Shirley's problems. I would do more at home."

Shirley has a great sense of humor and considers it crucial to success. Any formerly fastidious housewife will smile at her description of dropping her superwoman role: "Once I became committed to school, the floor no longer said, 'Gee, I feel so nice and clean, thank you.' It didn't matter; no one ate off it. If the kids didn't clean their rooms, I just condemned their space and closed the door."

Shirley went to school full-time when her eldest daughter did. The next two girls were in high school. The youngest child, Peter, a junior in high school, was the most dependent on his mother. Shirley quipped, "When I was doing my field placement with the probation department, I got a few whispered phone calls from my son: 'Where does a child go to report neglect?'"

Shirley's newfound assertiveness affected her relationship with the children. She would no longer tolerate incessant bickering: "I would tell them 'I quit!' and then go out for a walk. Miraculously, the kitchen would be spotless or the dishes would be done by the time I got back. They would be speaking to each other in civil tones."

Peter at 15 commented, "Before she went to school, she would just clean up after us, go shopping, and do the laundry. Now, she's helping other people. I'm proud of her. A lot of my friends' mothers just sit around and do nothing."

Justin and Shirley had always stressed the importance of education. Their four children have all gone on to college. Two daughters have master's degrees in social work, the third is a registered nurse, and Peter is in a graduate program leading to a law degree and a master's degree in business.

At age 57 Shirley shows no signs of slowing down. She and two other women opened their own travel agency in 1986. She also runs a bereavement group at a family service center. When asked how she divides her time between the travel agency and social work, she replied, "About 110 percent on the agency and 40 percent on social work."

Justin is more enthusiastic about Shirley's social work than about her travel agency job. "It takes too many hours," he commented. "I resent that. It puts too much of a strain on her. Through the bereavement work, she contributes more to society."

Shirley, however, feels her work is balanced. She enjoys her current life-style, her work, and the pace she has set.

PERSONAL GROWTH, MARITAL STRAIN

Lydia was 40 when she received her master's degree in fine arts in 1978. Her marriage was four years away from the breaking point.

"I had decided the degree was something I absolutely needed; if it cost me the relationship, I was willing to pay the price. I decided to finish school and pick up the pieces later," she explained several months after graduating.

"There were a lot of pieces to pick up. Had I stopped to work out the relationship, I never would have been able to keep going to school. I don't regret this very painful and costly decision."

Lydia's odyssey during her decade of tremendous loss and subsequent growth led to a faculty position she describes as "more perfect than anything I fantasized." The job has provided a safe harbor in which to cope with the end of her twenty-two-year marriage and the discovery that she had an alcohol problem.

In 1974 Lydia wanted to get her M.F.A. as quickly as possible because she felt she had been "on hold" professionally since she and Anthony got married in 1961. Anthony reasoned that if Lydia took the degree in three years instead of two, their family of four would not be thrown so badly out of kilter.

Lydia had been combining parenting with teaching painting, drawing, and art history part-time at the college level. However, these positions were becoming more scarce in the communities near their home.

Lydia also wanted more intense involvement with her art. The M.F.A. program would qualify her for permanent employment and place her in an environment where she could truly focus on her painting.

Lydia felt a desperate need to catch up. She had stopped painting from 1969 to 1973 while Anthony, a university professor, was completing his Ph.D. She assumed all family responsibilities so that he could work on his book, which she typed and edited.

"It would have been very easy for me to just help my husband, help my children, help everybody. Going back to school meant I wasn't going to do that. I was going to earn money and pay somebody to clean the house while I developed my career. I wanted to avoid a depressing pattern I could see developing in my life."

Lydia believed time was running out for her to have a career as a teacher and an artist. She had spent more than a decade ministering to her family's needs. It was her turn now, and she approached school with anger and frustration.

In 1978 Anthony perceived Lydia's single-mindedness as rejection. "She was so strident, determined, and uncompromising. She was living in a world that had nothing to do with a relationship with me." He saw her spending every spare minute on her artwork. She was greatly upset by any interruptions.

After five years away from the marriage, Lydia explained her sense of urgency. "If the marriage collapsed, I wanted to be able to support myself at a level that would allow me to paint."

Lydia hoped her student role would make Anthony take her artwork more seriously. "Prior to my returning to school, my husband thought of my painting as self-indulgent, but he understood the necessity to work hard in school. Once I was in school, he saw my painting as a professional, important activity. He supported it. That made an enormous difference in the amount of time and energy I could devote to it.

"As I began to grow professionally, he began to feel threatened. I think it violated his ideas of what the proper role of a woman should be in a marriage. He felt neglected. Our marriage didn't survive the stress. I'm not sure it would have survived in any case."

Lydia's and Anthony's sons were 9 and 12 when she went back to school. Although she was less available to them, she believes the tension between their parents bothered them much more than having a mother in school. "They were aware of the strain and troubled by it. Both of them now realize that their father and I were incompatible."

The boys were supportive of Lydia's artwork. "I don't think my being in school affected them so negatively that it outweighed their sense that it was a good thing for me to do."

Today Lydia's anger and frustration are gone. Reflection and self-discovery have paved the way to a new understanding. "There would be times when I would feel like my head would burst from the conflict. I felt sad and somewhat guilty about having neglected my husband. If I had it to do over again, I would try to be wiser."

Lydia was terrified that finishing graduate school would mean being trapped back in the house again. After graduating she devoted herself to helping a friend build a kiln. Now she believes that was a big mistake.

"The family had been waiting for me to finish school, come back home, and make cookies. I didn't do that, and I really regret it. I think I could and should have been more sensitive to the strain I caused them."

Today, Lydia's professional life is very comfortable. She is on a two-year leave of absence from a private art school where she teaches painting and drawing to be visiting artist at a prestigious liberal arts college. She has plenty of time left over for her own work, and for a new relationship. She said recently, "I never imagined there would be a place this exciting and satisfying."

At age 50, she is focusing more on her personal life: "It's important for me to develop myself as a painter, but I'm also working hard at being able to live as a balanced and contented person. Now the very simple things about living are the things that concern me: taking care of myself and enjoying the days as they unfold without needing them to be more or other than they are."

Graduate school made Lydia highly employable. She took a new look at herself. "Being honest with myself is what allowed me to discover that I was addicted to alcohol. From there, I could begin to recover."

Lydia now believes that during the years she was married she was probably incapable of having a good relationship. She explains, "Until I found myself by doing my work and doing it well, I was out of balance. I had such low self-esteem, I don't think I could have had a good relationship with anybody.

"I am living with more integrity now. My husband is happily remarried. We're all closer to the things that were true to us. Now I'm living the life I was supposed to live. I don't think I knew who I was."

In some recent correspondence, Lydia commented: "My single-mindedness and determination led to tremendous suffering. But now that some years have passed and I am beginning to feel comfortable alone, the necessity of having done what I did is clear."

Lydia hopes to maintain steady and consistent professional growth. "I hope to continue to become more wise, mature, and evolved," she added. "That's what I'm working on. A person's need to grow must be put first. Find out who you are and what you have to give. That's what your life is for."

TRADE-OFFS AND COMPROMISES: PART-TIME REENTRY

In May 1987, at age 44, Helen received her A.A. degree in humanities from a local community college. It took her ten years.

Helen had chosen an uncomfortable, sporadic reentry route full of the trade-offs and compromises of trying to follow her own course while maintaining a family relationship.

"I was tired of being the housewife, chauffeur, dishwasher, babysitter, and everything associated with being a homebody. I felt my mind was on the level of a 6-year-old.

"I got tired of hearing about what color my neighbors were going to paint their bathrooms and what wallpaper they were going to use in their hallway. I felt I was down the drain mentally. I wanted to do something productive, even without knowing what my goals were. Maybe I just wanted to get an education and prove to myself that I could do it."

Helen and her husband, Jim, had many arguments because she returned to school. "There have been trials and tribulations," she said in a recent interview, "yelling and screaming about what's more important: family, house, school, the girls, what? It goes back to the old-time Southern upbringing we both had: The wife's responsibility is to everyone except herself.

"There've been times I've wanted to walk out the door," she said, "but couldn't financially. Maybe I'm thinking this college degree and the opportunities it will offer me may let me walk out."

Jim, right from the start, had very definite ideas about how Helen should approach education. "I wish she'd find a general direction in which to head. I guess that's the one thing she finds hard to understand," he said. Jim holds a master's degree in mechanical engineering. His own educational experience was straightforward: he identified a major and headed straight through.

Helen says Jim was encouraging at times. When she began her studies, he said, "You need to encourage your wife. She has the chance to think about something other than being a mother and a wife. It's a chance to become self-reliant, happier, more well-rounded."

Helen knew her husband wanted her to develop clear-cut goals. However, in order to develop her confidence she felt she should take the classes that interested her—art, history, photography, design.

"I feel a lot of pressure from him," she said after her first semester. "He keeps asking me, 'What do you want to do? What goal do you see? What kind of degree do you want?' I still don't know. It's like looking down a tunnel and seeing rails going off in different directions. I'd like to do a hundred different things. I still lack the confidence to choose a major and get a degree by a certain date. I don't know if figuring out what you want to do takes time or hits you like a thunderbolt."

Helen wouldn't be pushed into identifying goals. Twenty years earlier her parents had insisted that she take a secretarial course instead of home economics. When Helen protested, her parents gave her no choice. She took the secretarial classes for a year so she could live away from home. This time she wanted things to be different.

As a secretary, Helen had helped finance her husband's education. Even so, she did not want to be financially dependent on him for her education. "I did not like asking my husband continuously for money for my books and classes. I wanted to feel somewhat independent with my own bankroll." She wanted to be able to provide extras for her two daughters, who were 15 and 23, without having to ask Jim.

Consequently, during her second year of studies, Helen decided to get a part-time job to cover school and other expenses. Working part-time and going to school part-time was difficult. She became a bank teller full-time, taking one night class each semester.

Helen was recently promoted to a management position at the bank and now earns $20,000 a year. Although she welcomed the salary increase, she doesn't want a career in banking. Helen dreams of starting her own business. She wants a B.A. in business and management and hopes to set up a photography or design studio.

"It's going to take a lot of hustle," she said, "but I want to be independent for myself and for my children. I don't want to have to ask my husband, 'Do you have the money?'"

When Helen graduated in May 1987, she shared the stage with her oldest daughter, Lynn, who was getting her second associate degree. They held a joint victory bash.

Lynn was 14 when her mother went back to school. Her feelings about Helen's student role evolved over the years. In 1977 she said of her mother, "She still has responsibilities at home. I'm doing all the housework. She's not paying as much attention to me as she did."

Helen admitted at the time, "I've put more pressure on my two girls to do more for me. At times, I feel this isn't fair to them. If I'm studying and the potatoes need to be put in the oven, I will insist that they help."

Now, however, Helen is sure her daughters are proud of her. The youngest, Katie, who was 15 when her mom graduated, has given Helen some academic pointers. "She's helped me with a literature course I've been taking," Helen said. "I had been thoroughly lost. She had just had it in high school. I know she's proud. I've heard her talking to friends about me being in school."

Lynn, 23 when Helen graduated, feels very close to her mother. "She understands my generation better. She's grown, and she's closer to me because she's been in school with kids my age. Our relationship has gotten better since she returned to school," she said recently.

Lynn wishes her mother could go right on for more schooling. "Instead of worrying about us, Mom should continue to a four-year college. She's really smart, and I'm really proud of her. . . . She has so much to teach everybody, and there's so much to learn out there for everyone."

Helen agrees that she would like to be able to attend the university full-time, and she is investigating scholarships that might make this possible. "Going back to school," she concludes, "has been the highlight of my life during the past ten years."

AFTER SOME ADJUSTMENTS, AN IMPROVED RELATIONSHIP

When Louise decided to pursue a college degree, it meant altering an unspoken contract between herself and her husband of fifteen years. Clarence was the wage earner, and she was in charge of the five children and the house.

Louise's five years as an undergraduate and subsequent fifteen years as an eighth-grade teacher changed the couple's roles. "I became more of a partner and less of the protected person," she commented. "There had to be a big shift in his attitude and mine."

Louise's family was not entirely happy when, at age 42, she enrolled at the University of Rhode Island. She said, "It was difficult for my husband to adjust to the fact; I had an outside interest that became totally time-consuming. It was hard for him; he missed the attention.

"My family, my husband in particular, expected everything to run beautifully at home and the meals to be the same. That was a problem. The children still expect you to go to their games and help out as you always have, even though you're studying for an exam. They know you can't do everything, but emotionally they want you there."

When Louise went back to school, the five children ranged in age from 7 (twins) to 13. Although she had less time to devote to homemaking, she and the children developed a very close bond at that time.

"We always studied together. They'd hear my questions before tests; I'd hear theirs. It brought us together. I understood more, having gone through the same ordeal they did."

Being responsible for five children and college meant that Louise had to budget her time wisely. "I studied French while ironing and stirred the soup while memorizing."

Clarence, an insurance agent, commented ten years ago, "The college degree is one of the best types of insurance for Louise. No matter what happens to me, she'll be able to do for herself. Think of a lifetime—five years out of it is a small price to pay for all the benefits our family has reaped from her degree and career."

Even though Clarence subsequently balked at the amount of time Louise spent on her studies, the lines of communication stayed open. "We successfully fought it out," she said. "We were both willing to make adjustments. Housework and money were our big issues, not whether we loved or trusted each other."

Working it out is a high priority for this family and their friends. "None of our friends are divorced," said Louise, "and all of our children married people whose parents are still together."

"I had a lot of qualms when Louise went back to school," Clarence recalled. "It would change our life-style. We couldn't entertain or do things together that husbands and wives usually do because she had to devote time to her studies and her work. It took a lot of effort on both our parts. Marital relations took a definite back seat! There was constant preparation for classes, which cut into her time as a companion to me."

In addition, he noted, "People think that schoolteachers work a 6-hour day, but that's a myth. English teachers have to prepare; she was on a 12- to 14-hour day."

Clarence and Louise became a household with two wage earners in 1970; both were actively involved in their careers. Clarence had always put a lot of time into his job, often six days a week and many evening hours. Once Louise started college, she stopped complaining about his never being at home.

Two years after Louise started teaching, she enrolled in a master's degree program at Rhode Island College. She took evening and summer classes and graduated in 1974. All five of the children have graduated from college; two are now getting M.B.A. degrees.

Clarence is the only family member without a college degree, but he is not self-conscious about it, according to Louise. He enjoys his work, is very successful in business, and has many outside interests.

"He seemed to find me more interesting as I delved into my own career and hobbies," Louise said. "Clarence is a very secure person. Going back to school, having a job I liked, and becoming more independent improved our relationship. We both had to change a lot, but we became more companionable."

Clarence saw their children benefiting from Louise's efforts. Her extra income helped finance five college educations. "It's given the children incentive and motivation to do well in school. They help one another. If Louise had not gone to school, the children would have missed out on a wonderful example of self-discipline; they might not have finished their degrees."

Victoria, second eldest, said recently, at 34, "She was getting almost all A's in her courses, running a household with the help of five teenagers, and was still sane. We all learned a big lesson from this driven woman: anything is possible if you put your mind to it. Of course, we could never bring home bad report cards. She would retort, 'If I can run this house and get A's, then the least you can do is to get good grades.' What could we possibly say to that?"

Victoria feels her mother redirected her life by going back to school. "She could have lived a narrow existence, which would have made her nuts. College gave her a chance to stretch, to mix with

Degrees of Success

people of all ages. My mother came out of herself more. She has a broader base of interest and renewed self-confidence."

In 1986, Louise retired from teaching at the age of 63. She's spending her leisure time enjoying life and her grandchildren, relaxed and pleased about what she was able to accomplish so late in life.

CHAPTER 4
NEVER TOO OLD

If coasting is what you think of when you imagine the "retirement years," the stories in this chapter should shake a few stereotypes.

Lee plans to work until she's 85 or 90. Diana graduated from college at the age of 70 and became a therapist. Ruth got her first full-time job at the age of 61.

These women were actively involved in a college degree program at an age when most people begin to think about retiring. Returning to school was *not* second nature to them, either; like most people their age, they hadn't seen the inside of a classroom for at least a quarter of a century!

There are a variety of reasons why people over 50 are redirecting their lives by returning to school. Gloria felt frustrated and undervalued in her volunteer work. Ruth's children had left home, and school helped her figure out what to do next. Lee, already working as a therapist, needed a master's degree in order to get a license to practice.

The years on campus helped Abigail to deal with the challenges of raising a developmentally disabled son. Diana was lonely after moving from one end of the country to the other; at 59, she wanted to finish the degree program she had dropped thirty-seven years earlier.

All of these women, except for Abigail, were preparing for employment. Is this unrealistic when you are closing in on your 60s? According to Carolyn Bird in "The Shape of Work to Come" (*Modern Maturity*, June-July 1987), futurists predict "a chronic shortage of workers for labor-intensive new jobs in teaching, training, coaching, healing, counseling, communicating, comforting, and creating." Gloria, Diana, Lee, and Ruth were preparing to work or already working in precisely such jobs.

Another frequently mentioned motivation for a return to school among middle-aged women is a desire for the ability to be self-supporting. Several women in this chapter speak candidly about the importance of being able to stand on one's own two feet in preparation for such eventualities as widowhood or divorce.

Frequently, the older students on a college campus are extremely worried that they will flunk out and/or stick out like a sore thumb. The grades of the women featured here ranged between an A and a B. Lee and Diana suggest that as long as the reentry student doesn't make an issue of her age, no one else will either. Friendship with younger students is a fringe benefit of academic reentry. Being around college students of the traditional age can also provide insight into the development and pressures of one's own children.

The youngest person in this chapter is now 65 years old. All five are active and in excellent health. Stagnation is nowhere in sight. Gloria and her grandson recently went cross-country skiing in Lapland. Ruth is auditing courses in political science and anthropology. Lee has just joined the Peace Corps.

For women over the age of 50, going back to school is an opportunity to learn new skills, confront new challenges, and gain a new perspective on life.

SHE WAS GOING TO WORK; HE WAS RETIRING

Gloria, at 50, was back in school to gather credentials for paid employment. Her husband, Ned, at 62 was a company president two years away from retirement. The potential for conflict was great.

At that time, Ned felt, "One thing you look for in a marriage is companionship. You dream about taking off and doing what you want. I thought Gloria's employment might interfere with a few of those dreams. She had had her fill of volunteer work, licking envelopes while someone less qualified was getting the money and responsibility. I just wish she had done it earlier so we could have retired together."

Gloria had become very frustrated with her status as a volunteer counselor for a family planning agency. "I had some strong feelings about the importance of this counseling. I wanted to learn a lot more about it, and I wanted to be paid. Why aren't volunteers paid to be trained, at least given some expense money, a token?

"A group of us at the family planning agency resented being in our own little class of stereotypes. Somehow you aren't expected to be as dependable or capable as paid personnel. Pregnancy counseling takes responsibility and sensitivity, and we felt recognition was due in the form of a paycheck. In order to get a paying job doing the kind of counseling I wanted to do, I needed a master's degree."

Both Gloria and Ned recognized that her student role would run counter to his expectations for their marriage. Ned's mother had had to go to work, and working mothers in his childhood had symbolized a family in which the husband could not adequately provide.

"Ned grew up as a macho kind of person," Gloria comments. "I can remember his mother telling me, and my mother telling me, that it was really bad for me to go off overnight to a League of Women Voters convention."

Despite these potential points of stress, and even though marital relationships often falter during significant changes—like going back to school—this couple feels theirs improved. Enrolling in the master's program helped the malaise that Gloria attributed to her life-style. "I had this vague feeling that everything would collapse with the nest empty," she said. "I wonder if we would still be married if I had remained a frustrated housewife. I used to keep so many things bottled up. My husband probably thought I was a little bit crazy, but I think he respected my interest and decision.

"Ned and I can put our finger on what kept us together: we have always been fairly independent. We've always given each other a lot of space. I suppose I never would have gone back to school at age 50 if I didn't feel comfortable going off by myself. I give Ned a lot of credit for putting up with what he has put up with. I'm no longer the girl he married. I think he's proud of me."

Trust has been ever present in their marriage of thirty-eight years. "In spite of unsettling words or behavior, we each believed the other meant well," Gloria explained.

Gloria had earned her bachelor's degree nearly thirty years earlier. She was petrified about entering the master's program at Kent State University. "I was scared my brain cells had rotted, that I wasn't capable, that I wouldn't even ask the right questions. I was scared to death. My knees trembled going up the stairs to my interview. Why would they want me in their program? Could I do it?

"There was a horrendous registration process involving four different buildings and many hours. I went to the first three classes, drove home, and panicked. I didn't sleep all night! I thought, 'What have I gotten myself into? I can't possibly do this.'

"In the middle of the night I decided to drop two of my three courses. The next Wednesday, I went to the one remaining class and ran into a graduate student in her late 20s. She said: 'Come on! You can do it! Take two classes.' She bolstered me. As soon as I got the first midterm and paper back, I knew I could handle it."

Gloria and Ned have five children, now 27 through 36. When Gloria became a reentry student, two sons were still at home, one in junior high and the other in high school. An unexpected fringe benefit of Gloria's student role was that the relationship between parents and sons improved.

Gloria was glad to get away. "I was a little tired of adolescents," she explained. "The boys were giving me the message that going back to school was a dumb idea," Gloria said. "They probably thought I couldn't be a good counselor if I didn't take care of them the way they thought best. Believe me, I enjoyed missing dinner with them two nights a week!"

Ned was left in charge of the boys, and he got to know them better. "I had a new role—having to listen." The couple's three daughters were particularly enthusiastic about their mother's return to school. They told all their friends about their mom, the student. "They thought it was cool," Gloria recalled.

Gloria identifies the pluses that resulted from her return to school: becoming more assertive, self-confident, and better able to communicate, to mention just a few. "Perhaps I was too outspoken at times," she said. "But I've also learned to listen, accept criticism, and try to understand rather than be threatened or embarrassed."

Gloria's grade point average was between a B+ and an A–. She took two extra courses so that her master's degree in education had a double emphasis—rehabilitation counseling and college counseling.

Before she received her degree, Gloria was offered a job as a university career counselor. Her dream had come true—she had a part-time job with summers off, allowing plenty of time for vacations with Ned. She stayed with the university for two years. Then she was offered a part-time position as a community organizer at a free clinic.

In 1978, at age 55, Gloria retired so she could spend more time with Ned. Together they enjoyed travel, tennis, and sailing. Gloria labeled and distributed family photographs to their children; she sorted out a very cluttered attic.

Soon, however, Gloria found herself taking a professional interest in the aging process. One of her daughters, a professor at the University of Michigan, told her about the university's Institute of Gerontology and encouraged her to enter its graduate certification program.

In 1980, at age 57, Gloria, who lived in Ohio, enrolled in a graduate program in Michigan. "You take a class for a week, come home, and write papers until you're blue in the face," she said. "I almost threw in the towel a couple of times because the courses were so hard." She managed to arrange the required field placement at her local county's Council on Aging.

For two years her life was a far cry from retirement. Gloria worked part-time as a counselor for older adults at a nearby community college. She also created reminiscing groups through the Council on Aging and co-facilitated seminars for adults with elderly parents. As part of her internship, she helped develop a plan for installing life-emergency response systems for frail elderly people living alone. She completed the course work for certification in 1981.

"One needs to keep the elements of one's life in a comfortable, meaningful, and sensible balance," Gloria commented as she began to feel a shift in focus. "I'm now feeling a strong pull toward spending time with my husband, who is 76," she explained in 1986. "I'm also helping out with and enjoying the dual-career households of my kids and their kids. I'm interested in my grandchildren, and they are all over the country. I want to be supportive and available. It's a stage I'm in now that I wasn't in ten years ago."

Currently, Gloria serves on the boards of directors of the Council on Aging and the Association of Specialists in Aging. She is also president of her area's Family Planning Association board, the same agency at which she volunteered before returning to school in 1973. She continues to do workshops and speaking engagements, mostly as a volunteer.

Gloria acknowledges that she has come full circle from her volunteer days. However, her perspective has changed dramatically. "I've become a different type of volunteer. Now I'm volunteering as a professional.

"Being able to earn money was important to me originally. I didn't need it to put bread on the table but to prove I could do it. I don't feel that need anymore. Now I choose to volunteer my services.

"My goals are essentially the same. I like learning and new experiences. Ned and I are taking computer courses at the community college, trying to figure out our computer. I like being out and around in the community, and I want to do a little something to make the world a better place.

"I think about my husband, what we do together, our relationship with our kids and grandchildren, and my professional volunteering. I like the balance right now. I look forward to getting older and feel kind of toughened up for the inevitable losses and adjustments we face as we age.

"I spent my first Social Security checks taking my eldest grandson, age 11, cross-country skiing in Lapland," she reported recently.

In order to increase their mobility and independence, the couple is about to trade their home of more than thirty years for an apartment. They are contemplating a move from Ohio to Wisconsin, where they'll be centrally located for all their children and grandchildren.

ENJOYING WORKING FULL-TIME AT AGE 68

The past ten years have not been idle ones for Lee. She was divorced, earned a master's degree in social work, relocated, launched her career, and became self-supporting.

Lee was admitted to a master's degree program in social work administration in September 1976. She and her husband separated four months later. She was 57 years old at the time. The end of this marriage was the end of a working relationship: she and Robert were partners in a therapy practice.

"Going back to school may have been my way of separating myself from my husband," Lee said. "We lived and worked together. My becoming a student was the straw that broke the camel's back.

"There was a lot of competition set up between my husband and me. We were already having a lot of difficulty in our marriage. School either gave an excuse for a divorce or hastened it. I think it would have happened anyway."

The couple's five children, now ranging in age from 24 to 38, were very enthusiastic and supportive of their mother's plans to go back to school. While Lee was in school, her daughter, Margot, told her that there was no one she felt closer to, nothing she couldn't tell her mother. Margot was also planning to return to school. "The older ones say that, because I have done it, they can do it too," Lee said.

"When I graduated, all five of them were there. It was a delight," she recalled. Staying in close touch with her children is one of Lee's top priorities and greatest pleasures. She was present for the births of her three grandchildren—right in the delivery room for the third.

Lee was a well-established, full-time therapist before returning to school. However, in 1977 her state put into effect a new requirement that all therapists be licensed and hold a master's degree.

Initially, Lee found it quite difficult at 57 to be one of the oldest students in the program. "I thought there would be a big difference between the other students and me," she explains. "I wondered how I would be accepted."

Lee and her younger colleagues would meet for lunch or drinks. "Age barriers were soon erased," she said. "I was accepted by my classmates. It was super. If you're worried about being older, just 'be yourself.'" Three of Lee's friends decided to go back to school after their involvement with her reentry.

The faculty and administration of the master's degree program at the university understood the needs of older students. Lee was assigned a special adviser who was very accessible, supportive, and encouraging. She was also involved with a women's group that met once a month.

For a while after her separation, the financial aspect of her master's program was a concern for Lee. However, she took out loans and did some part-time work. Knowing that she would be employed full-time after graduation, Lee felt she would be able to repay the loans without too much trouble.

Lee hadn't been in a classroom for thirty years and found it quite difficult at first to set a clear-cut time for study. She developed a system of incentives and rewards for herself. She would plan something special each day—a walk, a cup of coffee with a friend, watching a favorite television program. It helped her achieve a B+ average.

Before she went back to school, Lee was very apprehensive about driving on her city's congested downtown streets. But while she was in school she said, "If someone had asked me a year ago if I wanted to work downtown, I would have said no. I thought people who worked downtown were crazy. Now I drive downtown three days a week."

Lee graduated when she was 60. The most appealing job opportunities turned up at the other end of the state. So the same woman who was apprehensive about driving in traffic picked up her life and relocated. She also drove nearly 300 miles once a month to participate in a Gestalt training program. Her work as a pastoral counselor at a hospital and as a counselor for an employment assistance program was very satisfying. She was able to be self-supporting, earning $30,000 a year.

In 1988, Lee traded Ohio for the Marshall Islands. She has joined the Peace Corps and recently celebrated her seventieth birthday on an atoll in the western Pacific Ocean.

"I don't ever want to stop working," she says. "I'm not kidding. I'd like to work until I'm at least 85 or 90. I'm excited and filled with wonder. As a young girl I wanted to be a missionary. This is as close to that as I can come—a dream come true. A new chapter is beginning."

RESPITE FROM THE CHALLENGES OF RAISING A DEVELOPMENTALLY DISABLED SON

Abigail returned to school at age 45, just a few months after discovering that her newborn son, Roger, was severely developmentally disabled. Being on campus, with the full support of her husband and older children, turned out to be her mainstay as she confronted the special education system throughout the years.

Abigail had always wanted to complete her bachelor's degree. She spent a year and a half in college right after high school, dropped out to join the women's army in 1942, and served as a radio operator on a cargo plane.

When Abigail returned to school twenty-two years later, her husband was in the air force. She started with night courses on an air force base nearby, then took a few classes during the summer, and finally switched to Northern Michigan University.

Abigail describes what it was like to be a middle-aged woman on a college campus in the '60s. "Everyone automatically thought I was a member of the faculty. They'd open doors for me and stand back when I entered elevators. The professors were, for the most part, caught up in the 1960s and tried to be avant-garde in their thinking. I think they looked down a little bit on an older woman, a mother of five, especially one who had been a housewife all her life."

Abigail had planned to become a special education teacher. However, she soon decided that working with developmentally disabled children all day long in addition to caring for her son was not the right choice for her. "School provided something completely different to think about besides my son," she explained.

When the family moved to Arkansas in 1974, Abigail and her daughter Amanda began taking classes at the state university. "At first, I tried taking some courses with Amanda. But she wanted to reverse the roles and play mama to me. She tried to help me too much. I finally decided that it wasn't a good idea for us to be in the same classes. I got into the English department to get away from being Amanda's mama."

Abigail's second youngest, Janice, was a senior in high school while Abigail was a college student. She was very proud of her mother. "I was a great conversation piece," Abigail said. "Mothers get into the habit of pontificating. It was good for me to learn to sit and listen quietly, to have to consider other people's ideas.

"College kids in the '70s were very relaxed around me," Abigail recalled. "I enjoyed watching them and comparing them to my children. I glimpsed the pressure they were under."

She and her children had something in common. "I too felt pressure to excel," she said. "It's surprising how much your children can help you! I tend to be terrible with spelling and grammar, but my kids were great proofreaders."

Abigail believes that she sometimes overextended herself by carrying too heavy a course load. Occasionally, the balance between family life and school tilted. Then, she says, "My nerves were worn and my judgment wasn't always very good. My self-control wasn't as strong as it would have been if I had been better rested. You need to be realistic about what you can do—and how long it may take." And indeed, it took her nearly fifteen years to get her B.A. in English.

As Abigail felt better about being a student, things went more smoothly at home. "I was much more relaxed," she said, "with a better sense of humor." Her self-confidence improved dramatically, and she believes this made her much better able to deal with the problems and challenges of raising a disabled child. She became more assertive, less fearful of the roadblocks set in her path.

Abigail was determined to find good special education programs for her son. "I don't think I could have survived the pressures I was under if it hadn't been for the university," she recalled. "It was a beautiful escape from the painful realities I was facing in the outside world." In addition, she established close relationships with several professors with whom she could discuss the options open to her son.

Abigail says school also taught her to lighten up. "I learned to take myself more in stride. This was very constructive. I learned to take the world and myself a little less seriously. I had a streak of puritanism that made me think you had to do something significant in order to make life worthwhile. I don't feel that way anymore. Now I feel life is wonderful and is to be enjoyed."

With these new insights, Abigail eventually stopped battling the special education system, and she felt liberated. "I finally decided I wasn't going to be a force in changing the special education system. I took all the letters of protest, all the literature, and everything else I had accumulated out to the incinerator and burned it all. It was a rite of passage, and the end of something very painful."

In 1980, at age 61, Abigail graduated with a bachelor's degree in English. Three years later her husband died, and she returned to northern Michigan to be near two of her daughters. Now 68, she is thinking about getting a bachelor's degree in history during the summers. Her daughter Leah is a teacher and has offered to care for her brother so Abigail can live in the dorm.

Abigail took a few journalism courses while she was earning her bachelor's degree. She would like to write for publication. She said, "It's always a dream in the back of my mind. Perhaps I could do it if I had the time to concentrate in the dorm by myself."

Her return to school may or may not happen this summer, but, as Abigail said, "There are other summers. Life never comes to an end until it comes to an end. I intend to live to be 100, so there's lots of time yet."

AFTER THE CHILDREN HAVE GROWN: WHAT TO DO NEXT

Ruth's decision to go to college at age 54 was a part of her slow-simmering mid-life crisis. She had spent almost all of her adult life as a mother and housewife. The youngest of her three daughters was soon to leave home. The nest would be empty.

Ruth graduated from high school in 1935. "No one expected me to go further," she explained. "I wanted to get married, be a wife and mother, and be taken care of the rest of my life. I had no career ambition—it never even crossed my mind."

"Thirty-seven years after I graduated from high school, the last of my children was about to leave home, and I knew I would lose my major role. I would be out of a job. I had no training or skills except as a housewife. A person is defined in our society by what he or she does, so I had to find something to do. I felt useless, tense, anxious, desperate, and depressed."

Ruth's eldest daughter, Marissa, in her late 20s at the time, was involved with the women's liberation movement. She recommended certain reading to her mother, and the two had many discussions about life's crossroads.

Ruth joined a consciousness-raising group, where she met other women who were dealing with the same sorts of issues. Realizing that she was not alone was a relief. "There was nothing terribly wrong with me. I realized that most women of my generation had not been encouraged or expected to develop their potential as individuals."

When Ruth decided to earn a bachelor's degree and find a job, she had the support of her husband and daughters. Ruth was altering the life-style she and her husband, Joe, had adopted. Yet, Joe was exuberant about her plans. Like Ruth, he credited the women's movement with providing impetus and support.

As he said, "The women's movement helped her see she was not stupid or alone in having felt that way. When she realized it was culturally instilled, not true, she changed. It changed both of us and was the best education I've had in my life."

Ruth feels that her relationship with her children improved during her college experience. She commented just before her graduation, "We relate much better now. My daughters aren't my total concern since I've begun to develop myself. They are proud of me and happy for me."

Marissa is a second-generation reentry student. At 34 she received her master's degree in social work just as her mother received her B.A. (Marissa's story appears in Chapter 14.)

Marissa says her mother was her role model. She commented recently, "My mother tackled her fears rather than being paralyzed by them. Through watching her and interacting with her, I felt as if some limits were lifted off me as well. If my mother could go to college, then I could do things that were scary for me."

Nina, the youngest daughter, is back in school studying to be a court reporter like her middle sister, Aliza. Still a teenager when her mother began taking courses, Nina recalled, "I was glad she was keeping busy and off my back! I wish she had done it sooner because it was so good for her. She was very unhappy before that, and school helped her feel better."

Ruth began her college education by taking one course at a time, then two. As her confidence in her academic abilities returned, she decided to take a full-time program. She signed up for a degree in early childhood education because she believed that dramatic changes were necessary in the way that young children were being educated—especially in terms of sex role conditioning and racism.

Initially Ruth was very concerned about how she would do academically. It had been nearly 40 years since she had been inside a classroom. "I had no confidence," she remembers, "that I would be able to do it. I didn't know if I would be able to concentrate. I worried that I wasn't smart enough."

Ruth graduated at age 60 with high honors. Commenting on her personal growth, Joe said, "She has fulfilled a lifelong ambition. Ruth has always been extremely capable, but she never believed it. Now she no longer feels any difference in intellect at social gatherings. She speaks out, is much more assertive—a pleasure to be with."

When Joe was asked about any negative effects, he laughed. "The all-consuming business of keeping a house as neat as a pin, always having a meal ready on time . . . good grief, why these things were ever considered important, I will never know. They were, I suppose, for lack of anything else. Now Ruth is thinking about the kinds of contributions she might be able to make over the years. I can't think of any negative effects on our family."

While Ruth was in school, her career focus changed. She realized that, for her, working with small children might be too physically and emotionally draining. She transferred to a human services program and took her bachelor's degree in social work.

Ruth wanted to work part-time, but she was unable to find a job in her field right away. Then she heard about a part-time position as therapeutic recreation director at a nursing home. She was hired for this job and enjoyed it so much that she was able to turn it into a full-time job. "I was dealing with people," she said. "I could apply some of the things I learned in the early childhood program, such as crafts. The residents were so appreciative. It was very gratifying."

After seven happy years, Ruth, about to turn 70, retired. Joe had cut back his work, and the couple wanted the freedom to travel. Ruth is pleased to have more time to give to the causes and issues that are important to her. She and Joe audit university classes and attend Elderhostel sessions, continuing the satisfactions that Ruth so happily discovered at age 54.

GRADUATION AND A CAREER AT AGE 70

Diana was in her second year of college in 1936 when her father told her he no longer had the resources to fund her education, and didn't believe women should apply for scholarships. She dropped out immediately. Thirty-seven years later, at age 59, Diana returned to college.

Diana received a master's degree in human development in 1984; she was 70. Today, she has an active counseling practice. Besides doing individual counseling, she leads many support groups.

Recently, Diana sought special training for counseling adult children of alcoholics. She describes herself as a continuing education junkie, attending as many seminars, workshops, conferences, and training programs as she can. "I never thought I would be as busy and as involved as I am," she said.

Years earlier her daughter had advised her, "Just take one step at a time. Don't think about getting a graduate degree. Just take a couple of courses and see how you like them." That's exactly what Diana did. The school she attended in southern California made her reentry relatively painless. She received credit for life/work experience and for most of her previous course work, putting her only three courses away from her bachelor's degree. After getting her B.A., she immediately enrolled in a master's program.

Diana had been a volunteer counselor at a suicide prevention center before she went back to school. Her director was very enthusiastic about her starting a women's support group. Diana recalled, "I said to him, 'You're a Ph.D., and I have no credentials. If I do try to start a group, will you put your money where your mouth is?' He said, 'Absolutely!' and immediately sent me a client.

"I started the support group for some selfish reasons too," Diana said. "We had moved from the East to the West Coast several years earlier, and I felt lonely and isolated. I wondered what in the world women without connections did in this city. I figured there must be other women dealing with transition who could benefit from a support group. I had never seen or heard the term 'women's support group' before I started one and labeled it that. Now there are women's support groups everywhere."

When Diana went back to school, she wanted skills that would help her expand her group. Her family backed her decision, although her husband, an attorney, could not understand why she wanted to get the degree.

Her son's and daughter's enthusiasm was unbounded. "My mother has gained a whole new sense of who she is and what she wants from life," said Jenny, Diana's 34-year-old daughter. "She has become much more self-confident and is not nearly as dependent on my father. She has a career that she has always wanted, is capable of earning a living, and feels good about her skills as a therapist."

Jenny feels that her mother's life would have taken a very different turn had she not gone back to school. "When my mom moved to the West Coast at an older age, she knew no one, had no idea what she would do with herself, and was frightened. I would not have been surprised if she had moved back to the familiar and comfortable East Coast. She found a whole new life by going to school."

Diana's 38-year-old son, John, said, "I think she would have had too much time on her hands and would have wanted to do something worthwhile. Now, in her 70s, she has something fulfilling and satisfying to do."

Jenny added, "What my mother did gave me a whole new respect for her. She had the guts to go back to school when she was over 60 and start a new career. We shared experiences regarding college classes and psychology. I could relate to what she was going through."

Diana thinks that her husband viewed her plans as her way to deal with loneliness. "I don't think he realized how serious I was. When I got my master's degree, he seemed shocked to hear I was going to do something with it," she said. "It's been a slow process. Bill is a wonderful man. I think it's more my problem than his. I had always been the typical good wife of my era. Good wives take care of their husbands, cook their meals, and are always available.

"When I changed my schedule, I let Bill know I wouldn't abandon him. 'Remember, tomorrow night is my group night,' I would say. 'I won't be here when you get home. I'll be home at 9:30.' His favorite meal would be in the freezer."

Diana's major problem when she started school was fear of failure. "I'd always been a terrible student," she said. "I even got left back in high school. I worried about failing my master's program. What would people think? How would I explain it?"

Coming to grips with her fear was liberating. While still in school, she said, "It's OK to fail. I hope to make the grade, but if I don't, I don't. I'm not competing with anyone. Even if I don't get the degree, I've gained so much, there's no way I can think of myself as a failure."

Diana believes she has become an autonomous woman by getting her master's degree and launching her career. "I'm a woman of the '80s," she said, "in belief, philosophy, spirit, and action. It makes me laugh—I guess I was born a century too soon. Everything that has happened in my life was unheard of when it happened to me, but today it is commonplace.

"When I started school, I felt out of place; I was the grandma. I didn't want anyone to know how old I was. Soon I realized how ridiculous that was, so I announced my age. I expected everyone to be very surprised, but I was the only one making an issue of my age. I'm proud to reach this plateau of wisdom and feel youthful.

"I teach and preach that all women must be autonomous. Statistically, the majority of us will outlive the men in our lives. If we don't learn to develop autonomy, we're going to be in a boat without oars."

Concerning negative changes caused by her return to school, Diana mentioned: "My daughter says I overanalyze everything, and it's true. I'm working on that, trying not to bother figuring out why someone said what they said or why they did what they did."

Diana regards self-awareness as her top priority. She has been in therapy herself and feels it is also responsible for her intellectual and emotional growth. "I am more able to accept myself than I ever have been in my life.

"Most of my life I thought I wasn't 'enough,' that, no matter what, I would not be enough. I've learned that I'm quite enough. As a result, I'm easier on myself and less judgmental of others. I see myself honestly and project it. I no longer feel I need to be a certain way in order to be liked."

Diana is even able to turn a life-threatening event into a stimulus for new personal growth. "Six years ago," she recalls, "I was mugged at gunpoint and thrown out of my car. There was severe injury to my back. My back will never be perfect, but I'm grateful it's as good as it is.

"Something like this makes you look at your own mortality. I've always been vital. I look younger than I am, so I've always been able to push away these thoughts about mortality. But the mugging made me look at where I am. It's made me work through a lot around my own issues and those of my husband. That's been very good for me.

"I would say that in the last two years, after thirty-eight years of marriage, my relationship with my husband has evolved into one of openness, communication, and tolerance. This never would have happened without the therapy and the learning experiences."

Recently, Diana became a grandmother. "People say you don't know what it's like until you become one," she said. "It is a rare experience. I am close to my granddaughter, Sally, without having any of the responsibilities and worries. My own growth has made me a much better grandmother, and I think I'm a better mother to Jenny as well."

Diana finds great pleasure in her present life-style. She would like less traffic and smog, but she's content to continue her routine. "I've discovered my own natural intelligence, a logical mind, and creativity I never recognized or thought I had."

GOING AFTER THE JOB
YOU REALLY WANT

CHAPTER 5
APPROACHING COLLEGE WITH CLEAR-CUT GOALS

The women in this chapter had very specific career goals when they returned to school. Therefore, they were exempt from the main anxiety-producing question that confronts many mature students: Where is "all this" going to take me?

Adult students who have clear goals have an easier time assuaging the doubts of family members that the disruption in their lives will be worth it in the end—for all concerned. The stresses and strains of academic life are viewed within the context of the end result and the possible benefits for the entire family—additional income being the major one. For example, the second salary can make college a financial reality for one's children.

Responses from husbands in this chapter run the gamut from resentment to encouragement. Savannah's husband, for instance, did not understand her need to get a college degree as quickly as possible, and they were divorced by the time she got her degree.

On the other hand, Ellen's husband, an internationally recognized physician, was actually relieved when she decided to pursue a career as a middle school science and math teacher. Ellen's commitment to her goals allowed Charles to feel more comfortable about the time *he* was spending writing his textbook and going to evening meetings. He was interested in Ellen's major, and her studies added a new dimension to their lives.

Eleanor's schedule was absolutely grueling during medical school and her internship. Simultaneously, her husband, Ben, was just launching his own career as a lawyer. Ben, totally supportive of Eleanor and her goals, commented that together they "phased in the craziest time of our lives. . . . "

A common link between the women featured here is their certainty that careers can evolve as interests change. Maureen, a community college teacher of English as a second language, can see herself as a teacher in China or a roving language evaluator. Elizabeth, a therapist and an artist, has expanded her counseling practice to include art therapy.

Ellen, after nearly twenty years of teaching children, might like to teach computer skills to older people. Savannah is sure she has the potential to move up at the company for which she works. Eleanor's possibilities are unlimited: teaching, writing, private practice, the clinic. The only restraint is reaching the appropriate balance between home life and work.

Reentry students who are certain of their career goals are often in a desperate rush. Attempting to make up for lost time can cause alienation of one's family and friends. Setting aside time to nurture and be nurtured, no matter how rushed or urgent one feels, is critical. Keeping the end in sight can go a long way toward calming frayed nerves.

Exhaustion is often the constant companion of the reentry student who is trying to find the shortest distance between two points. Eleanor comments: "You have to have the wisdom to realize it's not going to be like that forever."

THE BEST WAY TO BE HEARD BY DOCTORS WAS TO BECOME ONE HERSELF

After her freshman year in college in 1958, Eleanor dropped out to get married and work as a secretary in a hospital. She resumed her studies a year later, graduating in 1962 with a B.S. in nutrition from a university in the west.

Eleanor's husband, Jack, was a naval officer. After Eleanor's graduation the couple moved east so Jack could do a six-month stint in naval intelligence school. They then moved to Hawaii with the military. During the three years they lived there, Jack worked in naval intelligence and Eleanor was a cereal chemist.

Their relationship was strained when they returned to the mainland in 1965. While Jack attempted a career in creative writing, Eleanor became a hospital dietitian. Almost immediately she decided to enter a master's program in public health. She graduated with a specialty in nutrition in 1967.

At that point, Eleanor, who was then 27, decided that she wanted to become a physician. However, she said, "Jack was adamant that I should not pursue a medical degree just then. Although I wanted to do it, I had some trepidation, so I put the degree on the back burner."

The couple made yet another 3,000-mile move in 1968. Jack was working with the navy, and Eleanor found a job she liked as a public health nutritionist at a neighborhood clinic in a low-income area. She discovered she had a special gift for understanding and relating to the people she was serving. As she became more knowledgeable, she felt little was being done to treat each person holistically. The more involved she became, the more convinced she was that physicians required almost as much education about nutrition as their patients. She concluded that the only way to influence the physicians she was working with was to become one of them, and she revived her old dream of medical school.

"The people I was serving," Eleanor explained, "had many needs that were not being addressed by people on legislative levels or by the medical staff at the clinic. I felt impotent."

Then, in 1969, Eleanor and Jack ended their marriage, and Eleanor's sister, Sharon, was diagnosed as having a malignant brain tumor. Sharon died the following year, leaving Eleanor convinced that her case had been mismanaged, at least from a psychological standpoint. She felt strongly that the quality of Sharon's life during those last months was not a major priority for the physicians involved. Eleanor said, "I wanted to learn whether my anger at her death was justifiable or was something I could somehow assuage and overcome."

Another motivation for deciding to pursue a career in medicine was financial. Eleanor wanted to provide for her divorced mother as well as to contribute to the many causes she considered worthwhile.

Thus, one year after Sharon's death, Eleanor, almost on impulse, signed up for the MCAT, the standard medical school entrance exam—eight days before it was to be given. Her scores and wait-list status at three good medical schools encouraged her to study diligently to prepare to take the MCAT again.

Eleanor did well on the next MCAT and was accepted at the medical school of her choice. In 1973, at age 33, she relocated nearly 3,000 miles away, leaving behind the man she would marry the following year. Ben, an attorney, was not able to join her until the end of the year.

In 1978 Ben said of Eleanor's medical school years, "You enter into this servitude that eats up all your time, takes all your energies, and imposes awful separations. Eleanor worked incredibly long hours and then stayed up all night studying. She was always afraid she didn't know enough. For the first time since I'd known her, she reached the extremes of her energy levels. Whoever devised medical training ought to be hung by their thumbs. What they do to people is terrible—awful."

Eleanor elaborated: "You're at school or the hospital all the time; when you're home, you're totally out of it. It's not normal. When I was in my clinical years, the most blissful thing in the world was passing out in bed. Ben would cook dinner, but I couldn't stay awake to eat it. I'd be falling asleep at the table."

Most reentry students discuss how important it is to find emotional support at home and among friends. Eleanor, on the other hand, says she tried not to require any emotional support. "I considered it one of my wisest moves not to suggest that I needed emotional support. I had already steeled myself for an unpleasant and lonely ordeal. I didn't let my guard down among my colleagues because people who did got stabbed in the back on a number of occasions. Women in particular would complain to their major professors or the people with whom they were doing rotations. It would always show up on their various clerkship ratings. I never let myself do that.

"I didn't want Ben to be involved with what was going on medically. There's no way to share that level of deprivation with someone. I wanted to be able to come home and talk about something unrelated. Talking about medicine would have been disgusting, because it was already total submersion. What I really wanted was a complete change of pace, and that's what Ben and I were able to provide each other."

The four years of medical school weren't as bad as the internship that followed. Eleanor said, "You have to . . . realize it's not going to be like that forever. You have to have an incredibly strong relationship to begin with."

Ben was entering the law firm where he is now a partner. He said recently, "When Eleanor was in medical school, I was working the hardest as a young lawyer. We sort of phased in the craziest time of our lives simultaneously. It wasn't a good time for either of us. At least, one of us wasn't always at home waiting for the other."

Ben was totally supportive of Eleanor's goal. He said in 1978, "She's filling out her whole being in this extremely positive way. She's delighted to be a doctor. Eleanor has the credentials and training to do what she wants to do the rest of her life."

Even though Eleanor's biological clock was definitely ticking, both she and Ben are greatly relieved they were not combining parenting with medical school. Ben said recently, "That would have been very difficult. I wouldn't recommend it to anybody."

Eleanor added, "It would have been awful to be in school and have a small child. One woman in our class had a child during that time and described her almost biochemical need to see her little girl. She'd come home late at night and have an irresistible urge to wake up the child."

At age 40, Eleanor began a practice in internal medicine with another physician, founded and directed an eating disorders clinic for high-risk patients, taught several classes, and began lecturing and writing on nutrition for physicians.

The following year, Eleanor and Ben became parents twice within seven months. "After working very hard on trying to procreate," Eleanor said, "we adopted two splendid kids."

In 1987 Eleanor reported working approximately 80 hours a week giving her patients the kind of time and energy she felt they deserved. This usually meant trips to the office or hospital on weekends and endless hours on the telephone every night. Her evolving practice and successful clinic attracted attention, and Eleanor was appearing as an expert in her field on national television programs.

The couple found a wonderful woman to be with Alex and Ariel during working hours when the children were not at preschool. Even though Eleanor was able to get by on 4 or 5 hours of sleep, balancing family and work was a constant challenge.

On the day of her tenth reunion for medical school in 1987, Eleanor decided to resign as director of her eating disorders clinic. She wanted more time with her family. While her colleagues at the reunion talked about their professional advancement, Eleanor beamed about her resignation.

Today, Eleanor works approximately 50 hours a week (not including the telephone calls). She enjoys activities with her two children, who are now in kindergarten. Frequent visitors include her mother, father, and stepmother and Ben's parents. Having worked so hard for so long, she finds that a 50-hour workweek seems to leave plenty of time for her family. The balance feels right to her.

In 1985 Eleanor treated a woman suffering from the disease that killed Sharon. This woman was under the care of some of the same physicians who had managed Sharon's case sixteen years earlier. Eleanor intervened at the critical moment when the team of oncologists at the university were about to prescribe maintenance of therapy despite clear tumor growth on that regime. Because Eleanor insisted on a protocol change, the patient had a wonderful, almost comfortable extra year and was bicycling on the beach with her family two weeks before her death.

Eleanor was available to this woman and her family throughout the illness, working with all of them to ensure a higher quality of life up to the end. During a home visit three weeks before her peaceful death, this patient and Eleanor watched the sun set together. To Eleanor, it felt as if a circle had closed.

A MANAGEMENT DEGREE LED DIRECTLY TO HER JOB OF CHOICE

Savannah is considered young by reentry standards. She was only 22 when she started a bachelor's program in management at Alverno College in 1977. However, she was combining her studies with full-time work, and she was engaged to be married.

Savannah was an administrative assistant at Alverno, a small private women's college in Milwaukee, but her goal was to work for a large profit-making organization. She saw the degree in management as her ticket.

Savannah entered the charter class of Alverno's Weekend College program geared specifically for working women. "I go to school on Saturday from 9 a.m. until 4:30 p.m. and on Sunday from 9 a.m. until 5 p.m. every other weekend," Savannah explained during her student days. "Since I work from 8 a.m. until 4:30 p.m. during the week, the only time I have for homework is after supper and on my free weekends. It doesn't leave a lot of time to do much else."

Faculty and staff members were very supportive. A major thrust of the program was to get mature women back into school and then out into the work force. Counselors made themselves available to discuss any problems: financial pressures, family difficulties, lack of child care, or rusty study skills. They provided much-needed guidance and information on how to achieve career goals.

Savannah's worries about fitting in were immediately dispelled. Instead of winding up as an "older" student, she turned out to be one of the youngest in the program. Tuition was expensive, but the college had a tuition reimbursement program that funded all her education.

Academic performance was also a major worry. She recalled, "I wondered if I could handle it. Did I want to put the time and effort into it? Could I? Would I find it a big disappointment? Would I find *myself* a big disappointment?" In fact, she did well.

More difficult hurdles were personal ones. She got married during her sophomore year. When she graduated four years later, she was divorced.

Just before her wedding in 1978, Savannah hinted that her fiancé was not as enthusiastic about her pursuit of a degree as she had hoped. "My family has offered me more support than my fiancé," she said. "He already has his degree, and he doesn't see it as a burning desire the way I do.

"Being in school showed me that my life's partner wasn't as supportive as I needed him to be. My marriage was short-lived, and that turned out to be a blessing. Staying married would have been an error."

While her life was turned upside down by divorce, Savannah's family offered her tremendous support. She said recently, "Of the eight kids in my family, I was one of the few without a college degree. My family helped me through a tough time. They thought I was doing something difficult and wonderful."

Believing that job opportunities would be greater if she had a double major, Savannah took her bachelor's degree in business management and professional communications. After graduating in 1981, she got her first job through an on-campus recruiting program.

Her entry-level position lasted for seven months, after which she moved to another position for the next year and a half. "Then," she explained, "I was promoted to management. I was a supervisor for two years before moving into my present job. There was an internal posting, and I was one of about ten applicants. My prior positions and education were extremely helpful."

Today, Savannah is enjoying her work as a quality assurance analyst earning $33,000 annually. In this position, she works on special projects, such as designing a computerized customer attitude survey or helping other departments to initiate changes.

Savannah believes her education continues to serve her well. She said recently, "I'm using it every day. I learned great techniques for dealing with people, whether at work or at home, in groups or one-on-one. I'm able to deal with my world as I find it." She would like to stay with the company indefinitely and believes that her prospects for continued promotion are excellent.

LIVING, WORKING, AND CREATING UNDER ONE ROOF

Elizabeth blends the personal, professional, and artistic elements of her life. The blue Victorian building she calls home is also a counseling center. Her painting studio is just outside her back door.

When Elizabeth and her husband separated in 1972, she was 43 and their six children ranged in age from 8 to 19. She was immediately confronted by having to find a place to live.

Elizabeth's response to this problem shows the resourcefulness she has exhibited ever since. She decided to purchase a home with Penny, her partner in a small counseling practice. Like Elizabeth, Penny was a divorced mother attempting to juggle family and career. The house they found was ideal—with plenty of room for the two women, the six children who lived with them, and occasional boarders.

The flexible living arrangement they created has accommodated extensive personal and professional development. As the children left home, Elizabeth and Penny leased space to other therapists. Elizabeth calls the building "a growth center." Four therapists work there, and four adults call it home.

A large room filled with big comfortable cushions is used for group sessions. Penny created a special area for play therapy. Elizabeth has her painting studio out in back. "This house allows both public and private space," Elizabeth said. "We each have our own space, and that makes this house work. We can each be by ourselves."

Back in 1972 the two families were able to alleviate a great deal of financial pressure by splitting expenses. Elizabeth earned money through her counseling practice and painting. But she knew she needed a degree and a license if she ever wanted to establish a counseling practice elsewhere. Therefore, twenty-three years after receiving a bachelor's degree in fine arts, Elizabeth applied for admission to a master's program in psychology. It was the only program within hundreds of miles. Her worst fears were confirmed when she was turned down.

After being rejected, she learned about a pilot project that was about to begin in her area. An out-of-area university had decided to offer a two-year master's program in counseling for adults and was actively recruiting students. Classes would be taught in the evenings and on weekends by local professors and a group from the distant university. Elizabeth was accepted immediately.

The program seemed perfect, but Elizabeth was very unsure of her intellectual abilities, despite her achievements. Like so many other women when they think of going back to college, she says, "I thought I wouldn't be able to do it."

The forty students in the program—ministers, welfare workers, probation officers—were an instant support group. Most were in their 30s and 40s; like Elizabeth, they were trying to fit the degree program into a full life.

Elizabeth said, "We all had jobs, so we weren't threatening to each other. One of the highlights of that program was the support. An isolating experience would have been hard. This situation was a change for me; I was bathed in support! We'd come over to my house after class and rap. We studied together and helped with each other's weak spots. It restored my faith in mankind."

According to Elizabeth, her children benefited from her student role. "I think it's a general rule that the better a mother feels about herself, the better her relationship is with her kids." Passive and dependent is Elizabeth's description of herself for most of her married life. She believes that it was very good for her children to see her emerge as assertive, independent, and outgoing.

Elizabeth graduated in 1976, just before her 47th birthday. "We were a cohesive lot," says Elizabeth. "I made a lot of friends. It turned out to be fun."

Elizabeth is now 57, and her approach to counseling has changed. "For many years, it was purely psychologically oriented," she said. "I've moved into what I call a transpersonal way of looking at our human condition, a more spiritual way. So, I'm adding that to my work.

"I'm a counselor here, and I'm an artist here. They flow back and forth, complementing each other very well." Elizabeth sees art as a connection to one's spiritual self. She hopes to combine her two roles in the years to come. In fact, she has been doing art therapy with several clients.

Elizabeth looks forward to continuing with counseling and painting well into her 80s. She believes a person's vision of himself or herself expands with age. She points to a friend who was a pilot until he went to divinity school in his late 60s, and to Grandma Moses, who didn't take up painting until her 70s. "You're never too old," Elizabeth concludes. "It's never too late to do something new or different. What's important is to keep going. If you maintain your curiosity and sense of aliveness, the sky's the limit."

ONE DEGREE AWAY FROM ACHIEVING HER GOAL

Ellen had a specific career goal in mind when she returned to school at age 40 in 1968. She needed a bachelor's degree so she could teach junior high science and math.

She was unsure of her academic ability. Except for taking a sprinkling of courses, she had been away from school for more than twenty years. She was so convinced her SAT scores would embarrass her that she had the results sent to a school her four children (10 through 15 years old at the time) did not attend. As it turned out, she had nothing to fear.

Ellen not only did well academically but hit her career goal right on the mark. She has taught eighth-grade science and math since her graduation in 1970, later adding computer classes to her repertoire. In 1980, she became chairperson of the school's science department. Recently, she became director of its computer education program.

Ellen's husband, Charles, is a physician at a prestigious medical school in New England and an internationally recognized expert in his field. Although extremely busy with his own career, he was completely supportive of Ellen as she charted her academic path and her subsequent career.

"I think Ellen would have been dissatisfied with the life of a doctor's wife," he commented. "Her return to school was the best thing she ever did for herself, and it was extremely important in our lives. Over the years, her identity as Ellen the teacher, then the beloved teacher, then the extraordinary teacher—I don't think I flatter her—has given her a role quite different from that of Mrs. Charles So-and-So."

Ellen and Charles had always shared equitably in the household responsibilities, consistently dividing chores by interest rather than sex stereotype. Consequently, Charles often cooks; Ellen shovels snow and does carpentry. Charles urged Ellen to go to school full-time rather than part-time and willingly increased his share of chores around the house.

In 1947 Ellen had earned an associate degree so she could become a lab technician. When she went back to college in 1970, she discovered that many of her science credits would not transfer. Consequently, she majored in American history because it would be the fastest route to a bachelor's degree—even though she wanted to teach science and math.

"I enjoyed the music, art, biology, and math courses," Ellen said, "but I hated the history courses. I'm not a good reader. I'm a much better problem solver. My husband helped me by editing my papers and correcting my grammar."

Viewing school as a means to an end helped Ellen strike a comfortable balance between home life and school. "I decided I would probably have to do some things I would not have suggested to my own children. I didn't read every recommended book or understand every word the professor said in class. I made a few compromises." Even so, she graduated with a B average.

The youngest child, in sixth grade when Ellen went back to school, felt her mother's absence more than the other three children (a son in ninth grade and twin girls who were high school juniors). Ellen said, "I asked my sixth grader, Anya, if she would help me because I had a lot of work to do. She said, 'Why should I help you? If I help you, you'll graduate, and then you'll go to work, and then you'll never be home.'"

Ellen and Anya struck an agreement. If, when Anya was in eighth grade, she still felt her mom wasn't home enough, Ellen would not work full-time. "She wanted me home, so we compromised. I started off part-time. It worked out well; as we both look back on it, we realize we both profited from the compromise."

The timing of her graduation couldn't have been more perfect in terms of launching a teaching career. A local private school was looking for someone to teach science and math, and they were agreeable to her working part-time the first year.

Teaching means long evenings and weekends of class preparation, not to mention having to grade papers and tests, but the couple's relationship thrived. Charles was working on a major textbook while Ellen was in school and during her early years of teaching. Once his book was completed, he became more involved with evening activities at the medical school and the university in general.

Charles sees nothing but positive effects. He said recently, "Ellen's having a goal, an occupation, a vocation has enabled me to continue to develop professionally. I have been able to travel and spend my evenings working without feeling too guilty. I have been proud of having a wife who has really been an educational force in the community."

Ellen's teaching position has also affected the couple's social life in a way Charles enjoys. "We have a number of friends whom we might not otherwise have had, largely from her school," he said. "Our closest social friends now come from Ellen's side of things rather than mine."

Ellen and Charles are at an interesting crossroads. Now 63, Charles has cut back at the medical school. He now has more time during the day to do some of the work he used to do evenings. However, Ellen, at 59, is busier than ever.

"I'm trying to wear too many hats," she said. "I'm feeling a little burned out." She is contemplating resigning from teaching and focusing completely on the directorship of the computer program.

"We're both getting close to retirement," she commented. "I ask myself, 'Do I want to stop working or don't I?' I'm not sure I know the answer. I have a lot of interests now that I would like to pursue, a lot to learn with my computer. I think whatever comes up, I'd just like to let it happen."

HER EDUCATION AND SUBSEQUENT CAREER BECAME HER ANCHOR

In 1975, Maureen returned to school at the age of 35. She already had a master's degree, teaching credentials, and solid experience as a high school teacher. Her academic and career goals were clear: a master's degree in teaching English as a foreign language would give her a specialty and make her more marketable.

Maureen began her hour-long commute to the university when her daughters were 6 and 8. Her husband, a pediatrician, was completely supportive of her entering graduate school.

"He arranged it so he could be there when the children needed him after school," she explained. "He was happy to see me widen my horizons." While Maureen listened to her Mandarin Chinese language tapes on the crowded freeway coming home from San Francisco, her husband ran the household smoothly. Maureen's mother and father were also happy to pitch in.

Shortly before she graduated in 1978, Maureen said, "I have a personal need to work. I don't have to do it for financial reasons, although I would like to pull my share of the load. I don't want my husband to always have to bring in all the income. Maybe it would mean he wouldn't have to spend quite as much time working."

Maureen's first goal was to teach half-time, and she was lucky enough to be offered a half-time position at a nearby community college immediately after graduation.

Thus, less than three years after her return to school, the balance between Maureen's family life and career was just right. She looked forward to the stimulation of teaching, being home each day to greet her children after school, and sharing the financial responsibilities.

Then tragedy struck. Maureen's husband—age 39, slim, a nonsmoker, and a runner—died of a sudden heart attack. Maureen's work proved to be a solid anchor. She believes the second master's degree and her subsequent career helped restore emotional well-being.

"I had already lined up a teaching job for the fall. The day my husband died I believe I told my boss I wanted to go ahead with that job. It was one of my first thoughts. When my children went back to school, I dreaded the idea of empty days. No matter how shocked I was by grief, I was very grateful to have that job to go to. . . .

"During the next year, or perhaps two, my teaching gave structure to my daily life. It helped me to continue to function. The job in itself was not a reason to go on living—my children were. But the rewards my students brought me kept me going and gave organization to my life.

"I can't think of another occupation that would give me such high interpersonal rewards. There's no part of my job I like better than being in the classroom relating to students. I have a very strong philosophical commitment to teaching. I don't think I will ever change professions," she said.

Confronting losses has been painfully frequent in the past ten years for Maureen. Her father had open-heart surgery in 1983 and died in August 1986. Her mother died one year later. A close friend of the family, a woman Maureen's age with children the same age as her children, succumbed to cancer in 1987. "When I can't stand to think about some of these tremendously sad events," she said, "I turn my mind to the constructive business of teaching."

Maureen's return to school served as a springboard for an intellectual reawakening. "It was a kind of reaffirmation of something I guess I knew about myself," she said, "which is that I will probably always be a student."

In 1986, at age 46, Maureen enrolled in an intensive Chinese language class. "Most of the students in the Chinese course were my children's ages. I was delighted to discover that I still learn languages very well." She also enjoys the many professional conferences, workshops, and seminars she attends.

For the past three years, Maureen was a guest teacher in one-month training courses for representatives who will be teachers of English as a second language. Currently, both of her daughters are in college, and Maureen is actualizing a lifelong dream—to live in the Orient. She is on a sabbatical and teaching in the People's Republic of China.

When she returns, she can imagine herself as a roving language evaluator, possibly working for the State Department. Or she might focus all her energies on an intellectual challenge and apply for a Fulbright.

Degrees of Success

"The more you learn," she said, "the more you learn about yourself, and the more willing you are to take risks—academic and emotional. The process of going back to school made me more willing to take risks."

With nearly twenty years' experience in the teaching profession, Maureen shows no signs of switching careers. However, at age 48 she is contemplating teaching in new and unusual ways.

CHAPTER 6
SETTING AND CLARIFYING GOALS

We live in a goal-oriented society. Consequently, many reentry women students feel anxious about attending college without clear-cut career objectives in mind. An academic setting is an ideal place to acquire skills and clarify interests. Identifying a career is easier amidst an assortment of interesting subjects and encouraging professors. Some of the women in this chapter had no idea what career they were headed for when they went to school. Others thought they knew, but they changed their minds.

Allison, for example, was majoring in natural sciences in order to become a scientific illustrator. Her interests were diverted, instead, to law school, and now she is a professor of law. The switch had to do with the ripening of goals toward the end of her undergraduate days. As she forged ahead, she realized she wanted to be in a position to have an impact on society.

Pat, master's degree in hand, headed off to Mexico to distance herself from a relationship. She came back bilingual and eager to serve the Hispanic population in California.

Natalie spent the first fifty years of her life without any career goals whatsoever. Volunteer work in neighborhood schools evolved into an interest to pursue a college education and a career as a special education teacher.

Reentry students often make career decisions for practical or mundane reasons. Marcia switched her major from psychology to social work because she could attend school only at night, and the social work building was the closest to the parking lot. Laura majored in sociology because the class scheduling conformed to her child-care arrangements. Now a city planner, she comments that at age 20 she would not have known what a city planner was. Sheila, a college counselor, was encouraged by friends to take a few classes because she lived on the edge of the campus.

Degrees of Success

Once they settle into an academic routine many reentry students renew old interests. For example, although teaching was the furthest thing from Allison's mind when she went to law school, she had majored in education before she dropped out of college in her teens. Teaching at the law school combines that old interest with a new one. Laura is enrolled in a Ph.D. program in philosophy—her minor as an undergraduate.

Going to college with one career goal and coming out with another certainly does not have to spell frustration. Besides, no one asks to see a student's career goal when he or she sets foot on campus. Keep your options open as you wend your way through the academic world. Something is bound to catch your interest.

CHOOSING AN UNDERGRADUATE MAJOR BASED ON CHILD-CARE AVAILABILITY

Laura dropped out of Vassar at age 19 in order to start a family. When her son and daughter were toddlers, the family moved west, and she began taking classes one at a time, trading baby-sitting hours with a friend.

Laura didn't have a career in mind. Her goal was to finish her bachelor's degree. During the first few years back in college, she enjoyed the life-style of a young mother and wife taking a class or two.

"I had little kids tugging at my skirts in the registration lines," she recalled. "For years, I tried to make school as trouble-free as possible for my family. I would get the catalog, go through areas of interest, and circle the classes that met between 10 a.m. and 3 p.m. Then I'd get together with my friend to see whether there was anything she wanted to take, so we could trade baby-sitting. My major was determined by when I could arrange baby-sitting. Sociology had classes over the lunch hour, and that was a good time." It took Laura twelve years to get her degree.

Although Laura did not have a career goal in mind as an undergraduate, she intended to work once she got her degree. Her family provided excellent role models: her parents and grandparents all had advanced degrees. In fact, her mother, a psychiatric social worker, had supported her children after a divorce. "I grew up thinking it was only prudent, if not necessary, for women to have an education that prepared them for work," she said.

Laura was introduced to city planning as a possible career when she became involved with neighborhood zoning issues. The staff from the planning office were friendly and open to input from the community. Working in that setting appeared to be really enjoyable.

Once Laura found a career to focus on, she entered a master's degree program in urban planning in 1975 at the age of 31 and graduated two years later. For the past ten years, she has been a city planner and she was recently named the long-range planning director, earning $54,000 annually.

Although Laura started thinking about going back to school from

Setting and Clarifying Goals

the moment she withdrew in 1964, in retrospect she is pleased that she was older when she decided on a career.

"I'm glad I had a chance to spend a lot of time with my kids in their younger years. I would not have chosen to be a city planner at age 20. I don't think I even knew what a city planner was. Now it's a job that fits me better than any other on the face of the earth. Going back to school as an adult was a good thing.

"My job is everything I could have wanted in terms of opportunities for creativity, using my skills with people, and a sense of accomplishment," she remarked. "I have a job that almost gives me more than I give it—a sense of being on the right track emotionally, being financially independent."

Because of her income level, Laura was able to afford to send her son, Seth, to a good boarding school when she wasn't pleased with his junior high school. "The boarding school was a great experience for him, and it got him out of a bad, defeating situation. I feel fortunate to have been able to help him in that way. I don't know what would have happened otherwise."

Currently, both her children are in college. Seth, an international economics major, is doing his graduate work in China, where he has already traveled widely. "A lot of these opportunities came about because I could afford it; I could let them follow their dreams. Without my finishing graduate school, it would not have been possible." In fact, Laura was able to pay off her entire graduate school tuition with her first two-week paycheck.

The personal growth attendant on settling into her job took a toll on Laura's marriage of thirteen years. Dwight and Laura began their marriage during her undergraduate days when she was a recently divorced mother of two toddlers. Gradually they grew apart and ended their relationship in 1984.

"The person that Dwight married was a young woman with two small kids and no job," Laura said. "By the end of our marriage, this person had become someone that not only had a job but earned more money than he did. I had many more commitments and demands on me because of my job. In some ways I was and still am in love with my job.

"I don't know whether our marriage would have lasted if I hadn't gone back to school and didn't have the job. As we grew and changed, as the years went by, he felt less important to me. The funny thing is that we're still good friends. Making that break has been important to him because it enabled him to look back and see what we did have. He cares about me now as the person I am."

"I feel proud of what she's done and happy that she feels capable," Dwight said the year after Laura graduated. Problems can arise, however, when one partner introduces a dramatic change: "There's potential for competitiveness. How does one view bright women getting good jobs with very high degrees? How does a man feel about that? It can be a problem.

"Laura's a smart person. She always did well in school. During my later years in school [while getting a bachelor's degree], I didn't do as well. I am comfortable in what I'm doing, and I don't need an M.A. in anything. But I guess I've always thought the man should have the M.A. and the woman should have the B.A. or both have M.A.'s," he said.

Laura's experiences as an undergraduate and graduate student were as different as night and day. During her undergraduate days, she scheduled her classes around the needs of her family. Graduate school, on the other hand, meant commuting an hour each way. In addition, the program required full-time study.

Laura knew she would need work experience in order to get a good job after her graduation. The school had an excellent internship program, and Laura had a series of very good work experiences. However, she was in school full-time and working practically full-time for two years.

"The first time I went back to school, I don't think anybody noticed. I went into some gear I didn't know I had—still filling obligations, baking cookies, reading fortunes at the PTA carnival. I tried not to change anybody's routines. The second time, they couldn't help but notice, because I wasn't around for great blocks of time.

"I think of those years in graduate school as kind of hyperactive and sort of a mess. I wasn't really able to focus on any of my commitments fully. It was hard on everyone. I was doing the best job I could, which wasn't always the job I wanted to do. I don't have good memories of it. But in the long run, getting the degree that led to the job has been pivotal in my life and absolutely the right thing to have done. It is a leap of faith," she said, "to start something and be able to find a way to believe that in the end it's going to lead somewhere."

Laura is now enrolled in a Ph.D. program in philosophy focusing on values and social policy. Ultimately, she will be able to teach in planning and architecture schools. Some of her subjects might include ethical decisions, planners' roles, and social equity. At the moment, she is able to attend school only sporadically, because of her time commitments. Completing the program and teaching are part of her long-range goals.

There are many changes in Laura's personal life. She is involved in a new relationship. Over the past two years, she has happily lost nearly 50 pounds without much effort or thought. She is also reserving more time for travel, recently joining Seth in China, where he has been studying for a year.

Laura would like to stay in city planning for the foreseeable future. Then, at some point, she would like to join the Peace Corps in Nepal, where she has spent time trekking.

FROM NATURAL SCIENCES TO LAW

In 1975, at age 27, Allison went back to school to complete her bachelor's degree. She was interested in being a scientific illustrator. After majoring in natural sciences, she graduated in 1977. Ten years later, however, she is a law school professor who graduated at the top of her class.

Setting and Clarifying Goals

In high school Allison said her major goal for college was to be married within six months of graduation. "I had no idea in 1965 what my goals were," Allison comments, "although I pretended I did. I knew I was wasting a lot of time in school at that point." After trying several different majors, she settled on education. Her grades fluctuated wildly: one semester she had a 4.0 GPA; in another, a 1.0.

Allison left school in Maryland to join her fiancé, Eric, in Virginia, where he had received a fellowship. Although she planned to transfer her credits, the couple needed additional income, so Allison did office work during their first year there. "In 1971 I applied to school and was accepted," Allison said. "We had saved money; I didn't need to work. I got my acceptance letter one week, my positive pregnancy test the next. I postponed school."

After Eric completed his Ph.D., the family spent a year in Stockholm, where he was on a postdoctoral fellowship. They settled in Boston for several more years of postdoctoral study before moving to the Midwest, where they have remained ever since.

Allison had not wanted to become a full-time student in Boston while their daughter, Emma, was young. However, she took several art courses and worked part-time for a biology professor. Scientific illustration seemed like a logical career choice, as it would combine her interests in science and art.

In 1975, she says, she "did a lot of thinking about who I was and what I wanted to do. I concluded I couldn't just go along attaching myself to my husband and defining myself that way."

Once they moved to the Midwest, conditions were ideal for Allison's return to school. Because Eric was a university professor, her tuition was free. Also, they joined a parents' cooperative day-care facility. All three family members were enthusiastic about the co-op.

Although Allison had completed three years of college, the university required two more years of course work for graduation. "I could pick and choose the classes," she recalled. "I mixed technical classes like chemistry with courses in American studies and art. It was fun. Shifting from one mode of thinking to another was a very rich experience."

As Allison's focus on a career in scientific illustration became sharper, she began to see that it might not be appropriate for her. The job market was limited where they lived, and Eric's job meant staying put.

She also sensed that, in the long run, the kind of problem solving demanded in this field would not be engaging enough. She doesn't regret spending those years preparing for a career in scientific illustration. She said, "When you're going to school, you have to aim for something; it seemed like a good target at the time."

The summer before Allison graduated, she did an independent study project with a consumer action agency, researching and editing a medical directory. This experience was the beginning of a new focus: she felt she wanted to be in a position that would enable her to use her skills to impact various social issues.

Law school seemed like a reasonable option, so she applied. She recalled thinking, "This is what people do if they're decent with words and they want to solve the world's problems." She was accepted, but because she still wasn't certain of her own ultimate goals she decided to postpone her decision for a year.

During the academic year 1977–78, Allison worked under contract for the consumer action agency and was co-coordinator of the alternative school Emma attended.

"I wasn't sure that going to law school was a good decision," she said. "I kept sending in the tuition deposits to keep my options open. I showed up for orientation and was still not convinced that this was right." She finally gave it a try. "I found myself a successful law student, and three years later I graduated. I went through the bar exam, and suddenly I was a lawyer."

After her first semester in law school, Allison had found out about a child advocacy organization and was able to get a position with them during the summers. After graduating, she went to work there full-time for several years. Then she wanted a change

When she told some of her former law school professors that she was looking for work, she was astounded when they recommended her for a faculty position. "Much to my surprise, I got hired, and I've been doing it ever since," Allison said. "It's very unusual for them to hire a graduate of our law school. It's also very flattering and very gratifying. It had never occurred to me to consider teaching."

Eric said recently, "Allison's going back to school was very positive. She's exceedingly bright, and to apply that to a career seemed like a natural move. All three of us have always been quite busy. No one felt neglected or left out."

The couple was somewhat unsynchronized during the early years of their marriage when Eric was a graduate student and Allison was neither in school nor in an intellectually challenging situation. Allison said, "Eric has always been an overworker. He's always defined work by what there is to do, not by what fits from 9 to 5. My being in a similar situation gave him free rein to continue without feeling guilty."

Emma's excellent day-care situation helped everyone. The co-op was open during hours that suited the family's schedule. Through day care, they were able to, as Allison put it, "establish a network of friends all of whom also had an overcommitment of their time and energy." These friends became extended family, and eventually some of them formed an alternative school.

The life-style Allison described during Emma's preschool years was comfortable. "We'd all three leave in the morning," she said. "Eric would go off to teach, I'd go to school, and Emma would go to day care. We all spent time with each other. Sometimes Emma would come to classes with me or spend time in Eric's office.

"Eric and I spent time at the co-op. We were each involved with what the others were doing. This gave Emma a sense that her family was composed of individuals, each with something important to do. None of us felt isolated or alienated."

Allison finds teaching challenging. As a relatively new teacher, she is dealing with the pressures of publishing and qualifying for tenure. The sheer mechanics of preparing for a class is a huge drain of her time and energy.

"There is never a time when I'm done," said Allison. "Eric and I are in these jobs with no end to the week and no end to the work. It doesn't matter if you work a 60-hour week. Basically, you're probably further behind than you were at the beginning of the week."

Allison has been forcing herself to cut back, realizing that the stress of falling behind will be there even if she devotes 24 hours a day to her work. In 1987, she decided to take Emma to the world figure-skating championships during her spring break. She said, "It will be a good time to be off together. It'll be fun. I should be here writing around the clock, and when we come back, I'll be stressed out. But, I'll be stressed out anyway, so why not go?"

Allison derives tremendous satisfaction from her family's busy life-style. However, she hopes that she and Eric can both learn, at some point, to plan on taking time away from work. The family has many spontaneous good times together, but planned time away from work is rare. Allison's recent promotion to associate professor may take some of the pressure off this busy family.

KICKING BACK IN MEXICO CLARIFIED HER GOALS

Pat was fed up after working for five years as a county probation department counselor. She thought her bachelor's degree in psychology might be limiting her career options, so she decided to pursue a master's degree in social work at California State University at Sacramento, even though she was not sure what she would do with it.

When she graduated two years later in 1979, at age 30, Pat and the man with whom she had been living decided to separate. Unsure of how to utilize her degree, Pat went to Mexico for two years and supported herself by teaching English.

Pat said recently, "I thought speaking Spanish would help me advance in the field of social work. But the major part of my decision had to do with how difficult the ending of the relationship was for me. I wanted to kick back before going ahead with my career.

"I was totally immersed in the Mexican culture. This was the first time I had done something completely on my own. We tend to be very busy and goal oriented, and we don't really reflect on who we are and what we want. This was a time I came to know myself better, and it was a very powerful experience."

During the first year in Mexico, Pat could see no correlation between what she was doing and what she had prepared herself to do in graduate school.

In the morning, Pat was paid to help engineers and executives become bilingual. In the afternoon, she voluntarily taught English to any interested children in the remote town where she lived. "I managed to con my boss into giving me books for the kids," she said.

"Women who were in a crisis sought me out. I did some counseling, networking, and resource finding for quite a few different people. I took kids on weekend outings."

Pat, completely bilingual when she came back to the United States in 1981, had new confidence in herself. "Having been totally independent in Mexico made me feel like a whole person," she said recently. She emerged from those years with a much better picture of who she was and what she wanted to do.

Pat looked for a job through which she could serve the Hispanic population. She settled in Sacramento, lived with her mother, and taught English and living skills to Cuban refugees. She also worked on a state-funded program aimed to keep senior citizens out of nursing homes.

She decided to seek employment in the mental health field and maintain her interest in Spanish-speaking people. Because more bilingual jobs were available in southern California, she decided to relocate.

In Los Angeles Pat quickly found a job as a bilingual case manager at a community agency program for the elderly. She was soon offered a job as a medical social worker in a hospital. Most of the people she served there were elderly Hispanics. During the two and a half years there, she was part of a multidisciplinary team involved with dialysis, pediatrics, and the emergency room. "It was a mixture of counseling, resource finding, crisis intervention, and working with families facing illness and death."

In addition, Pat worked toward her clinical license (LCSW) and was also a consulting therapist for the agency where she first worked. Part-time, she interviewed cancer patients for a university-funded project and worked as a home health-care specialist. In 1985, she was promoted to supervisor at her primary job.

Although she loved her job at the hospital, it consumed all her energy. She wanted to spend more of her time at home—just relaxing. Her companion, Keith, a corporate bank officer, was dissatisfied with his job of sixteen years, and the couple wanted to leave Los Angeles.

Moving several hundred miles north, Pat quickly found a position as a psychiatric social worker with a county department of mental health. The area has a large Hispanic population, and she is the only female psychotherapist on the staff who is bilingual. Her starting salary was $30,000. Keith, with Pat's full emotional support, is exploring new options.

The balance between home life and work feels really good to Pat. She works an 8-hour day, a drastic cutback from the hours she kept in Los Angeles. She and Keith are enjoying their new home and like hiking by the ocean and through the area's many parks. Pat does long-distance running on a regular basis, watches what she eats, and is careful to get enough sleep.

"It sounds like I'm pretty boring, doesn't it?" she asked, "—sleeping at normal times, not staying up till the wee hours on the weekend, keeping a regular schedule. Actually, I feel so much better about myself. I have a much more positive outlook; before, I was more up and down. I don't feel the moodiness like I used to.

"My last job gave me a lot of pressure and more responsibility. Right now, I'm enjoying my job. It's not easy, just a lot less stressful. I'm not sure I want to climb the ladder and wind up in the management rat race again. My work life and my free time are balanced."

In the back of her mind, Pat is weighing the pros and cons of going back to school for a Ph.D. in psychology. She would probably do the same kind of work she is doing now, but she would be paid more. "I'm not sure whether that would be worth it to me or not," she said. As she spends more time on her job, she believes the deciding factors will become clear.

PURSUING A CAREER IN SPECIAL EDUCATION AFTER AGE 50

Natalie graduated from a commercial high school program in 1943 and did secretarial work until she and her husband, Sam, started a family. She didn't enjoy either her high school classes or working in an office.

Going to college never entered Natalie's mind. Her father died when she was 8, and her mother supported Natalie, her sister, and her grandmother. "I always had the feeling in my teens that I just wanted to go to work and let my mother stay home," she explained.

Thirty years later at age 48, Natalie mustered up her courage and enrolled in one psychology course. Now, with a master's degree in special education, she is a highly respected and confident teacher of learning-disabled children.

For fifty years Natalie had had no career goal. She said recently, "When I was growing up no one ever asked me what I wanted to do. I never thought about it. Times were tough. Fulfilling life dreams was not on my mind. I didn't like office work, but where I came from, that's what you did. I never entertained the idea of teaching."

Natalie has always enjoyed helping young children, and for many years she volunteered at her children's schools, working with youngsters who were having difficulty reading. When her son, Brad, went to college in 1971, she needed "something more than the PTA and volunteer work."

Fortunately, her school district in a suburb of New York City decided to hire paraprofessionals to work with students whose learning skills were below grade level.

One "para" was hired for every school in the district, and Natalie was an ideal candidate. The program coordinators sought people to whom the children would relate, people who were genuinely interested in children. Preference was given to people without college degrees, in an attempt to attract those who would pursue degrees in that field. The job was part-time and low paying but ideal for someone interested in helping learning-disabled children.

The position provided funding for college tuition and released time from the job. Natalie knew several paras who enrolled in college courses immediately, but at first she couldn't imagine following suit.

She said, "My greatest fear was that I couldn't pass courses after being away from school for many years. I saw the kind of work my own children were doing, and I thought I would never be able to do it."

For the next two and a half years, Natalie worked with a reading laboratory program. The paraprofessionals took the children out of the classroom and helped them on an individual basis. The job involved specific training and materials.

In 1973 the district set up a reading diagnostic center at which a psychologist, a neurologist, and a reading specialist planned programs for individual children referred to them by local schools. Natalie was one of the three paraprofessionals selected out of twenty-nine applicants. She became fascinated by the evaluation process and desperately wanted to take a few psychology classes.

"I thought about it for a year. I was a chicken; I just didn't have the guts. Finally, I decided to take one course in psychology. If it went well, I would take courses that looked enjoyable and wouldn't worry about taking math and biology."

Natalie's mother was completely perplexed as to why Natalie would want to work and go to school. She thought Natalie and her family must be very comfortable on Sam's salary as an office manager for an import business. Why wouldn't Natalie want to stay home? Similarly, Carol, a ninth grader at the time, thought it strange that her mother wanted to take a college class.

Sam was unconditionally enthusiastic. He holds a bachelor's degree in economics and has always placed a high value on education. The couple's son, Brad, who was away at college, was equally excited that his mother had decided to take some classes.

For the next year and a half, Natalie took one course at a time at Queensborough Community College. Her fears dissolved. She discovered she was a good student, and she was enjoying the younger students.

As Natalie gained confidence and experience through her academic success and her work at the reading diagnostic center, she began taking two courses a semester. During Carol's last year in high school, Natalie decided to work for an associate degree and then a career in teaching.

"As I went along," she explained, "I decided I needed direction; I started taking education courses." She saved the dreaded math requirement for her last semester. "I was convinced I couldn't handle it, but I got an A–. Unbelievably, I understood it. What a feeling of accomplishment!"

It took Natalie four years to get her associate degree in education. She graduated in 1978, the same year Brad graduated from law school. Carol was in her second year of college. With both children away from home, Natalie had fewer obligations and more time to pursue a bachelor's degree.

Sam was completely behind her. "He was proud of me when I was going through it and proud I became a teacher," Natalie said. She completed her bachelor's degree in education from Queens College, cum laude, in 1981. Although Natalie continued to work as a para that year, she took a break from the course work in order to have time enough to fully enjoy the preparations for Carol's wedding.

The following year, Natalie worked as a special education teacher in the school district of her choice. She entered a special education master's degree program at Adelphi University and graduated in 1984 at age 59. Sam threw an enormous celebration.

Natalie said she is in her infancy as a teacher, only having been at it for six years. "I love working with the children. I love the rewards of teaching—seeing the growth, the progress."

Sam recently retired and assumed that Natalie would follow suit. However, she commented, "It took me so long to get here, but I'm here, and I'm enjoying what I'm doing." She feels she is in her professional prime and plans to work at least another five years.

THE THIRD DEGREE

Marcia decided to follow in her father's footsteps in 1950 by choosing engineering as her undergraduate major. She applied, but not a single woman was accepted by the school's engineering department that year. After briefly considering a premed major, Marcia switched to physics. That department did not welcome her or the only other female student either. In 1953 she dropped out of school, got married, and supported her husband through his engineering degree. He launched his career; she became a full-time homemaker and mother.

Nineteen years after leaving school and getting married, Marcia ended a marriage she describes as miserable. She could not possibly support her three children—ages 7, 12, and 17—and custody was awarded to her husband. At age 39, Marcia needed skills, knowledge, employment, and a decent income.

She was not terrified of a college campus. "I went back to school because it was the only thing I had been successful at," she said. "School was a safe place for me, a place where I felt good."

She went to a state university not far from her home. Although she intended to major in psychology, she switched to social work for practical reasons. "I could only go nights. The honest reason why I changed to social work was that the university is in the woods, and I didn't want to walk through the woods to night classes. The social work school was located alongside the parking lot."

Although Marcia saw her children frequently, she often disagreed with their father. She felt he left them alone at night too often, yet she was powerless to change the situation. "Going to school seemed like the logical way of putting myself in a position to get my children back," she said in 1978.

The college was very sensitive to the needs of reentry students. With the school's help, Marcia was able to locate various grants and loans. She graduated magna cum laude with a bachelor's degree in social work in 1974 at age 41.

Immediately after graduating, Marcia volunteered at the state psychiatric hospital. Within six weeks she was hired as a social worker there, an interesting but low-paying position. She concluded that she would need a master's degree to command a decent salary.

The nearest school with a master's program in social work was prohibitively expensive and too difficult a commute. Marcia worked instead, on a part-time basis, for a master's degree in education with a counseling emphasis. She was awarded an assistantship, which paid her tuition and gave her a stipend. Soon she was able to have her daughter, the middle child, live with her.

Just after her graduation in 1978, Marcia decided that an associate degree in nursing might provide her with an even better income than she could command with the credentials she had just earned. She attended school at night for certification as a registered nurse.

Marcia had an interesting series of jobs during her nursing school days. She spent a year as a field supervisor at a home health-care agency. She worked as a counselor at a day treatment center. Her third job was as a state social worker with a new agency for neglected and abused children.

In 1981 Marcia received her associate degree in nursing, but she decided to stay in her position as a social worker for six more years. The pay was very good, and she liked the work.

In 1984 Marcia and Ed, a physician, decided to live together and bought a house to renovate. Ed did not want Marcia to work. The couple didn't need her salary, and he did not understand why she wanted to support herself.

Remodeling the house was a shared project, and the tasks were endless. Marcia quit her job in 1985 to work on the house. Then, in December 1986, Ed died of a heart attack.

Marcia immediately decided to go back to work. After a brief job hunt, she became a nurse at the psychiatric hospital where she had worked previously. To pay the mortgage, she took a second job two nights a week as a nurse in a detoxification center.

At age 54, Marcia is considering the possibility of going back to school once again—for a master's in nursing. Since she works for the state, her tuition would be paid for her. By the time Marcia is 60, she hopes to be able to teach, at the community college level, within the profession she truly enjoys.

GIVEN NO COUNSELING, NOW SHE PROVIDES IT

Sheila, a Canadian, earned a bachelor's degree in home economics in 1960. She married an attorney several years later and had four children.

In 1975, when she returned to school, she was 36 and a single parent of three elementary school–age children and one preschooler. Sheila planned to study psychology.

"I had always been interested in it," she said. "One of my friends talked me into going to school by saying, 'You live right on the edge of the campus. You might as well be taking courses.' It wasn't a career-oriented decision."

Sheila spent her first year picking up the necessary courses to qualify as a psychology major in a master's program. By the time she applied, the program was full.

She didn't want to wait another year, so she switched to a master's program in education with a counseling emphasis. She took several graduate courses in the psychology department just because they were interesting.

In 1978, Sheila was almost done with her thesis. She had decided on a career as a university counselor. The academic route that she chose turned out to be ideal for acquiring the knowledge and credentials she needed. Today, she is a psychologist and counselor at the very university that granted her degree.

Sheila identified the lack of counselors as her primary problem when she returned to school. "No one told me it would be difficult to do what I was doing," Sheila said. "I immediately set out to do it, then wondered why I was tired all the time. No one said, 'Right, you are having a problem, and you need a lot of support.'

"I wanted specific encouragement, assurance that there was a way of doing it, a counselor to talk things over with. You need some support. You might have given up a job or other arrangement to enter a new situation."

Sheila had to find day care for Ted, the youngest child, during the year before he entered school. After that, there was a steady stream of baby-sitters once the elementary school day ended.

"I don't know how I did it. I would get Ted off to day care, the other three off to school, and myself to an 8:30 class. I was preoccupied with organizing them. I had to get over the feeling that all of that was my responsibility. I felt I wasn't being a good mother if I wasn't home all the time, making all the sandwiches, getting all the clothes ready. It was a painful time. I couldn't allow people to help; I couldn't ask for help."

Her children, Sheila reports, initially thought their mother was funny. "You're this old, and you still haven't finished school?" one of them asked. Sheila's strongest supporter was her mother. She was happy to stay with the family when baby-sitters, day care, papers, exams, and classes became overwhelming.

Now the children are proud of their mother's accomplishments. Chris, the youngest daughter, attends the university where Sheila works. She brings her friends to her mother for counseling.

Chris said, "My mother is a very understanding person, outstanding when it comes to making people feel that they can go on. I look to her in times of trouble and happiness. Many people cannot communicate. She's good at relating to people. It's a precious trait."

Sheila's job now requires a master's degree in psychology and registration as a psychologist. The degree she earned in 1978 did not meet the qualifications, but her graduate course work and extensive work experience did.

She said, "There was a brief period of time when people with a mixed bag of qualifications could be registered. In my case, they gave me credit for having a master's degree and the three psychology courses I took in graduate school. They required me to take two more psychology courses." She enrolled in these classes during 1979–80 while she worked at the university.

Sheila is a strong advocate of counseling. "I think it's helpful to talk to someone who is knowledgeable about occupations and guidance," she said. "Or just to talk to someone who is knowledgeable about you—to help you clarify goals. Talk to people in similar situations—people with children, people in the same program. Constantly tell how you're feeling. Don't try to do it on your own."

In recent years Sheila has involved herself in organizations specifically focused on women's issues. She helped create a women's health education network and has served as its president. She is also president of a network of over 8,000 Canadian women that helps fund women's projects in African, Asian, Latin American, and Caribbean countries. She presented a workshop at the 1985 United Nations End of the Decade conference for women, held in Nairobi. She was also involved with an international conference on women's health, held in Costa Rica.

All Sheila's children will soon be away from home. The eldest daughter teaches school in Costa Rica. A son is in law school. Chris is in college, and Ted has only one more year of high school.

Sheila expects many changes in her life-style and career focus. She said, "I hope to work in a developing country. I imagine going into another branch of my interest in people, probably something to do with women and health, women and community development, setting up women's centers, or establishing outreach programs in a developing country." As of the moment, Sheila has obtained her teaching credentials and is contemplating teaching overseas, perhaps with her daughter in Costa Rica.

CHAPTER 7
ENSURING JOB SECURITY AND ADVANCEMENT

This chapter features four women who went back to school so that they could keep jobs they liked. A diploma, license, or certificate was the route away from limbo to job security.

Ten years ago, Lucy was the only professor at her university with a lowly B.S. after her name in the catalog. Tenure was impossible without a Ph.D. Alice and Kay were hired by elementary schools on the condition that they earn specific degrees. Anna, an RN by training, could see the handwriting on the wall: a B.S. in nursing would soon be required for the job she had as operating room supervisor.

Going back to school while employed in the job of your choice eliminates a nagging feeling that can be a constant companion of the reentry student: "Will this degree get me where I want to go?" It's a lot less agonizing when you know beforehand that you've already got the job you want.

The women featured here all had very supportive families. Perhaps the assurance of tangible results makes family members more likely to endorse this type of reentry—even when the results create a further problem, as in Lucy's case.

CERTIFICATION: BEING ABLE TO AFFORD ALL THE EXTRAS

Alice loves her job. A former kindergarten teacher, she became a librarian and sixth-grade remedial reading specialist in 1971. She was hired on the condition that she go back to school for certification as an associate media specialist.

The school system, which paid for her education, did not put pressure on Alice to get the degree quickly. As a result, she took classes at Trenton State College in New Jersey part-time for five years.

Alice took one course each semester; classes met one night a

Degrees of Success

week. The days when she was both student and teacher were long—get her kids to school in the morning, work all day, drive an hour to school, try to stay awake in class.

Alice studied on weekends. She spent most of one weekend day on schoolwork and the other with her husband and four children. "You can trade quantity of time spent with your family for quality of time," she explained.

Alice was careful to explain to her family how they would all benefit from her degree. "They knew I had to go to school in order to keep my job," she said. "I had to work so that we could afford some extras. Everybody understood and cooperated. They all pitched in and helped so we could have more time together."

"It helps to have an understanding husband," she said. When she first entered the program at age 35, the children were 6, 8, 10, and 12. She and Ken, an elementary school teacher, had always shared household responsibilities. The time she spent on schoolwork was not considered a major disruption.

Certification brought a dramatic increase in Alice's salary. In 1978 she earned $12,000; last year, she earned $27,500. She can measure the difference in tangible results. "We can afford college and weddings for three daughters.

"Even taking one course a semester for years and years will get you where you want to go eventually," she said. She cautions against taking a large course load; in her case this would have upset the balance of home, school, and work.

Alice would like to continue working as a librarian and remedial reading specialist indefinitely. She is not considering a master's degree, because it is not necessary for her job. She and Ken are very comfortable with their present life-style. They hope to travel more and possibly remodel their home.

ONE PARTNER'S JOB SECURITY CAN PUT THE OTHER PARTNER IN A JOB WASTELAND

In the university's catalog, Lucy was the only teacher with a B.S. after her name. All the other professors had at least an M.A. In order to keep her job, she entered a Ph.D. program in social psychology, graduating in 1978 at age 34. Lucy had publications to her credit, and she was awarded a research grant; tenure looked promising.

Her husband, Leo, was experiencing a career slump. "He's struggling along in a very difficult area," Lucy said ten years ago, "and he's meeting closed doors." Leo is a documentary photographer; for almost fifteen years it has been nearly impossible for him to find work in his field near their home.

Lucy needed a Ph.D. both for job insurance in her current position and in order to be marketable at other universities. Job security was a top priority because, until two years ago, she was the family's primary breadwinner.

Lucy viewed the advanced degree as the final step in her education. In 1965, the couple had moved from New York to the Midwest to enter Ph.D. programs. Leo had dropped out of his program in 1967, and Lucy quit school because she assumed Leo would be happier if they moved back to the East Coast. Later, she realized that Leo would have felt comfortable staying put while she finished her studies. Reentering a Ph.D. program nine years later was a particularly weighty decision because she was determined not to quit this time around.

Lucy found an ideal program through the Union for Experimenting Colleges and Universities in Cincinnati. Students design and direct their own course of study. Each student is assigned an advisory committee, and, aside from a minimal residency requirement (such as a three-week symposium), students don't spend time in classes.

"It was an unstructured program," Lucy explains. "That was nice because there were very few pressures on me, very few hurdles. I didn't feel like an oddball. It's a program aimed at working people who want to get a degree. Most of the students are women.

"On the other hand, I felt isolated. I kept wondering if I was doing OK. I didn't get the feedback you get when you're in a classroom with peers who are going through the same thing. I was just out there. I had my committee, and I did my work."

Lucy explains that during the year and a half it took her to get her Ph.D. she was very preoccupied with teaching and her family life. The children were 3 and 6 when she began the program.

"I have no memory of it," Lucy said, "but Leo tells me that I would come home from work, we would have dinner, and then I would go into my study. I made tremendous demands on Leo. He really had to bear most of the burden of taking care of the kids and the house. However, he knew this was important to me and that I would have to spend a lot of time on it."

Lucy credits much of her success to Leo's willingness to take on more than his usual share of child-care and household chores. The couple had always tried to share equally in these responsibilities, depending on their work loads.

Lucy recalled, "We had always pitched in, depending on what was going on at the time. I think it would be horrible if you didn't have that kind of relationship. I don't think you can establish that kind of relationship just because you are going to school."

The Ph.D. and a tenured position gave Lucy and Leo more financial security. They could count on at least one solid salary. But tenure actualized Leo's worst fear—the family had to stay near Lucy's university. She slowly realized that it would be extremely difficult for her to get a tenured position elsewhere.

Although Lucy teaches in a social work program, she is not a social worker. Her degree is in social psychology, and she has never taught in that field. Because she defines herself primarily as a teacher and not a researcher, her publications are few, a drawback to finding another position in a highly competitive academic environment.

"I'm not attractive to other universities because I am neither here nor there," she said. "I don't feel very confident about my abilities to sell myself elsewhere, so I'm holding on to this job," she admitted recently. She enjoys her position very much and likes the city they live in.

In 1985 Leo was offered a teaching position at a university more than 600 miles away. He realized that the three-year contract might not lead to a permanent position.

Lucy felt she should not give up her job. The children, 13 and 16 at the time of Leo's job offer, did not want to move. The couple finally decided that Leo should take the job, but that the family would not relocate. Eight months out of the year, he is away for ten days, then home for four. His work in photography requires a lot of traveling at other times as well. For example, he spent a month in Central America in 1987.

While Leo is teaching, he is uprooted from family and friends. A large part of his salary goes to pay for rent and travel expenses.

"We are fractured," Lucy said. "We try to meet our [professional] needs, but we only do that with a great deal of loss. Our relationship *is* stable—but we've lost a real family life."

Lucy is sure that without her tenured position she would have been more inclined to relocate and find another job. "One of the issues is power within relationships," she said. "My education gave me independence. I was able to get a job that satisfied me and would support us. This kind of job gives some power, which is a good thing, but not an unequivocally good thing.

"I'm not saying I wish it had turned out otherwise. I'm saying we've had a lot of strife and pain. If I didn't have the job, we would go where it would be good for Leo. I feel guilty about that. It's confusing, and I don't know what's the right thing to do." If Leo's position becomes permanent, the couple will face a hard decision.

JUST ONE MORE YEAR OF SCHOOL MADE ALL THE DIFFERENCE

Anna is a reentry pioneer, returning to college in 1967. Most of her friends thought she was unwise to give up a secure nursing position for the rigors of academic life at age 44. They questioned her ability to study and pass tests after twenty-two years away from school. Besides, Anna's position as a nursing supervisor of an operating room gave her great responsibility and satisfaction.

However, the hospital where Anna worked merged with a university medical school and changed the qualifications for supervisory jobs. Anna said, "I knew that eventually they would require a B.S. degree for my job." Discovering that her status as an RN was worth about three years of college, she hoped that she would be able to complete a B.S.N. in one year.

Her year in college, 1967, was a rough one. Anna's husband's shop was not doing well. Her father's health was failing, and he came to live with the couple. The first semester was especially difficult—there were financial hardships, her study habits were rusty, and she had a nagging feeling that being in school might not even be necessary.

Counseling services were unavailable at that time. Fortunately, Anna's family was supportive, and one of the deans encouraged her. She managed to complete the degree in one year and return to her former job.

Anna gained self-confidence. "I developed an ability to stand on my own two feet and be articulate," she said. Back at her old job, she was no longer intimidated by physicians or colleagues.

Her associates noticed a dramatic change in her interactions with hospital staff. One physician observed, "The surgeons began to respect her more. Her word carried weight. When she went to a meeting with the other supervisors, she was on an equal footing. This boosted her ego. She knows she has the respect of her coworkers."

Anna decided to pursue a master's degree in guidance counseling. She attended school part-time and received the degree in 1973. The additional degree increased her earning power and responsibilities. She was promoted to clinical director of all the operating rooms. Anna said recently, "When I went into nursing in the '40s, I never thought I would wind up with a secretary and an appointment book."

Her increased salary proved critical for her family. In 1970 her husband suffered a stroke and became disabled. Her father was also disabled, and Anna provided for him until he died in 1977.

Additional degrees helped Anna advance. She said, "Within the organization, there have been enormous changes involving shuffling of key personnel. I feel strongly that, had I not gotten the additional degrees, I would have been shuffled out the door along with many of my colleagues. I continue to urge young men and women to continue their education, for without it, earning power is greatly diminished."

Degrees alone do not ensure the ability to keep a position, especially in a field like nursing. "One has to grow, develop, and change to meet the needs of the hierarchy as it changes," said Anna. In the fifteen years since she received her master's degree, Anna has designed postgraduate education programs. In addition, she has supplemented her salary by consulting in her field.

Anna is convinced that women need a good education and good training to be competitive in their fields. "Women will be discriminated against only if they sit back and allow it," she said recently.

Now 63, Anna plans to continue work until she is 71. She enjoys what she does, and it allows her and her husband to have a comfortable life-style.

STAYING "CURRENT" IS A LIFELONG PROCESS

Kay completed three years of college before she dropped out in 1962. Her husband, Jerry, had just graduated with a bachelor's degree in business administration, and the first of their three children was born. Family responsibilities and school were too much for Kay to handle.

In 1975 Jerry entered the hospital for what the couple thought would be a routine appendectomy. Peritonitis and complications prolonged his stay for 108 days. Within the next twelve months, Jerry underwent thirteen operations.

Jerry's battle to regain his health lasted several years and served as a catalyst for a family decision: Kay should complete her college degree. She had worked at a preschool, but she had always wanted to be a special education teacher. For this, she would also need a master's degree.

Kay postponed resuming her education until Jerry's condition stabilized late in 1977. When she registered at East Central University in Oklahoma, her husband was full of encouragement.

"It offers me some security about the future," Jerry said of Kay's plans. "She can make a living in case she needs to. I wanted her to go back to school ever since she quit when I graduated and the kids were small. It's a positive step for her and for our whole family."

Kay, age 37, was anxious about details: finding a parking spot, registering, buying textbooks, and locating classrooms. A good friend who was already a student at East Central offered to walk Kay through her first bewildering days. It made all the difference. Later Kay was able to provide the same support for other friends who were afraid to cross the threshold of the registrar's office.

The challenge for Kay was juggling her home life and studies. Jerry was recuperating, but his illness was still a cause for concern. The three children were 11, 14, and 17 when Kay went back to school. There were adjustments. Jake, who was 11 at the time, said, "I don't like it sometimes. If I forget my lunch or my books, there's no one home to bring them to me."

"You cut a class to take a daughter to the orthodontist," said Kay. "You do the best you can with the time you have. I had a tendency to do too many things for them. Yet, my children are more independent than they would have been had I not gone back to school. Being in school has enriched our family life."

Kay balanced obligations hour by hour and day by day. She got used to it. During her senior year, Jerry was in and out of the hospital three more times, and the hospital was 90 miles away. "I was going to school, driving back and forth to see Jerry, and raising three kids," Kay recalled.

Kay was able to complete her degree in four semesters and a summer. In 1979, at age 39, she graduated and was hired immediately by an elementary school to work with multiply handicapped children. As expected, her employer required that she also get a master's degree.

Incorporating the master's degree into her busy life-style turned out not to be a hardship. Kay took her time, attending school at night and during the summers. In 1982 she received her master's in learning disabilities.

Kay has been able to help many children who are developmentally disabled, visually impaired, or physically challenged. She was named Teacher of the Year for her town in 1985. And there was a side benefit to her accomplishments: the woman who stepped up to receive her award was a happy shadow of her former self. She had shed 60 pounds while concentrating on her work and her studies.

Kay has continued her studies in order to teach many types of disabled children. She said recently, "School will always be a part of my life. It's very easy to go to summer school and very easy to be part of the college campus. It's an important part of my life. I can't think of a year that I haven't been in some type of class since I finished the master's degree."

In her eighth year of teaching and president of her town's education association, Kay is at full stride. "Our lives are very comfortable," she says. "I love teaching. I have the time now to become involved not only with special education students and their families but also with other teachers. I can raise the public's awareness of what the schools mean to our state and country. I can crusade for better working conditions for my coworkers, many of whom are raising children on very low salaries. That could have happened to me."

CHAPTER 8
CLOSED DOORS, REVOLVING DOORS

What if your very worst fear is actualized? What if you go to all the trouble of completing a degree program only to discover that you can't find a job in your chosen field? Or, what if it slowly dawns on you, midway through your academic program, that the career of your dreams no longer interests you?

For most reentry students, "closed doors, revolving doors" has to be the worst of all possible scenarios. The six women featured in this chapter met with disappointment after they finished their educational programs, yet none claims school was a waste of time.

Architecture school gave Donna the personal validation she needed to call herself an artist and designer. Although she is not working as an architect, she is an award-winning costume designer, does theatrical set designs, and makes jewelry. She and her husband are involved in an amazing array of creative projects, including the remodeling of their home.

April was midway through an associate degree in electrical engineering when she realized wiring and circuitry were no longer of interest. She completed the program anyway. Now, although she does entirely different work, she has the satisfaction of knowing that she completed a very difficult program.

Often, closed doors are a result of actively choosing to leave certain options unexplored. Donna and April could have found jobs in their specializations but chose not to. Likewise, Carolyn, the recipient of a master's degree in public health, concluded while still a student that bureaucracies were not responsive to people in need. She found a job in her field immediately after graduation but then chose to leave public health altogether.

Florence could not find an elementary school teaching position. She switched to educational administration and curriculum design and concluded she was better suited to this type of work.

Career changes affect family life, and vice versa. Five out of the six women here have experienced a change in marital status during the past ten years. Florence and Carolyn are now mothers of toddlers. Both these women have chosen to stay home during their children's preschool years.

Sarah, also the mother of a toddler, has been divorced, remarried, and divorced since going back to school. Even though her attempts to find a permanent teaching job have spanned six years, she remains optimistic. In fact, the most recent news from her indicates a permanent position is on the horizon. Mary, remarried just before she went back to school ten years ago, recently realized that, between teaching and union activities, she has devoted little time to her home life. She was ready to shift the personal-professional balance in her life.

Mary's story is perhaps the most unsettling. She has consistently confronted roadblocks to her attempts at switching from teaching to school administration. Yet, frustration aside, she has identified many pluses resulting from earning a master's degree in school administration: increased self-confidence, the skills needed for union work, and the respect of her colleagues.

Academic and career counseling might have saved all of these women a considerable amount of wear and tear. Carolyn thinks counseling could have steered her to a public health program that had an emphasis more compatible with her beliefs. Florence and Sarah both knew, ahead of time, that elementary school teaching positions were scarce, and they might have been helped to switch goals.

To avoid "closed doors, revolving doors," check out the number of jobs available in your field of interest. To make sure that an academic program is going to meet your personal and professional needs, talk with as many people as possible *before* you enroll: faculty, students, career and academic counselors, and people already working in that specialization.

UNABLE TO FIND A POSITION AS AN EDUCATIONAL ADMINISTRATOR

Ten years ago, Mary entered a graduate program in school administration. She had twenty-two classmates. All were reentry students; seventeen were men who were already working as administrators.

Mary thought at first that being a woman worked in her favor. "Being a woman is an advantage because you can turn on the smile," she said in 1978.

Ten years later, however, Mary was bitter and angry. Neither her credentials nor thousands of hours she has volunteered in an administrative capacity nor her smile has gotten her a job as a school administrator. She believes that she is a victim of sex discrimination.

Mary had seemed destined for success. She was a cyclone of activity with solid organizational skills, which she refined through the master's program. Running her household was a feat in itself when she went back to school at age 30. She had recently remarried, and her household included five children, ranging in age from 5 to 15. Mary went to school at night and was an elementary school music teacher by day.

Ten years ago her goals were clear-cut. She wanted to move into a supervisory position at the county level. After teaching for five years, she was ready for a change: "I can't stand working for no money. In education, you work very hard, and you're underpaid. In order to get into a position where the pay is equal to the responsibility, I'll have to move into another area. I want room to move up, to earn more money, and to get out of the classroom."

Mary's first administrative attempt involved reorganizing her music program. Through this successful project, she eventually became responsible for all the special area teachers—those involved with music, art, and physical education. "If there was a problem, the teachers would come to my room and say, 'Mary, would you go out and see these people, figure out what to do, then let me know.'

"I was an informal leader, like a department head. As long as I had assumed that job, I decided to ask for the title. I didn't want any money for it, just the title." The administrators said they couldn't possibly—it would put Mary in a position of authority. "You have all this energy and you wind up working for free to help your peers. Somebody's got to do it," Mary said.

She continued her unpaid involvement in administrative roles, such as serving her district's teachers union as president, chief negotiator, and chairperson of its grievance committee.

As negotiator for the past ten years, Mary has been responsible for handling contract disputes between teachers and administrators. She provides teachers with legal advice and defends them at various administrative ranks.

Mary also became interested in effecting change through political action. She was appointed to the municipal board of adjustment and served as secretary. She also was elected to her county's Republican Committee.

However, these experiences did not bring Mary closer to a paid administrative position. Today, she is still an elementary school music teacher with an annual income under $30,000.

"I haven't gone anywhere," she said recently. "I'm still in the same place. I kept the goal, but it didn't pan out." Mary believes she was unable to move up because she was willing to assume a leadership role without increased pay or official recognition. She thinks this is often the case with women, especially those in education.

She said, "You find yourself doing these jobs, without recognition from the administrators, but with the blessing and respect of your peers."

In retrospect, Mary thinks she should have been more perceptive. She believes that unless there is an administrator in the school district who has you in mind for an administrative position, there's no sense going back to school. She also thinks that it is not uncommon for men in education to have trouble handling assertive women.

Mary has applied for at least twenty-five administrative jobs in her area since she graduated in 1980 with a 4.0 GPA. At least half the time she is called back for a second interview as one of three or four finalists.

"I make a tremendous presentation," she said. "That's why I make it to the second round of interviews. I'm qualified. But I think you get beat in the end because you're a woman. You don't have the connections. You don't have the clout."

Mary says that it seems that many districts like to make a show of interviewing women. "They do this," she said, "so they can have a token in the finals. I'm a good token candidate locally."

Mary could interview for an administrative job in a different county; there are several possibilities within a reasonable commute of her home. But she is convinced that a lot depends on whom you know. When all the candidates are considered, three or four might have the same qualifications, but she feels the successful candidate inevitably is friendly with the superintendent of schools or someone powerful on the school board.

Mary has concluded that her active role in the union also works against her when she applies for a job. Although she denies being a troublemaker, she admits she might look like one on paper. She's modified her résumé to reflect less union experience.

Howard, Mary's husband, is as upset as she is. He said recently, "The course of study she undertook was a waste of time. She's still doing the same work she did before she went to graduate school. Her sister told her she was wasting her time getting a degree in school administration. Maybe if she had listened to her sister, she'd be in banking now."

Although Mary continues to serve on various committees, she thinks she's at a dead end in terms of paid administrative employment. Five years ago, in addition to teaching, she started a successful interior decorating business. For several years Mary earned more through her business than she did as a teacher. At its peak, the business had six employees and a waiting list of six to nine months for contracted work. Although she achieved one of her goals—to earn a great deal of money—this business unfortunately added 40 hours to her workweek.

When she turned 40 in 1986, Mary decided to slow down. Her husband received a considerable raise, so that Mary's income was not as critical as it had been. Only two children still lived at home; the other three were self-supporting. As a result, she closed her business.

"I've resigned myself to the job at school, so it hasn't been so hard to go there every day," Mary said. "I've come around to thinking that being an administrator wasn't as important as I used to think it was." Despite this thought, she applied for another administrative position in June 1987. Again, she came in second.

If she had it to do over again, Mary would take a different approach and try to be less threatening to the district supervisor. "He's the only boss I've got," she said. "Maybe if I had selected a different major, he would have been more helpful. Or maybe if I had moved to another system, I could have made the connections."

Although Mary believes that her schooling failed to bring career advancement, she points to several benefits. She proved to be a good student. When she got her bachelor's degree in music education in 1969, she had a 2.7 GPA. In 1980, with a full-time job and a family of seven, she managed to earn a straight-A average.

Mary used to be intimidated by administrators. Now, even without the paid recognition, she feels on a par with most of them. The organizational skills she acquired in school have carried over into her personal life, her teaching, and her work with the union.

A MASSEUSE WHO GOT A DEGREE IN ELECTRICAL ENGINEERING

April was a reentry student twice. She went back to school three years after graduating from high school. When she received her second degree, she was 33.

She was only 21 when she began her studies at a state university in New England, but she nevertheless felt self-conscious about being older than her classmates. She was married and working full-time. In fact, she and her husband were both juggling school and working. Luckily, the university had support systems for reentry students, and she soon felt at home.

April went back to school the first time, she said, because she "couldn't stand working in the real world." She was hoping for personal enrichment and decided to major in psychology. She had no particular career goal in mind.

To finance her education, she continued working at a copy center. After getting her B.A. in 1978, she took another job supervising a copy center, this time at a university. It didn't matter a bit to April that the job had nothing to do with what she had studied.

Although she enjoyed her job, April said, "You couldn't eat on what that university paid. There were wonderful benefits and nice people, but I got tired of chicken liver and fried eggs."

Because she maintained the university's copy machines so well, the next thing she knew she was hired to do repair and maintenance by a leading copy machine company.

April soon learned she had hands-on experience but lacked real knowledge of what she was doing. She said, "I could fix the copiers, but someone would ask, 'Why are you replacing the capacitor?' and I'd say, 'Capacitor? You mean this object in my hand?' I knew nothing but the nuts and bolts of fixing. I had no idea what I was fixing or why it worked."

At age 29, April went back to school for an associate degree in electrical engineering. The company for which she worked provided partial funding for her education.

She finished her A.A. in four years. Halfway through, she was positive she would never work as an electrical engineer. "I certainly wasn't going to wire a house," she said. "And I wasn't interested in being an engineer for Electrolux or GE, much less sitting somewhere drawing up wiring plans. All the technicians wind up with bad backs, bad knees, and bad ankles. They practically live at their chiropractor's."

When April realized she did not want to be an electrical engineer, she decided to try earning her living doing something she enjoyed: massage. She quit her job—even though she stayed in her degree program—and became a masseuse. Yet she's glad she finished her degree in electrical engineering. She feels a sense of accomplishment and confidence in mastering something complicated.

She had never even taken a shop course in high school. "Suddenly I was faced with Kirchhoff's voltage law and network theory. I loved the challenge, but it was hard."

School was also a welcome respite from her personal life; April and her husband divorced in 1979. School, the second time through, provided an opportunity to meet many new people, and her social life blossomed. "I'd say that some of the people who are most important to me personally and socially I met through school," she said. She remarried several years ago.

April was certainly the only student in the electrical engineering program who was making ends meet by working as a masseuse! She is enthusiastic about her present work.

"I'm not a mystical type of person who talks about auras and feelings or asks your sign. Physically touching someone does something to that person, and it does something to the masseuse, too. I know I'm good at this. Knowing that I'm going to make people feel good, knowing that I'm going to improve their day, that they may even feel good for many days, means a lot to me. Massage is a talent I can take with me wherever I go. I'm actually using my psychology degree because people tell me a lot about their problems."

Some of April's clients have health problems, and others, such as aerobics teachers and body builders, are very active. Some of her favorite clients are "little old ladies" she works with at a community center. April is also the operations manager of the center. She puts in a 60-hour workweek between the community center, a health center, and individual clients, up from a 20-hour workweek a year ago.

She likes the busier schedule because, she says, the more she has to do, the more she gets done. However, she would like to become more involved with volunteer work. She has enjoyed doing recording for the blind during less busy times.

April would like to go back to school again, perhaps for a degree in English literature. Although she does not have career plans that would utilize the additional degree, she thinks that learning for the sake of learning is enough incentive.

She also views the university as an ideal place to meet new people. She commented: "Whatever courses you study, you meet people who make you feel better, make you realize you are not alone, make you feel worthy of being included in their circle. One of the real advantages of being in school is the feedback, the positive reinforcement."

COMBINING SUBSTITUTE TEACHING WITH WAITRESSING

Since deciding to become an elementary school teacher in 1976 at age 28, Sarah has divorced, remarried, added a third child to the family, gotten her teaching credential, divorced again, and moved from the Northeast to the South. Currently, she is supporting her family by combining substitute teaching with waitressing jobs and has yet to find a permanent teaching position. Although she has had several long-term subbing jobs since her graduation in 1982, she has not been able to depend on teaching for a steady income. She also works as a cashier, bartender, and cook.

"I want to be an elementary school teacher," Sarah said recently. "People keep suggesting that I go back for a special education degree since it is difficult to find an elementary teaching job. I enjoy elementary school teaching more than anything else and I have accomplished my goal of getting a degree. But I may be forced to consider a different field."

Sarah felt that the Northeast was a particularly competitive area of the country in which to look for the job she wanted. Consequently, in 1986, she and her youngest child moved to the South to live near her sister and brother-in-law. Her middle child lives with Sarah's first husband, Scott; the eldest child is out on her own.

A family crisis originally sent Sarah back to school. Scott, a junior high school teacher, became ill in 1975. "I suddenly realized," she said, "that I had nothing to fall back on except his income. I had no education, no training, not even in a secretarial field. I could have done baby-sitting for the rest of my life—that's about it."

The following year, with her youngest child in first grade, Sarah volunteered as a classroom aide and quickly discovered that she enjoyed teaching young children.

The teacher with whom Sarah worked had gotten her teaching credentials while combining studies with family responsibilities. She offered Sarah support and advice while Sarah decided whether or not to work for a B.A. in elementary education.

During the summer of 1976, Sarah eased back into school by taking one course. When she registered for 9 1/2 units at a community college in the fall, she was combining school with working as a teacher's aide 35 hours a week. It was too much. "I was falling apart," Sarah said. "The family was falling apart.

"Every night, Monday through Thursday, I was gone from 7 till 10. When the kids saw me for half an hour in the morning, I'd be saying, 'Come on. We have to hurry.' At night, I would come home exhausted. I would have to do homework, make dinner, and be out the door by 6:30. It put an awful lot on their father."

Sarah and Scott decided that her education was more important than her job. When she quit working, her schedule became much more manageable. Sarah was surprised she could do well in school, and she was pleased that her husband was supportive.

Having a student for a mother was a major adjustment for the two older children, 6 and 8 at the time. "My kids had always had me at home, ready to do just what they wanted me to do. I would drop almost anything to do something for them," Sarah said.

Her relationship with Scott weakened. "My growing independence made my husband feel I should act *more* independent. The more independent I got, the more he pushed me. Instead of growing together, we grew apart. Soon he never cared where I was or what I was doing, as long as things were taken care of at home," Sarah said.

The marriage ended after she received her A.A. degree in 1978. By 1979 she had remarried. She continued with her studies during the academic year 1979–80 and then took a year off from school. She and her new husband, Fred, had a baby. She received her bachelor's degree at the end of 1982.

During the last three semesters of the bachelor's program, Sarah commuted 100 miles round trip daily to the state university. If problems arose, Scott and Fred handled them as best they could. While she was student teaching, Sarah also had a toddler to care for. Her older daughters helped run the household.

Fred had not gone to college. Although he was supportive of Sarah's student role on a day-to-day basis, she believes he felt threatened by her goal, the B.A. degree. "He felt that once I got it, I wouldn't be happy with him," she said. The couple separated in 1985.

Sarah reports that her two older daughters are very proud of her. Kari, now 19, is thinking about college after spending two years making sandwiches at minimum wage. Sarah said her own reentry inspires her daughter. "She saw me go back and do it after I had been out many more years than she has," she said.

Kari wishes her mother could find a permanent job as a teacher and said recently, "She went to school to get a degree so that she could teach. Now she can't find a permanent teaching job. It's depressing."

Sarah, now 39, is a long way from giving up. She believes she is making a good impression at the schools where she substitutes and hopes it is only a matter of time before she will be offered a permanent slot. Recently, she reported that a position teaching fourth grade was opening up soon and she was definitely in the running for it.

AN ARCHITECT WORKING AS AN OFFICE MANAGER

In 1977, at age 32, Donna entered a master's degree program in architecture at the University of California, Berkeley. Just separated from her husband, she was adjusting to being a single parent to Jason and Aaron, ages 3 and 8.

Just a few weeks after entering the program, Donna said, "I need a skill, something I can do well. At age 30, I wondered what I would do with myself when I grew up. I began hoping for something that would become more than itself when I interacted with it, something to get excited about."

Architecture seemed a reasonable choice. Her prior academic background lay in science, and her friends had been telling her for years that she should explore her artistic talents. She saw architecture as a tangible way to blend artistic and technical abilities.

During her first semester, Donna commented that she hoped to integrate her work life and her personal life. She wanted to find a stimulating work environment where teamwork would provide personal satisfaction.

Donna definitely did not want to continue working as an administrative assistant in a family business that manufactured laboratory equipment. Architecture school felt like her last chance to get away from the family-owned company.

Donna found a roommate who helped with child care and empathized with her goals. Instead of spending all her time at school, Donna put a drafting table in her bedroom so she could work at home.

During her second year in the program, she and a contractor bought a house to remodel and sell. "We didn't make much money," she recalled, "but it was a fantastic education in the politics of building—dealing with planning commissions, codes, partnerships, and termites."

Although architecture did not turn out to be something Donna was passionate about, her degree program led her to course work in theatrical set design.

She said, "One of my survival rules in graduate school was to take one course in something I loved. In looking through the catalog, I discovered that the dramatic arts department offered a course in set design, a recognized subfield of architecture." Donna had always been interested in the theater. She had done a considerable amount of acting in high school and had made drama part of her student teaching.

She became one of four advanced students in set design and studied with a professor she greatly admired. She took costume design during her last year in school. Her thesis for the master's degree in architecture emphasized her emerging passion for design; she created a set for a dance performance.

"School did something important for me," Donna said recently. "It gave me license to be creative. Prior to school, I did a lot of dabbling. Now I know more about the creative process. I can take an intellectual concept and translate it into reality."

Halfway through graduate school, Donna met Wesley, an electrician. At a party he overheard her talking about architecture school. "Our first conversation was about remodeling," Donna said. "He told me he was doing some remodeling at his place and asked if I would like to see his kitchen counters. It was certainly a unique line, and it worked!" Donna and Wesley were married a year before she graduated in 1981.

Donna went back to her parents' company while she looked for opportunities to do free-lance set design. Soon her parents hired Wesley as an engineer. The couple has been there ever since. Except for several remodeling jobs for friends and family, Donna has not been employed as an architect.

Although working for her parents' company was not what Donna had planned, it offered advantages. She said, "It's not true of a lot of people of my generation, but I like working with my husband. I really like spending time with him. We lost enough time getting married this late."

Donna worked her way from an administrative position to her current job as operations manager. In this capacity, she is involved with personnel, troubleshooting, and technical problems, and she oversees two departments. "I wear a lot of different hats, not all of them becoming," she said.

Donna and Wesley now work as a team on a number of creative projects. They have become involved in costume competitions at science fiction conventions. Their work has evolved into small theatrical productions complete with music and voice-overs. They won first prize in a regional master competition in 1986 with four costumed characters. Donna did the design and handwork while Wesley did the machine sewing. In 1988, they won Best in Show in the masquerade competition at the World Science Fiction Convention.

Donna has joined the costumer's guild, and costuming has blossomed into a family affair. Her oldest son, Aaron, produced computer music for their last competition. Jason appears in the competitions and is taking acting classes through the American Conservatory Theatre. The conventions form the core of family vacations, and they have made firm friends of the people they've met.

In 1983 Wesley and Donna bought a home built in 1914. Renovating the house is a never-ending project. "We're constantly remodeling," Donna said. "We could never have moved into this house if we didn't have the skills we do. We did our kitchen down to the studs. We're working on a hot-tub room. We've walled in the yard. Next we'll add a costume room in the attic." All their work is true to the house's original style.

Donna has also done a stint as a resident set designer for a local theater. Her salary barely paid for the gas it took to commute to the theater, but it was an opportunity to design sets, costumes, and jewelry, her new interest. "If nothing else," Donna said, "we will never get bored! Jewelry and costumes have the advantage of being much more portable than sets."

Donna is ambivalent about the time she put into her architecture degree. She is disappointed she isn't using her degree to earn a living, and self-conscious about this fact. She said, "I tell people I'm trained as an architect. They ask me what I do. I hesitate. I shrug it off and mumble 'Managerial.' I live in Berkeley, and all of my professors and some of my fellow students are here. I don't go over and say hello when I spot them on the street. I sort of pretend I don't see them because I'm ashamed of the fact that I'm not doing anything."

On the other hand, Donna is very reluctant to take the critical steps toward the type of architecture that interests her—single-family dwellings. She doesn't want to work for a large firm drafting toilet stalls, gradually moving up to drafting other people's designs. Nor does she consider starting her own business. "You have to be able to go out and sell yourself," she said, "to toot your own horn, say that you're better than anyone else. I just can't do that."

Donna and Wesley have many financial commitments. The mortgage payments on their home are substantial. Aaron is a college freshman. "We don't have a lot of discretionary funds. If I were to stop working for the company and try to follow something else, we might lose our house."

Yet Donna sees many pluses from having gotten the architecture degree. It has definitely given her more confidence in her abilities as a designer and as a creative person. "There are several areas where I can say, 'This is something I'm good at.' It's one thing to dabble and another to have been successful in an environment that is heavily competitive. The degree made me officially creative or artistic, and a professional trained in design."

Her partnership with Wesley has deflected her urge to leave the family business. "If you're working with the right people," she said, "it almost doesn't matter what you are doing. Wesley is always involved with the costuming and has always helped with the practical aspects of the set designs. This is something I think I wanted more than anything else, more than a specific career goal—to be working with and spending a lot of time with the person who is most important to me."

LACK OF TEACHING JOBS LED TO A CHANGE IN CAREER PLANS

Florence's goal when she went back to school at age 27 was clear. She entered a one-year master's degree program in education at Wheelock College so she could teach young children, a goal she had set when she was in her teens. She graduated in 1975 but couldn't break into elementary school teaching in Boston.

Instead, Florence found an enjoyable job as an associate director and curriculum coordinator for an education program that brought together inner-city and suburban high school students. Later, she became promotions coordinator for one of Boston's major tourist attractions. Although she designed materials attractive to children, this shifted her interest from classroom work to public relations.

Florence's prior work experience, when she was fresh out of college in 1969, was in television production for National Educational Television and WNET/13 New York. However, she became disenchanted with film and television production, and commented in 1978: "I didn't have the 'driven' personality it took to excel in the New York film world. I didn't have the total commitment to compete successfully. After a couple of years of free-lancing, I needed to change my work and my life completely." As it turned out, the skills she gathered through this work, coupled with her master's degree in education, made her very marketable as a curriculum coordinator.

Florence did not experience many of the conflicts that confront reentry women students. Her parents helped finance her education. The major adjustment was going from working woman to student.

"I was a woman living alone. I didn't have to answer to anyone. When you're a student, your time is not your own the way it is when you're a working person. You have less control over your life. There were all kinds of things I wanted to do, but I had to study. The obligations don't end when you leave the campus."

Florence acknowledges that she gave up working in a field in which there were not enough jobs only to land in teaching—another field where there were not enough jobs. Nonetheless, Florence is glad that she got her master's degree, even though she was unable to find the job she wanted. She reports that she became more assertive after going back to school. She also feels good about having done well academically.

"My goals were affected by reality. I couldn't get the job I set out to get. However, I was very happy with the work I found. I also came to realize that I was probably not well suited to elementary classroom teaching. Now that I look back on it, it was a fortunate turn of events that I did not get a job in that field."

What Florence learned in the early childhood education program is coming in handy during the most recent chapter of her working history—motherhood. She married a psychologist in 1979 and the couple now has two preschool-age children.

Florence said recently, "This is what I want to be doing now. It's a very self-sacrificing role, but the rewards are enormous. I literally could not be doing it any other way. I need and want that total commitment to bringing them up. If I were to have a job outside of the home, I would feel tremendous separation anxiety; I would feel I was missing something I really don't want to miss."

Florence recommends a comprehensive examination of the job market before heading back to college to prepare for employment. "It seems a bit misdirected to prepare for a job that ultimately does not exist. Had I been more on top of things, I would have realized how difficult it was going to be to get the job I wanted," she said.

Concerning her own plans for working outside of the home, Florence is in a holding pattern. She feels satisfied with her present life-style and plans to keep her options open.

SCHOOL HELPED RENEW HER SELF-CONFIDENCE

The fatal skin-diving accident of the man with whom she lived precipitated Carolyn's return to school. She felt a pressing need to do something to make the world a better place. She decided to pursue a master's degree in public health.

Going back to school meant leaving San Francisco, a city Carolyn adored, and moving back to Los Angeles to live with her mother. She sold her car and all the furniture she had collected. She left all her friends and made a drastic switch in life-style. As a social worker she had earned a good salary. As a student she had to get by on $300 a month.

Carolyn wanted to work with severely developmentally disabled children. Almost as soon as she entered the master's degree program, however, she realized her philosophical approach differed from the one advocated by the school.

She preferred to focus primarily on prevention and education rather than on providing health services. She swiftly concluded that a master's degree in public health might prove irrelevant. "From the very beginning, I realized that I was going to be bucking the system," she said.

"I've become very pessimistic about the world we live in, knowing that one individual can do nothing. Even though we feel that we can, in the long run we can't." That is obviously a very sad commentary on our world. Government and bureaucracies are not responsive to the health-care needs of people," she says now.

Carolyn is convinced that counseling would have helped her realize ahead of time that the M.P.H. program was not for her. Similarly, she thinks that a career counselor or academic counselor could have offered suggestions for alternative degrees.

Carolyn had promised herself she would stay in school no matter what. Now, however, she says that, if she had it to do over again, she would switch programs. Despite these feelings, she believes the time she spent in school was worth it. "I went back to school because I lacked direction, I was unhappy, and I was trying to fill a void," she said. "While I was in graduate school I learned to cope with the real world." Carolyn became more self-assured while she was in school, and graduated with a 3.7 GPA.

When she returned to school at age 27, Carolyn was one of the oldest students in her class and she soon assumed a leadership role. "The other students thought of me as a grown-up," she said. "They looked to me for information they hadn't been around long enough to gather. I had been out in the real world working. Having other students think of me as a leader was an unexpected fringe benefit of being back in school."

Carolyn was able to effect some changes in the public health degree program. She served on the admissions committee during her second year. In this capacity, she discussed the students' counseling needs with professors and staff.

Immediately after graduating in 1978, Carolyn got a job as director of a facility for developmentally disabled adults and children. The work only confirmed her sense of incompatibility with the field. "The goal I had set for myself—to help developmentally disabled children—was an impossible task because of the financial and bureaucratic problems," she said.

"I decided to get out of the field of public health and developmental disability, having been burned out by it." Carolyn found part-time temporary employment, working as a secretary in various medical settings. She had done this type of work previously.

That same year, Carolyn met Ron, her husband-to-be. She began to focus more on her personal life and less on her professional one. She and Ron, an administrator in the county welfare department, were married in August 1979.

The following year, Carolyn's brother was diagnosed as having multiple sclerosis. He came to live with the couple, and Carolyn was able to use her knowledge of the medical field and health-care systems to improve her brother's life while he came to grips with his disability. In 1981, with her brother stabilized, she accepted a full-time job as administrator/secretary in a doctor's office.

Carolyn and Ron adopted a newborn, Harry, in May 1984. Since then the family has been Carolyn's major focus. On a very part-time basis, she manages a friend's psychotherapy practice and helps her brother, who is now living on his own.

"In the past year," she said, "my attitudes toward career and motherhood have become clear. I've chosen to put my energies toward motherhood. That's where I feel I want them at this time."

Carolyn reports that she has maintained the self-confidence she gained in school, even though she has not utilized her degree in a career. She is also able to offer help and advice about how to deal with various health-care systems and with medical matters in general. She serves as a major resource for an impressive number of family members, friends, and callers from the community. If she can't answer a question, she usually knows how to track down the information or to whom the person should be referred. "This has a direct relationship to my having gone through the public health program," she comments. "People think I am a knowledgeable person, and that makes me feel good."

Time at home with Harry is letting Carolyn rethink her career plans. She has become interested in environmental health, where she feels it is possible to work outside of the system. "I'd like to find something part-time in this area. I'm willing to start over again with an entry-level position and work my way up to management. One's career goals are constantly changing."

THERE'S MORE TO A COLLEGE DEGREE THAN FINDING A JOB

CHAPTER 9
SEEKING PERSONAL
DEVELOPMENT

A diploma is something tangible that can be framed and put on the wall. In many cases, it establishes instant credibility. It symbolizes the completion of a specific program of learning, the acquisition of skills and knowledge, a readiness to go out and get a job.

Statistics indicate that college graduates earn more money than nongraduates and spend less time unemployed. Going back to school in order to prepare for employment is the most common reason for the "graying of the campus."

Back in the 1940s, after the war, working mothers of children under age 18 were the glaring exception rather than the rule. Women were supposed to be completely fulfilled by activities centering in their homes. But today, women often feel guilty if they don't have a job-oriented answer to the question "What do you do?"

In the 1970s people simply assumed that if you were an older student, you were taking classes for intellectual stimulation. Nowadays, when older students say personal development and intellectual stimulation are their reasons for returning to college, some people wonder about their hidden agenda.

Although most students are career oriented, others have found plenty of good reasons to take college classes. Some are in degree programs, while others are not at all concerned about accumulating credits. The five women featured in this chapter have reaped the intangible benefits from taking on a student role as an adult.

Ninety-one percent of the women interviewed for *Degrees of Success* reported an increase of self-confidence as a direct result of returning to school. Marilyn, the mother of ten, has come such a long way since she thought of herself as "Miss Stupid of the World." Annette, valedictorian of her high school graduating class in 1950, was hospitalized after a complete nervous breakdown ten years later. School helped her restructure her life.

For many reentry women, going to college and graduating is the completion of unfinished business. Rachel, for example, attended college from 1946 until 1948, when she got what she calls her "MRS." degree. Twenty-eight years later, the last of her children had left home, and she decided it was her turn to go to school. Being able to achieve something that she really wanted has convinced her that she is now fit to face life's challenges.

Adult students are very conscious of their grades. Tests and writing assignments can be viewed as an indication of how a person is doing. There are no finals in a woman's role as mother, for example, no quantifiable way of being sure you are doing it right. Grades can be a relief and a pleasure for adults who have been grappling with tests whose results are intangible.

School can help serve as a tremendous resource for women in a mid-life crisis. Libby, for example, said she was in a rut. Her husband was busy being successful, her children were busy growing up, and she felt useless. Not only did she find self-confidence and independence through her reentry, but she and her husband reported an improved relationship.

Terry's marriage was dissolving while she was back in school. School gave "some forward movement" to her life, as she put it. "I had a feeling of gain during a time of loss," she said.

All five of the women whose stories are told in this chapter associate college with "forward movement." In fact, all continue to take classes—for the mere joy of learning.

The process of going to college can be just as valuable as the actual degree. Carol Aslanian and Henry Brickell point out *(Americans in Transition)* that 80 percent of adults who return to school do so because their lives are changing. College can be a wonderful place in which to experience life's transitions.

THE KEY WAS SELF-CONFIDENCE

Imagine this as your first job out of college at age 51: driving a shiny one-ton truck, ordering pilot burner tips for dehydrators, serving as liaison between two oil-field workers with your shortwave radio.

What was an honor student in English doing in an oil field? "Enjoying my work," said Marilyn. "I'm interacting with people, supporting myself, and feeling part of a company I like." Marilyn believes that it was precisely going back to school that gave her the confidence to get a job as field coordinator for a major gas company. Previous job experience: part-time hostess and cashier at a restaurant. "Self-confidence was the key for me. It was so satisfying to do well in school. I used to project a scatterbrained image, and people didn't take me seriously. School changed that," she said.

Marilyn dropped out of college in 1948, after one semester, in order to get married. When she enrolled at a state university in 1974 at age 45, she was the mother of ten children, ages 9 to 25. Her husband was a professor at the same university.

Seeking Personal Development

"I thought I was Miss Stupid of the World," Marilyn commented. "Many women my age feel they may not have the capacity for school. A lot of my friends—faculty wives—wouldn't dream of going back to school because they didn't want their husband's friends to see how dumb they were. They didn't want to embarrass their husband. That's exactly how I felt at first."

Marilyn was so frightened that she audited only one class the first semester. A friend helped her through the registration process. The next semester, she took a class for credit. As her confidence built, so did her course load. She graduated with a 3.9 GPA.

Before returning to school, Marilyn had felt completely defined as a wife and mother for years. She had happily chosen those definitions for herself. She said, "I delighted in making my husband happy. That was my biggest goal—just pleasing my husband. I was in love."

By the time Marilyn decided to take classes, she was fighting depression. In 1978 she said she felt inferior to her husband and many other people she encountered.

"The depression was a gift in a way because it showed me how unhappy I was with things the way they were. I had to pull myself out of that depression," Marilyn recalled in 1987. "I discovered I could be recognized for myself instead of as my husband's wife. Sometimes my self-confidence is lower than it should be, but never again will it be as low as it was. After I got out of school I was a person. Before that I had been pretty much asleep."

Marilyn wanted an identity separate from her husband. "One professor was a great fan of my husband's. The first semester I worked with him he always asked what my husband was doing. The next semester he was asking what I was doing, what I was writing or thinking about. That was a wonderful exchange."

Bernard, Marilyn's husband, was proud of her for taking courses and pursuing a degree. In 1978 he said, "I am delighted to have my wife in school. I think it has broadened her interest in everything, and she is excited about learning. She has a different range of interests—not exclusively home and children."

At that time, Bernard also discussed some of his concerns: "She tends to overachieve and to become desperate about doing well on tests. She has a tendency to announce, 'I am going to study four days for my test, so I won't be doing anything else.' This does disrupt things a bit. I think we all resent it, although we have gotten used to it."

When Marilyn began taking classes, she used her husband's office as a "security base." Bernard recalled, "It helped her at first, but I felt she was intruding in my territory. This didn't make me feel comfortable about her being in school." Both spouses adjusted. Bernard said, "Now she has interests in other departments and spends most of her time away, but I feel we are doing the school thing together."

Marilyn believes, however, that Bernard continued to resent the time she spent on school-related activities. And as she grew more confident, she said, "I needed him less. I was meeting other people. I don't think he ever liked that."

In 1987 Marilyn said she wished she had combined her reentry with better parenting. "It was hard on the kids," she explained. "My interest was more with school than with family; everyone suffered. I didn't have as much time to read them stories at night. I was trying so hard to do well in school. It took time. It took me from the kids."

Marilyn believes that all of her children are very proud of her, especially the older ones. "But I don't think the younger ones will ever forgive me, although I'm a much better mother to them now than I would have been."

One of the children still at home when Marilyn went back to school was Heather, 24 at the time of her interview in 1987. She was ambivalent about Marilyn's student role. "I remember feeling embarrassed that my mother was going back to school. It seemed like she was trying to act like a young adult," Heather said. "When she was studying, I couldn't or wouldn't bother her. I felt Mom was more concerned with herself than with me and the other kids. I was hurt that she chose studying over helping me, being with me. I felt like I wasn't good enough for her—that the family wasn't good enough for her."

Yet Heather is proud of her mother: "She seemed to change her whole outlook on life. It's almost like she grew up, opened her eyes. She seems interested in studying everything. It's wonderful. She's interested and interesting.

"When Mom went back to school, her marriage and mental health were falling apart. School was all she hung on to. I don't think she would be alive today if she hadn't gone back to school and learned she was OK.

"I'm very proud of my mother. She did something really important for herself. Going back to school takes a lot of courage. I'm dealing with many of the same choices now."

Marilyn wishes she had gone back to school before she had children. "If I were to do it over again, I would better integrate my student role and family life. I wouldn't make the student part so prominent or what I was hanging on to for survival."

Marilyn believes that things might have worked better if she had devoted one day a week exclusively to her children. She wishes she had shared her student experience with her family.

"If I were to do it again, I would recruit the family so they could feel important and part of the experience." She suggests taking children to the university library, concerts, and other campus-related events. She also thinks it's a good idea to set up specific times for mother and children to study together.

Heather offered a good suggestion: "I wish she had explained to us why she was going back to school. I wish she had told us where she was going, what it was like, and what it felt like to be older. It would have been better if she had told us what she was learning and what that meant to her. I was confused about what was going on."

Heather commented on the changing relationship between her parents: "She changed so much and grew to be a different person. I don't think my dad could handle that. Maybe he felt threatened, or maybe he felt uncomfortable that Mom was smarter than before, and she knew it. Dad seems really liberal about women's equality, but I believe he didn't like the thought of Mom being equally intelligent. He didn't want to talk with her about intellectual things."

In 1979, near the end of her junior year, Marilyn and Bernard separated. For the first time in her adult life, Marilyn was job hunting—at age 50. She found work as a part-time hostess and cashier at a restaurant. "It was a perfect step between working and not working. It gave me critical experience working with people."

Marilyn enjoyed talking with the customers. Just after graduation, a customer told her about the oil-field coordinator position, urging her to apply. She began her new job in January 1981 and earned enough to live comfortably. "I'm proud of that," she said, "especially considering how dependent I was for so long."

Marilyn left that job in 1983. She had always wanted to travel. She covered a lot of ground during the next few years, including a five-month stint in Greece. She has now settled in a small town in the Southwest. "This town has artists, music, bookstores, and people who are interested in more than small-town gossip and their husband's job and new car," she said.

"The first day I came to town, I was hired by an art gallery because someone overheard me talking to a friend about art and about needing a job. He came up to me and said, 'Would you like a job?'"

In 1987 Marilyn was unsure of what she wanted to do next. She was thinking about creating and marketing walking tours of several towns in the area or going back to school in anthropology or archaeology (an outgrowth of her volunteer work at a museum). "Or I might take early Social Security, buy myself a pickup truck and trailer, hit the road, and visit all my kids and the national parks."

Marilyn's desire to learn is voracious. Scattered throughout her home are books on aging, myths, Greece, photography, poetry, and the Spanish language. "I'll always be learning things," she said. "And, there are so many places I want to see."

"What I gained from school was self-confidence, the knowledge that I could do a good job, complete an assignment. It made me aware of capabilities I didn't even dream I had before I went back to school."

NONCREDIT COURSES CAN STIMULATE PERSONAL DEVELOPMENT

Terry received her bachelor's degree in art from Southern Methodist University in 1965 at the traditional age of 21. Eleven years later, she decided to audit a few classes and has been in school ever since. The time she now spends in college has nothing to do with degree programs. Terry is in school for stimulation, personal development, and knowledge.

"Everything I have studied has enriched my life in ways I am realizing every day," Terry commented at age 43. "I remember when my psyche lived like a pale shoot under a rock, which was my sense of my own limitations; it blocked out the sun. Those limitations were of my own making and were in my power to remove."

In 1978, Terry and her husband, an artist, were in the process of separating. Terry, also an artist, thought the stimulation of a college campus would help her through what she called "the emotional morass." She said recently, "My life had kicked loose. I went to school to engage my intellect and establish a schedule. I also began exercising regularly. My aim was survival and enjoyment rather than a practical reward. I wanted to go back and get an education, without the hassle of degree requirements, or grade point averages, or other distractions."

Terry had already established herself as a craftsperson and was able to support herself by selling the jewelry she designed. "I needed other interests. My identity was bound up in one area. I wanted to experience other things, learn other things, get out of the rut I was in." The first few semesters she took t'ai chi, poetry writing, art history, and life drawing.

Asked if there was anything she had to give up in order to take classes, Terry responded, "I lost a sense of security based on always doing the same thing, always knowing where I would be. But I got some forward movement to my life. I had a feeling of gain during a time of loss."

School was 100 miles away from her home in Texas. Yet Terry did not view time away from her studio as a problem, even though it meant less time for making jewelry. She commented at the time: "If you make a living as a craftsman, you need a lot of hours in the studio. Suddenly, at least two or three days a week, I was not there. But it worked out. I am so stimulated when I am away that I can work more intensely when I get back. The whole financial thing worked out all right."

One reason Terry took classes in 1978 was because she wanted to develop her own identity when she and her husband were growing apart. She said, "I feel good being in the city half the time and being in the country half the time. I have a better idea of who I am and what I need to do in my life. I have a better sense of self than I had before."

Terry reports that she feels more comfortable in unfamiliar situations as a result of the wide variety of subjects she has studied. She said recently, "It accounts for my feeling of ease and competence in starting a business that I'm learning from the most elementary levels." Terry, her mother, and her sister have started a construction business, and Terry's jewelry business continues to do very well. Her work is sold in a number of fine galleries nationwide.

"This last year," she said recently, "I bought a computer and learned word processing. I learned accounting and put my business accounts on computer. I have a graphics package that lets me design my mailers and print labels.

"When I can afford a really good graphics printer, I'll design jewelry on the computer. Last night I started a class to learn how to read blueprints. In the morning, I'll pick up plans for two projects and learn how to estimate and bid. I love finding out how things work, how they go together. I can't imagine ever deciding I know enough."

Terry also takes classes that have absolutely no connection with her work. Not long ago, French and Spanish were on her to-do list.

Because Terry characterizes her jewelry business as "successful but not one that will put me in the money," she hopes the construction business proves to be more lucrative. What she is aiming for is a balance between creativity and a business offering financial security. She has remarried. She and her husband, an attorney, would like to travel more in the next few years.

When Terry started auditing classes at age 32, she was looking for enrichment. In the process, she has become more confident, met many interesting people, and learned a lot.

She commented recently, "I didn't begin to set myself free until I was in my 30s; before that I was just getting by. Of course, some women never get out from under the weight of their own helplessness. Maybe men, too. Who knows? Little girls are encouraged to make their way manipulatively, depending on the kindness of other people. I think it's hard for women to change, to realize they can become the people on whom they depend."

SELF-ESTEEM AND A NEW PERSPECTIVE ON LIFE ACCOMPANIED THE DEGREE

Annette's reentry story is an odyssey toward mental health. After a nervous breakdown in 1960 at age 28, after fourteen electric shock treatments, she was determined to restructure her life. The price was a divorce in her 40s, living apart from her eight children, and selling the family farm.

Today, Annette is strong, stable, and competent. She has achieved her lifelong goal of obtaining a college education. Her relationship with her children gives her pleasure and satisfaction—four of them were in college while she was. She is self-supporting and doing work that both interests her and allows her time to pursue another lifelong ambition: to become a writer.

When Annette graduated from high school in 1950, she desperately wanted to go on to college. "My father didn't believe in educating daughters, so I wasn't able to go to college even though I graduated at the head of my class. I got married. I was expected to get married," Annette said.

One thing she learned in high school was determination. During her junior year, she set her sights on becoming valedictorian. "I made it by three tenths of a point. Over the years, I've thought back on that experience, that achievement, and it has carried me over some rough ground."

Annette settled into family life in the same rural area where she and her husband had been raised. Their eight children were born between 1951 and 1964. Annette's husband was a construction worker until the couple bought a dairy farm in 1963, just three years after her nervous breakdown. They worked the farm until their separation in 1978.

After the separation Annette decided to actualize her dream of getting an education. A friend of hers wrote to her about his experience as a reentry student. "That set me to thinking," she explained. "I got that letter in March, and I started school in September."

Annette had a specific goal. She wanted to write and speak about actualizing human potential, based on her own battle with mental illness. She decided to major in sociology—"in order to better understand the world that had 'driven me mad'"—with additional emphasis on creative writing and journalism. After a few months in school, she broadened her goals, deciding that she would earn a living as a county social worker.

She had determination and stamina, but a major hurdle before she even began was money. The farm's net income in 1977 was under $12,000. When she inquired about financial aid at the admissions office, she was told that there was none for adults.

But Annette didn't give up. One of her sons had given her the toll-free number for information on federal grants. "I called them. They had someone there 24 hours a day. I talked for half an hour. The person there filled out a new financial aid form for me. Just thirteen days before classes started, I got a notice saying I was eligible."

Annette was terrified. Having been out of the mainstream for the past twenty-seven years, she worried about getting back into the routine of studying, that her brain might have "rusted." She also felt awkward about interacting with other students.

"The first semester I did not smile or look at or speak to anyone in the coffee shop," she said. "A friend, a nontraditional student, pointed this out to me. I was determined to go back in there with a different attitude. I walked into that coffee shop with a smile on my face, and three people that I had seen every day spoke to me. From that frozen, closed-faced beginning to the time I was a senior, I made a number of friends who verified my self-worth and my growth."

The four years in school changed Annette. She evolved from someone who was afraid to approach people to someone other people sought out for moral support. The self-confidence she felt on campus began to permeate her off-campus life as well.

Being with a new group of people was a relief for Annette. Almost everyone she knew before college was aware of her precarious mental health. At school, she started with a clean slate. "I was interacting with people who didn't assume I was crazy. They had no concept of me in that life. This helped me see myself as a competent human being."

In 1978 two of Annette's children were running the farm, another was a teacher, three were college students, and the two youngest were in seventh and ninth grades. There were rough times to come. The three youngest children chose to live with their father after he convinced them that their mother could not possibly support them.

The youngest, Grace, was angry with her mother about the divorce, but she decided to attend the same college as her mother. Soon Grace's roommates were calling Annette "Mumsie" and would come to Annette with various problems.

Four of Annette's children were in college while she was a student. In fact, all eight children attended college; five graduated. The children took pride in their mother's accomplishments. "I was doing exactly what I had always told them they could do—anything that they set their minds to. I was out there doing it at the same time."

Her second-oldest son, a successful insurance salesman and investment broker, said to his mother, "I tell my employees that my mother has given me the edge on confidence."

Annette secured a journalism internship with the local newspaper. Each week, she received an interviewing assignment from the editor, who said that he would print some of her stories if they were good enough. He used every one of them.

Annette's first practical experience in the field of social work resulted from one of her writing assignments. She had interviewed the head of a support group for parents who had problems relating to their children. Shortly thereafter, a new facilitator was needed for the group, and Annette volunteered (under the guidance of a social worker). The outcome of another assignment was an informal counseling situation with a woman who had had a very difficult childhood. Through these experiences Annette gained a new perspective on her own childhood.

Although she had been worried about her abilities, she graduated with a solid B average. However, even before she graduated, Annette realized a traditional social work job was not for her. She had wanted such a job because she sought financial independence, but she could imagine being intensely frustrated by how little she would actually be able to do for her clients.

"I knew that the starting salary, $13,000, would offer basic survival," she explained in 1987. However, a county social work job would also involve buying a new car and living in town. She could not afford the car or the town home.

Instead, Annette found work as a live-in person providing care for elderly women who wanted to stay in their homes rather than move to a nursing home. Annette believes that this type of employment was ideal for her at that point. She could do useful work and sharpen her communication skills in the process.

At the home of her last client, Annette began to feel very isolated. "One step at a time, I began correcting it. I used the problem-solving skills I had learned in college. I applied those skills to daily reality."

As a live-in attendant, Annette earned $75 a week plus room and board. There was an attractive fringe benefit: lots of time to write. "I have never, for one day, lived without my pen and my journal in my hand. I have never for one moment doubted that I will write."

Since 1985, Annette has been a member of a self-help group for adult children of alcoholics, which meets at a nearby college. She says that this is helping her understand her childhood, her marriage, and what she calls "the disease of the family where alcoholism forms the center, the focus."

The day after her last client died in April 1987, the pastor of the local Roman Catholic rectory asked Annette to come work as a cook. There, she prepares meals for the seven priests and has been told she's the best cook they've had in twenty-four years. Her job provides her with a beautiful apartment in a thirty-room building adjacent to the cathedral and $105 per week plus board. In addition, she doesn't have to worry about the sense of isolation her previous jobs sometimes created.

"I moved into a new world—just one block away! From $20 per week for food to a charge account at a supermarket I'd never been able to trade at. I get such satisfaction in using my shopping skills, planning menus, and serving grand meals. The pastor has a great garden, and there are such beautiful vegetables to serve. It's a beautiful atmosphere. No isolation here."

Although a college degree was not necessary for the life-style Annette chose, she says, "I wouldn't change anything about my experience at school. It was difficult, but overcoming difficulties was part of the education as well. It was a new phase of growth, of seeing myself as a worthwhile, competent person.

"College is not just going to a classroom to learn written material. It's about interactions and getting along with different people. I learned how to live for myself, how to become my own best friend."

Last year, at age 54, Annette said of her future, "I am looking forward to the continuation of a life of quiet happiness based on reasonable expectations."

ONE SUCCESS BUILDS ON ANOTHER

Rachel attended college at the traditional age from 1946 to 1948, but dropped out to get married. However, she never stopped wanting to finish her degree. Twenty-eight years later, the last of her three children went off to college. She realized she had plenty of time to take classes.

"You get to that stage of life where you don't know what's going to happen. What if something happens to your husband? Right now, our life-style is tied up in sports. What if all of a sudden something happened and we couldn't play tennis or golf? What would I do with my life? I think I found myself running a little scared," she said in 1978.

"I wasn't worried financially. I was worried about me as a person: What would I do with my time? How would I find satisfaction? I don't think there's anything worse than having a day where there's nothing to do."

Rachel took stock of her life. "All three children were out of the house. Suddenly no more car pools, no more orthodontia. Then you take a look at yourself. More time allows motivation and interests to surface."

Rachel soon realized that she wouldn't even be able to find satisfying volunteer work without some expertise. "Otherwise, you have to start as a stamp licker or an envelope filler. You can't just all of a sudden say, 'I want to do meaningful volunteer work,' and find something—unless you've had experience."

Although she wasn't interested in finding a career, Rachel began her studies by taking a career-planning class. She quickly discovered that there were many women who were going through the same process of reevaluation. In fact, a lot of the students already had degrees and were thinking about going back to school again.

It was through this class that she learned about adult college programs near her home. Rachel decided on Adelphi University, which had a program for people over age 35.

The admissions process and registration were easy, and class scheduling was arranged with the needs of adults in mind. Going on a part-time basis was the norm rather than the exception, and many classes met in the evening. Counselors were readily available to give advice on course selection and degree requirements.

Rachel's family was enthusiastic about her decision to go to school. Her husband, Jeff, holds a bachelor's degree in engineering, and the children were either in college or had graduated. When asked in 1978 whether her student role benefited her children in any way, Rachel laughed. "My daughter was in from college in San Diego for ten days. She took one of my papers from a science course and my whole notebook back with her."

Rachel went to work as a buyer for her husband's store shortly after returning to school. "Five years ago, I would never have done it," she explained in 1978 at age 50. "I'm out in the market. I love it. I got the feeling that if I could master school, I could master buying, even at this stage of the game, and I could master anything that's going to cross my path.

"The first step was going back to school. I guess I felt inadequate before—without realizing it. After I took the business course, I decided to work for Jeff. School gave me the confidence. Jeff went with me once. Then he said I was on my own.

"Going to school has been stimulating, working has been stimulating, relationships have been great. The whole thing is tied together. If I hadn't gone back to school, none of the other things would have followed. I'm very happy. When all three kids were out of the house, I think I went through a depressed state."

In 1982, at age 53, Rachel graduated with a bachelor's degree in psychology and a great deal of fanfare at a celebration staged by her family. She had a 3.8 GPA—all A's except for two B's.

Five years after her graduation, Rachel commented, "I was able to achieve something that I really wanted. Therefore, when I'm up against something new, I can say, 'Well, I did it once, and I'm going to be able to do it again.' You create a tremendous amount of confidence in your ability to go out and meet a new challenge."

She and her husband retired in 1987. Rachel is now exploring various avenues of volunteer work. Her approach is one of confidence. "I seek things out faster now, rather than hide behind my front door. I say to myself, 'Well, if that doesn't work out, I'll find something else. And if that doesn't work, I'll find something else.'"

Jeff and Rachel are considering spending their winters in California. She thinks they will continue as before—each pursuing individual interests as well as ones that they enjoy together.

Rachel plans to continue taking courses—art, education, writing, computer science. "A list of courses always offers something you never thought of, something fascinating. I need mental stimulation to acquire knowledge," she said. "I don't want to sit and stagnate."

A TWO-YEAR SECOND HONEYMOON

The thing the spouse of a reentry student might fear most is that his wife, with her newly acquired self-confidence and independence, will leave him.

Leaving her husband is exactly what Libby did—with his full encouragement and support. She spent the last two years of college at a school an hour and a half from home, seeing her family only on weekends. Rather than deteriorating, Libby and her husband agreed, their relationship actually improved. Their story is an example of how a family that can truly flex will spring back instead of snapping.

Neither Libby nor her husband, Wally, had ever considered going to college until 1976. The last time Libby had seen the inside of a classroom was 1953, when she graduated from high school. Wally, who owns a business, never completed secondary school.

When Libby decided in 1976 to take a few classes at the community college near her New England home, the couple's two children were both in high school. She explained that she was trying to get out of a rut. "My husband was running a successful business, and he was busy. The children were growing up. I was basically discontented with myself," she said.

Libby had been working part-time as an inventory and records clerk in a doctor's office, a job she did not particularly enjoy. "I felt more or less useless," she commented. When she decided to go to college, she didn't have a career goal, nor was she aiming for a degree. She was delighted to find that she had plenty of company at the community college—other women like herself who were back in school for stimulation and personal development.

After taking one course per semester for several years, Libby decided to enroll in the educational assistant program. For many years she had wanted to work with children, and this major seemed ideal. She soon learned that employment in this field was very limited, so she switched to the early childhood education major, receiving her A.A. degree in 1980 at age 45.

She wanted to go on for a bachelor's degree, but she was ready for a real change in her life. "The more I thought about it, the more I wanted to be off on my own. I thought: 'As long as I'm going to do something like this, I might as well try it in a warm climate.'"

"I think you've just blown my mind," was her husband's initial reaction when she explained that she wanted to get her bachelor's degree in Florida. After thinking about it, however, Wally felt it was a good idea for Libby to pursue her plan.

Libby's and Wally's daughter was away at college, but their son, Jay, had just graduated from high school and was still living at home. "His first reaction was, 'Who's going to do the laundry?' I told him I'd show him which buttons to push and he'd be all set."

Libby headed south, accompanied by Wally, who wanted to help her settle in. "We looked at the university, I found a place to live, and I was told by the dean that I would be accepted as an upper-division transfer student. I assumed that meant my community college credits would all transfer." Wally went home, and Libby went to registration day.

Although Libby was accepted by the university, many of her credits turned out to be nontransferable. If she wanted to graduate from this university, it would take her three years instead of two, and she would have to go to school all year round. She had no intention of spending her summers away from her family, so the Florida plan fizzled.

Libby decided to make the most of a disappointing situation, however. She had rented her apartment on a month-to-month basis. "I figured that as long as I was there, I might as well have a vacation." She came home after a month, refreshed and eager to start a bachelor's degree in early childhood education elsewhere.

Still wanting to live on her own, Libby enrolled at a state university an hour and a half away from her home. She found an apartment and went to school full-time, graduating in 1983 at age 48.

"What it did for our marriage was amazing," Libby explained. "Because we were away from each other, we didn't have conversations like 'Who's going to cook dinner?' Wally came every weekend to visit; it was like courting again—just like starting the marriage again. All the excitement and all the feelings of years gone by came back.

"The minute he came in the door, I was so glad to see him. It was wonderful. I wonder what would have happened to the marriage if I hadn't done this; we were in a rut, and I was so displeased with myself."

Wally agrees that Libby's going away to school was a positive experience for both of them. He said, "She has a lot more confidence in herself. She can function with people on a much higher level than before she went to school." Concerning their separation, he said, "It was kind of like a honeymoon for us."

Libby got so much more than just the degree out of her experience. "It's going to stay with me for the rest of my life. My husband agrees. It's changed me, the way I function, and what I am able to do."

Libby says she always worried that she was too dependent on her husband. She wondered how she would manage if she found herself a widow. "Having done this," she explained, "I know that I can make it on my own.

"It's the best thing I could have done for myself. And my self-assurance means a lot to my husband. He has a lot of business contacts, so he's always seeing people. I didn't, so I had very little confidence in myself. School gave me that. My husband used to tell me quite often how much of a difference he thought it was making. He told me he was really proud of me."

Even though her son complained about having to do housework, he and his sister were both proud of their mother. And Libby said that being in school with the younger students helped her to understand her own children better. "You can listen to your own children, and they can tell you things, but to hear the same things from other children their age helps you really hear it.

"I was able to come home and talk about what was going on in the world. You become more aware of what's going on out there, rather than what's happening in your own small home environment."

Many of Libby's and Wally's friends thought the couple was destined for divorce. "Friends said, 'How can you do that?' and they said to my husband, 'How can you let her do that?' One acquaintance said to him, 'You know, if you let her do that, she'll become very independent, and then she'll be wanting to do more things on her own.' I guess that's the way a lot of men feel," Libby said.

After graduating, Libby returned home and got a half-time job doing exactly what she wanted to do: preschool teaching. She loves her work. "I have friends who don't want to go to work in the morning. They're not happy with their jobs. I love doing what I'm doing. To me, it's not work. Three- to 5-year-olds are wonderful."

CHAPTER 10
COLLEGE AS A
FAMILY AFFAIR

Many women who return to school confront resistance from family members. For others, however, the desire for education turns out to be contagious and spreads throughout entire families. One person's return to school can pave the way for others.

Often, the children of reentry students are so proud of their student parent, they duplicate career and academic patterns. Carla and her son, Glen, set off together to become teachers, eventually earning master's degrees in related fields. In Lois's family, all four children chose the teaching field, following in the footsteps of both parents. Anne's daughter and husband followed her to law school.

Many reentry students from the 1970s report that their children are now second-generation returning students. In this chapter, Harriet, the daughter of Lois and Paul, is juggling work on her doctorate with seeing to the needs of her teenage children in much the same way her parents did. Kate, back in school at age 37, was able to provide motivation for *three* generations—her daughter, her sister, and her mother.

Vivian and her husband had fifteen children in sixteen years! It's impossible to sort out who influenced whom academically, since they all went to college. Vivian graduated with her eighth-born. This couple paid college tuitions for nearly twenty-five years and were delighted to have the opportunity.

Families in which everyone gets into the academic act haven't always been the ones with a strong focus on education. Linda was the first among her relatives to receive a college degree, and her husband was the first in his family to chart a professional career. Carla's husband left school after the sixth grade, and she was the only one among her many siblings to graduate from high school.

All six women in this chapter have a common link: they included their families in their decision-making process. They met less resistance than many other women because the family was a team determined to attain a mutually beneficial goal.

For example, Lois's income as a teacher was critical. The couple would not have been able to afford college for their four daughters on just one salary. Carla's husband was ill when she went back to school. Her preparation for employment was considered a family project to prepare her for a time when she would be on her own.

The women featured here came home to supportive environments each day. Linda's husband empathized with her law school experience because he had gone through the same ordeal. Carla, her husband, and their son used to sit around the table after school discussing what had happened in class. Anne and her husband, Stephen, felt their marriage benefited because of Anne's new interests and challenges. In Vivian's household seventeen people were rooting for each other.

These women believe their stable home life made their student role easier. They derived moral support and inspiration from their family. Their success inspired other relatives to follow in their footsteps.

TWO EDUCATIONS FOR THE PRICE OF ONE

Education was considered a luxury in Carla's family in the Arkansas hills. The goal of completing high school paled against the more basic needs for food and shelter. The family of nine was "rich in love," she says, but living below the poverty level established during the depression years. Although Carla (born in 1926) dreamed of an education and a job as a schoolteacher, it was hard for her family to imagine her doing it.

Carla clung to her dream, and was the only one among her brothers and sisters to graduate from high school. Thirty-two years later, at age 49, she resumed her education with the full support of her husband and children. After graduating in 1979, her dream of nearly half a century came true.

Carla's return to school was instigated by her husband, Earl, a disabled veteran of World War II. His left shoulder joint and forearm were destroyed by a mortar shell in the Battle of the Bulge. He was in very poor health; in 1973 he nearly died twice due to heart problems.

Earl was deeply concerned about how Carla would support herself if he died. A college degree, he reasoned, would be a valuable asset. He also hoped college might help Carla develop confidence in her ability to make decisions on her own.

Earl had known Carla since she was 14 and he was 20. To know her was to know of her intense desire to teach. He believed the time had finally come for her to take the necessary steps to achieve that lifelong goal.

In 1975 Carla took their 18-year-old son, Glen, to register for classes at the new community college near their Arkansas home. "I called my husband to tell him that we had completed Glen's registration. Earl instructed me to go back and register myself, too. He said he had been doing some figuring, and he was going to send us both. That's how I got on the learning bandwagon," she recalled.

"After I attended classes for two weeks," Carla said, "I tried to get Earl to let me turn in my books and get our money back. He said, 'No.' That was the end of that. I'm glad he knew me better than I knew myself.

"My return to school was a family endeavor. Earl was our staunch supporter and gave us the encouragement we needed when we felt low. While we were in classes, he kept the home fires burning."

Although Earl had left school after the sixth grade, Carla noted, he pursued an education on his own and had an especially keen interest in history. He knew a great deal about Arkansas, traveled all over the United States while in the military service, and had been in nine countries before he was wounded in the war.

Carla describes Earl as having been a modest, private person. Only a few family members and close friends are aware of the thirteen medals he received because of his military service—including the Purple Heart and the Bronze Star Medal. Carla said proudly, "His life could be the subject of a book!

"He had a self-made education," she commented. "Glen and I got it from a book. Earl saw history firsthand. He was very interested in my courses. It was a topic of conversation every day. We would get in around 2, and I'd start making the meal. We'd all sit around the table and discuss the courses. My return to school made my husband feel terrific."

Carla and Glen commuted to college together every day. While the two were at school, Earl pored over the books that weren't being used that day. Daughter Faye was living in Indiana but also offered her mother a great deal of encouragement.

Carla's many sisters and brothers remembered her childhood determination to become educated and were pleased that she was working to make her dream come true. They recalled how she began school at age 5, considered very young in her era, and was forced to repeat second grade after battling scarlet fever.

When Carla was 9, her family relocated to an area where they could pick cotton. Carla and her siblings went to school only when there was no cotton ready for picking. At other times of the year, they might miss school because of bad weather or impassable roads. In the winter, the sleet was so bad that she had to wrap a bandanna across her face for protection. One time, her feet froze. The summers brought swarms of buffalo gnats.

"One winter, a new wooden bridge was being built over a ditch of deep water that cut the road to school. I would walk before daylight to a teacher's home. Her husband would row us across and then drive us on to the elementary school in his Model T Ford," she recalled.

The constant absences proved too much for her brothers and sisters, who eventually dropped out of school. However, Carla graduated right at the top of her class in 1944 at age 17.

She married Earl, who was on his way overseas to fight in the war.

Teachers were in short supply, and, despite her lack of college, Carla was able to get a job teaching grades 1 through 5 in a small community 7 miles from town. She adored her job, and she took 12 hours of credit at the state college during the summer.

Earl returned in 1945. Carla continued to teach until she became pregnant with their daughter, Faye, in 1946. Glen was born ten years later, and Carla enjoyed focusing on her family. All the while, however, she jumped at any opportunity to teach. She did a two-month stint as a fourth-grade substitute teacher when Glen was in the first grade. And for twenty years she volunteered at her church's preschool.

Carla had wanted to get an education and become a teacher for nearly half a century. But when she suddenly had the chance, she was terrified at first. She lacked confidence in her ability to study and pass the courses. She felt she stuck out like a sore thumb at the community college—the oldest student by a good twenty years.

Carla was part of the first class to enter the new community college, and the instructors were energetic and helpful. "They took a personal interest in me. They gave a lot of encouragement and wiped away all my fears. At times, I felt like a mascot. With the help of my husband and my son, I did my very best." Carla tutored English at the same time that she was taking classes.

After graduating in 1977, Glen and Carla pointed their car toward a state university where they both majored in elementary education, receiving their bachelor's degrees in 1979. Carla had a perfect 4.0 GPA.

During her last semester in school, Carla did her student teaching under the supervision of a third-grade teacher who had been her close friend since their teenage years. At the end of the term, in January 1979, she was offered a paid position as an aide in the same classroom.

In the spring, there was an opening for a special education teacher at the school. Carla got the position for the following fall. During the summer she earned 12 credits in special education. September found her happily ensconced in her new job teaching children with learning disabilities in grades 1 through 5.

A year later, in 1981, Earl died, but he had had the profound satisfaction of knowing that Carla was happily employed as a teacher and that he had set her on her successful path. He had actively helped nurture Carla's development into an assertive and outgoing person.

Their son, Glen, speaks with fondness of the four years that he and his mother spent in school together. "She is more outgoing, more open-minded, and more decisive," he said. "If Mom hadn't gone back to school, I think she would have fallen apart after Dad died. She's been remarkably strong as a widow. Men have tried many times to take advantage of her in business matters. Mother hasn't allowed anyone to treat her unfairly. She has a good business sense."

Shortly after Earl's death, Carla completed all the course work required for certification in her field. But her career as a special education teacher was short-lived; she had to retire within the year because of a heart condition.

Although she is not in good health, Carla continues to involve herself in teaching. She tutors learning-disabled children. She volunteers her services to a youth program that seeks to help underprivileged children learn more about nutrition, grooming, and citizenship. She works with the children and is on the advisory board that plans the activities and curriculum. She is an active member of her church and helps distribute surplus food to people in need.

Glen, who lives near Carla, is a sixth-grade teacher. He started a master's degree program in school administration in 1984. Carla said recently, "I was able to lend him the books for his first two courses, and that made me really proud. Our experience as students together has resulted in each of us having a deep respect and understanding of each other." Glen received his master's degree in 1985.

The same year, Faye announced to her mother that she was returning to school to become a registered nurse. "If you can do it, I can too," Faye told her mom. In 1987, at age 40, she graduated from the program. To honor the occasion, Glen presented his mother with tickets for her first airplane trip; she was with Faye and her family for the graduation. The next day Faye started working, and she is now enrolled in continuing education classes in her field.

Reflecting on the past ten years, Carla commented, "The rewards come when I meet a student and can feel that I have had a real part in laying the foundation for his or her academic experience. I hope I can keep on helping children reach higher goals in years to come.

"I would not have been able to cope if I had not returned to school. I used to like to be alone, but now I am happiest when I am with people who share mutual interests. I feel that I have come full circle."

THREE LAWYERS IN SIX YEARS

In 1978 Anne, who was 44, decided to pursue a law degree at a university an hour from her home in New England. Her husband, Stephen, supported her enthusiastically. Anne's success in law school led Stephen to reevaluate his career aspirations. Anne graduated in 1981; Stephen enrolled at the same law school in 1982.

In June 1982, their daughter Emily received her bachelor's degree at age 21. She decided to follow in her mother's footsteps along with her father. She lived with her parents during her first year at law school, and there was one car pool of future lawyers heading to school at night and another during the day.

The family was the first wife/husband/daughter combination ever to enroll at this law school. "No, we did not get a package deal on tuition," Anne says, laughing.

Before law school, Anne had been combining volunteer work with part-time editorial positions for university publications. She found that the jobs were dead-end or not intellectually fulfilling.

"I wanted to obtain a law degree in order to have interesting work I could do at my own pace," Anne commented. She also concluded that the degree would improve the family income as well as her own status in their academic community.

Anne had enjoyed getting her bachelor's degree at Wellesley College twenty-two years earlier and looked forward to being a student again. She was not disappointed. "I liked the experience of being back in a classroom setting, making new friends, fitting all this into my ongoing life. I was a heroine of sorts in our group of friends," she said.

The process of retesting her academic abilities proved tremendously satisfying. She said, "I felt much more interesting as I moved into a new intellectual area." Although her student role meant spending less time with Stephen, he felt the quality of the time together made up for quantity: "Time is precious, so we use it more intensely. We talk more. She is less hesitant about expressing opinions and wishes."

Anne's and Stephen's children were 16 and 18 when Anne entered law school. Both were away at boarding school. Consequently, the couple did not have children's schedules to contend with.

The children, according to their parents, were enthusiastic about their mother's pursuit of a law degree. Stephen believes that Anne's academic role served to motivate both him and the children to take on new challenges.

When Anne started school, she wasn't particularly interested in practicing law. She enjoyed editing and intended to market herself as a legal editor. Soon she decided she wanted to make direct use of the degree. As she went through school, she identified specialties on which to focus once she was employed.

Finding a job proved challenging. There were only two major law firms in their community, and the family was determined not to relocate. Anne said, "Finding a job was tough unless you were at the top of your class or already 'connected.'" Anne obtained a judicial clerkship and then joined a practice of six attorneys specializing in personal injury litigation. She was hired, she believes, because of her writing ability and courtroom clerking experience.

However, personal injury litigation was not her primary area of interest, and she left in 1985 to form a partnership with another woman. "My present goal," Anne explained, "is to establish our practice in real estate, estate, and immigration law."

At age 53, Anne is enjoying her practice. However, she was surprised by how much time and energy it took to launch her business. Social life and leisure activities are still definitely on the back burner. But she and Stephen believe it is only a matter of time until she gets "the mixture right: a balance of interesting work, income, and leisure."

According to Anne, her daughter Emily has the temperament to make her the best lawyer in the family. She married in June 1983, graduated from law school in 1985, and works in administration for a major corporation.

Stephen's reason for taking on law school was similar to Anne's. He had been involved with university administration for seventeen years, but without an advanced degree he found it impossible to move into the highest positions. "Stephen insists that his work be fun, by which he means intellectually challenging," Anne said. "He prefers a job no one has had before, one that will be filled by two people when he leaves. These jobs are hard to find in an era of university budget constraints."

For five years after leaving the university, Stephen had written and published a newsletter focusing on management consulting for medical practices. He expected the law degree to serve as a credentialing device for dealing with physicians. Legal training is essential to understanding the regulatory processes and liability issues involved with running a medical practice.

With his law degree almost complete, he became a consultant for a large New York law firm that contracts with health maintenance organizations. He believes the degree he received in 1987 will be an essential credential for a permanent affiliation.

Anne thinks that Stephen's time in law school was more disruptive than hers. Although they each attended school at night, Anne had her days in which to catch up on household activities and plan social occasions. During Stephen's law school years, Anne worked full-time; Stephen went to school at night and worked during the day.

The family's firm roots in their community helped them find balance during the years of juggling school, careers, and home life. "After twenty-seven years of marriage, twenty-four in the same academic community and eighteen in the same house, going to graduate school just doesn't rank as that dramatic a change," Anne explained. Stephen fondly labels the couple's academic scenario a "dual mid-life arabesque."

MAGNA AND MATER CUM LAUDE

Vivian wasn't the only member of her family to receive a college degree on her graduation day in 1979. She and her daughter, Theresa, graduated together—both magna cum laude. Within the month, other family members graduated from high school and law school.

Vivian and her husband, a criminal court judge, had fifteen children in sixteen years (1950–66). All fifteen have attended college, with all but one graduating. One son and one daughter have finished law school, three have earned master's degrees, and another is in drama school.

At last report, ten children were married; Vivian and her husband, Hugh, were the proud grandparents of twenty-five grandchildren, with three more expected before the end of the year. All fifteen children live within a 10-mile radius of their parents' home.

About having so many children while going to school, Vivian said, "You have hectic times anyway. It's hectic whether you're working or going to school or staying home. It's hectic now, and there are only two children still at home, and I'm not working."

All family members were happy to help in any way possible. Vivian said, "My husband was wonderful. He encouraged me to do it because he knew I wanted to.

"But there were days when I was really up to my neck in kids and homework and term papers and dinner and cleaning that made me think of giving up. I would begin to feel guilty. I considered withdrawing, but my husband and children encouraged me to stick it out. We all pulled together."

Theresa, child number eight, encouraged Vivian to take a few extra credits so that mother and daughter could graduate together. Vivian recalled, "I laughed. I said, 'Forget it, Theresa.' But she told me to give it a try, and I did." There was a huge family celebration for the four graduates that year.

Celebration is what this family is all about. There is a steady stream of births, christenings, graduations, birthdays, and anniversaries. Vivian is quick to point out that one of the most meaningful family events was Daniel's graduation from law school in 1978.

"Daniel went totally blind at age 17. He continued his high school education, then went to college and law school. His graduation from law school was a day never to be forgotten. As he approached the podium, his classmates and the entire audience stood and cheered until Daniel returned to his seat." Daniel, now in his 30s, works as a law secretary for a Supreme Court judge. He and his wife have five children.

In 1978 several of Vivian's children discussed their mother while she was out playing tennis: "I wish I had one third of her energy. . . . She has a lot of spunk, a lot of drive. . . . She's motivated. She gets a lot done because she wants to. . . . She enjoys it. . . . She has a desire to learn more. . . . She's more understanding about not doing well in school. . . . My mom is terrific."

Before Vivian went back to school, she was completely in charge of preparing meals, cleaning, shopping, and doing laundry. Hugh and the children willingly did chores in the evenings and on weekends, but once Vivian started taking classes the rest of the family had to do more.

Vivian said, "At 5, I'd leave notes on the refrigerator—'Colleen: It's your night. The chickens are ready. Slip them into the oven at 5:30, and put the baked potatoes in. Timothy and Patrick: You have the kitchen to clean up tonight. Don't expect the girls to do everything.' By the time I got home, everything was hunky-dory. They learned how to take charge. It was good for them."

Getting her college education was something that Vivian had always wanted to do. "I was determined that one day I would have a college degree," she said. "It's as simple as that. Some of it is ego. I think getting a college degree is a great accomplishment."

Even though she had a house full of children at the time, Vivian knew, at age 46, that soon they would be on their own. As her responsibilities at home lightened, she wanted to have career options.

"I didn't have any skills other than typing and steno, and I knew I didn't want to do office work. I figured the best thing to do would be to start school, take my time, and prepare for the work force so that I could get a job if I decided I wanted one."

Vivian's biggest fear when she started school in 1974 was that she might be a "Dumb Dora," as she put it. She said, "You have visions of everybody in school being smarter than you. Then they open their mouths. When I went back, I thought I would be thrilled to get C's. I found myself getting A's."

Although Vivian's major was liberal arts, she chose gerontology as a minor. She thought she would like a job in that field, something part-time. "It's an up-and-coming field," she said in 1978. "And I'm very involved with the aged. My aunt is in a home. For a couple of years I took care of an elderly woman who was very sick and had no family. I was concerned about my mother and father when they were sick. It made me recognize that the aged have needs society hasn't even delved into. Somebody has to start someplace to see what we can do for them."

Almost immediately after graduation, Vivian interviewed for the position of assistant personnel director at a nearby nursing home. They were looking for someone with a gerontology background, and Vivian, at age 51, got her first job outside of her home since she married in 1949. She is certain she would not have gotten the job without the degree and her newfound self-confidence.

The job was ideal. Vivian worked three days a week. Although she was officially responsible only for personnel, she became very involved with the residents. "It was wonderful work," she commented. "It really was a very satisfying position."

After seven happy years she resigned. Recently, she said, "I was in an emotional dilemma. With twenty-one grandchildren and Hugh's mother spending four months each year with us, I was needed, needed, needed. That's a good feeling. I couldn't do everything; something had to give.

"The decision was not made lightly. I spent many hours in prayer and contemplation. I liked working, but my family was more important. It was just that simple when it came to the nitty-gritty. I miss working, but my soul and heart are happier and more at ease."

Now that she has more leisure time, Vivian is developing an avid interest in opera. She also enjoys matinees and museum visits. She continues to play tennis and bridge, but they are taking a backseat to her interest in the arts.

Vivian says that she and Hugh look forward to a life filled to the brim with grandchildren. Soon they will complete nearly twenty-five years of college tuition payments—with no regrets.

HUSBAND AND WIFE SHARE FIVE REENTRY EXPERIENCES

Between the two of them, Lois and her husband, Paul, returned to college *five times*. The first time for Paul was in 1946, with Lois following in 1950. Both had interrupted bachelor's degree programs in order to serve in the navy during World War II. When they resumed their studies in Oregon under the G.I. bill, being in school actually helped take some of the financial pressure off their family.

"Our funds were low," Lois explained. "Under the G.I. bill, we received funding not only for our education but also for housing and day-to-day living." The couple had two small daughters by the time Lois started taking classes. Their solution to the child-care dilemma: Paul went to school in the mornings, and Lois attended in the afternoons.

In 1951 Paul got a teaching job that necessitated moving. They were still in Oregon but too far away from the college Lois was attending for her to commute. Paul combined teaching with working on his master's degree, which he completed in 1956. Lois settled into the role of full-time mother and housekeeper.

In 1962, with two daughters in their teens and two still in grade school, the family left Oregon for Indiana so that Paul could enter a doctoral program. They soon realized it would be impossible to send four children to college on Paul's salary alone. With only three years of college, Lois's potential to find intellectually and economically fulfilling work was slim.

Since the time she had begun her college studies in 1942, she had always wanted to be an elementary school teacher. While Paul pursued his Ph.D., Lois worked for her bachelor's degree and teaching credential. Their daughter Harriet was just starting her own college career as a 17-year-old freshman. Mother and daughter headed off to school together.

The entire family rallied behind Lois's decision to complete her studies. She explained to her family her reasons for wanting to get her degree. They understood what it meant to her and what long-range benefits it would offer them.

"My husband kept propping me up emotionally," Lois recalled. "My children provided a lot of practical help. They taught me how to take notes. When I was buffaloed by new math, my third grader helped me. My daughters seemed proud that I was willing to take a chance and enter a new area."

Lois believes that Paul was relieved she had taken on a student role and was heading for a teaching career. She would be able to lighten the financial pressure on the family. Paul was also completely sympathetic to the growing frustration she had been feeling as "just" a housewife. "I think he was happy to see me enthusiastic and involved mentally," Lois said.

Paul was teaching at the same university where he was pursuing his Ph.D.; he graduated in 1964. The next year, Lois received her bachelor's degree, and at age 44 she got her first teaching job. The entire family was homesick for the West Coast, so in 1966 they moved to San Francisco. Paul landed a position as a professor in a graduate education program, and Lois found a job teaching kindergarten and first grade.

Focusing on the same field added a special dimension to their relationship. Lois said, "We've had such a compatible background as a result of my returning to school. I could empathize with his problems as an administrator and teacher. He could understand my problems as a teacher." Paul agreed, "It gave us much more to talk about. She has been her own person and made a contribution outside the family life. That's important for any person."

Lois believes that the two oldest daughters did not suffer from the life-style of a dual-reentry couple. However, the girls who were still in grade school got less of her time than their older sisters did at the same age.

"I didn't have the time to be the Camp Fire Girl leader, be the homeroom mother, make the extra cookies, and go to all the basketball and volleyball games," Lois commented. "I did my best. My husband and I took turns."

Harriet, a college freshman when Lois resumed her studies, had mixed feelings about having a student for a mother. She commented in 1978, at age 33, "I was glad she was fulfilling a goal she had talked about for such a long time. She was obviously happier than she had been in years. However, I resented the inconvenience of having to share the load of household responsibilities. At the time, I had a hard time understanding her constant need to be encouraged and supported."

However, twenty years after she and her mother were on campus together, Harriet is herself a reentry student. She is back in school, combining work on a doctorate with her obligations as mother of two teenage daughters. She's almost in her mother's shoes—right down to her major in education.

"My mother's going back to school provided a role model for me. I completed my master's degree while my first daughter was a toddler. My second daughter was born three weeks after I got the degree.

"My mother's return to school has strengthened my relationship with her. My doctoral work is in an area she knows a lot about; we have many discussions about it. Also, I can certainly understand how my children feel about having a student mother."

Harriet said that being a student and teacher helped Lois let go of her younger children when they needed independence. "Her preoccupation with her student life helped reduce the 'mother hen' syndrome that plagued our relationship in my high school years.

"The reduction of these tendencies came at just the right time for me. My mother was able to continue her love of mothering young children through teaching, transferring it to her students once we had grown into young adults."

Lois and Paul anticipated sending four children to college. All four graduated, and three completed master's degrees. All four were teachers at some point in their working life, and three continue to work in related fields.

Lois said, "I think my returning to school and becoming a teacher affected my daughters. All of them rejected the idea of being only a homemaker. Early on they decided they were going to have careers and interests of their own."

Degrees of Success

Lois's reentry took her beyond her bachelor's degree. Ten years later, at age 53, she decided to get a master's degree in education so she could teach child development at a community college. Tuition was free because she was attending the university where her husband taught.

In 1976 the couple relocated an hour north of San Francisco in order to be nearer to Lois's mother. Lois took a sabbatical in 1976–77. She continued to commute to the university and completed her master's degree program in 1977. Because of the long commute and her desire to be available to her mother, Lois retired at age 55. Paul continued the long drive until 1980, when he retired as well.

After about a year, Lois missed being in the classroom and decided to volunteer her services as a reading teacher at a Catholic elementary school. "I was asked to stay on as an educational consultant in reading," she explained. "That was definitely as a result of my having a master's degree.

"The faculty accepted new ideas—using teaching machines, cross-age tutoring, and a number of other things I instituted—mainly, I believe, because I had M.A. after my name. The master's degree gave me authority."

In 1985, Lois and Paul returned to Oregon—the twenty-third move in their marriage. Once again missing the contact with children in a classroom, Lois now volunteers as a catechism teacher. She said recently, "I love this situation because I can enjoy the once-a-week class with ample preparation time. It's enough for a retired lady!"

HELPING FAMILY AND FRIENDS RETURN TO SCHOOL

In 1974, twenty-one years after graduating from high school, Kate finally got up enough nerve to drive over to the nearby community college. Once inside the administration building, she was so apprehensive she bolted back toward the door. She actually bumped into another woman. After taking one look at the expression on Kate's face, the woman asked if she could be of any help.

What would have happened if Kate had not collided with Beth as she ran for that community college's door? According to Kate, it probably would have been years until she built up enough nerve to try reentering again.

Kate had been recently divorced and was the mother of four children ages 7 to 17. She had worked as a travel and booking agent but was convinced that she would never find fulfilling work without a college degree. "I felt like life had passed me by," she said.

"I saw an ad in the paper about a college's women's program, so I drove over on that Sunday. On a Sunday with no traffic, the college is about a 7-minute drive from my house. In my head, it seemed like twenty-one years. I was so scared.

"I remember gripping the steering wheel. Everything seemed foreign to me. I was so scared I was numb. You would have thought I was walking to the electric chair instead of to something I had really wanted to do for so many years.

"When I bumped into Beth, I must have looked very scared. She said, 'Can I help you?' I said, 'Yes. I've been away from school for twenty-one years. I want to take a class, and I'm frightened.' She said, 'Have I got a class for you!' And she did."

Beth turned out to be the teacher of Psychology for Personal Growth, an entry course designed to build confidence in students. For Kate, the class was the beginning of what she described as "the opening up of all kinds of worlds."

Two years after accepting Beth's help, Kate created a position at the community college that would enable her to provide the same kind of help to other reentry students. As the community outreach coordinator, two of the people she especially enjoyed serving were her own mother and sister.

At one point, Kate and her daughter, her mother, and her sister were all taking classes at the college. "My mother and sister were resistant to the idea of coming back to school," Kate explained in a recent interview. "They were scared like I was. I was able to pave the way."

Kate was instrumental in establishing and running a senior adult program in which her mother participated. Noncredit and credit classes were offered at convenient hours in accessible locations such as libraries, senior centers, high schools, churches, and community centers throughout the district. Televised courses were also available.

Kate was also responsible for a very popular improvisational drama program for senior citizens. This troupe received national attention when they were invited to perform in Washington, D.C., in 1982. Troupe members write and perform their own work.

Other programs Kate created have served as models nationwide. One is a weekly series of free films, lectures, and discussions focusing on growth and development starting with mid-life. Another matches grandparent-aged volunteers with day-care centers. Off campus, Kate and three friends formed an organization that involved at least fifteen ongoing self-help groups. These programs are over ten years old and are still going strong.

Kate's mother, Amy, enjoyed such classes as public speaking, theater, and medical ethics. In class, she was usually the oldest person by many years. The young students admired her energy and zest for life and looked to her as a role model. In addition to taking her classes, Amy was also a volunteer grandmother.

Because of her age, Amy is no longer able to participate in these things actively. "Now that my mother is in her late 70s," Kate said recently, "living in a retirement hotel and unable to do those things that she used to do, I'm especially glad I was able to make opportunities available to her. Those were some of the best years of her life, and that means so much to me."

Kate's sister, Liz, seven years older, had dropped out of college after completing one year. She opted to resume her education by taking one class each semester for eight years and received a bachelor's degree in art history. According to her younger sister, Liz is a born student and researcher. "She'll probably go on for her master's degree," Kate commented. "While she has no career plans, reaching her academic goals has given her a sense of fulfillment and accomplishment."

Kate encouraged many friends to resume their education. They profited from some of the programs she coordinated: the adult orientation program, student support groups, a special reentry class, remedial and study skills courses, and financial aid specifically geared toward reentry students.

Families going to school together were not an uncommon sight at the community college while Kate was outreach coordinator. A newspaper clipping from 1982 describes one couple in their 60s who enrolled in a painting class together and a mother and daughter who were both reentry students.

Kate feels that it is only natural to give something back to the family members and friends who supported her. She said, "It's kind of sad: many of my friends knew I was worthwhile and that I had something special, but I didn't know it. Not that I was a complete dump before! I was OK, but I'm at a whole different level now.

"I wanted to learn to be comfortable with myself. I took advantage of every seminar and class that was available. Those years gave me the confidence I had lost somewhere along the line. I rediscovered that I was smart, that I could do anything I wanted. Through school I emerged as who and what I am today."

After two years as a student at the community college, Kate transferred to a "university without walls" program. She received a Bachelor of Arts degree in theater management in 1978.

Kate feels fortunate to have worked within the same environment that nourished her intellectually and emotionally. "When things are good, it's great to be able to give back," she said. "I had the chance to help other people who were returning to school. The programs I developed for them, the classes, the help I was able to give—this was so meaningful for me."

In 1983 Kate left her position at the community college in order to become Midwest director of a national advocacy and service organization.

The job and Kate are a perfect match. "I work with wonderful people. I travel. I have great autonomy. Every day is new and different, and I am a jack-of-all-trades. I'm always going to meetings and seminars. There are opportunities to write, to speak, to do all the things that I enjoy doing. And my office is 5 minutes from home."

At age 50 Kate said, "I can't think of a nicer life-style than the one I have. I have good relationships with my children and a wonderful man in my life. I am able to take advantage of theater, movies, books, seminars, and all the things I like to do. Thirteen years ago I would never have believed that I could be so serene and content, yet so involved and comfortable facing new challenges."

RECEPTIONIST AND GAS STATION ATTENDANT ARE NOW PRACTICING ATTORNEYS

When Linda met Matthew in 1965, she was a recent high school graduate working as a receptionist and typist. Matthew, 22, was pumping gas to put himself through a bachelor's degree program. Sixteen years later they were both practicing attorneys.

Linda and Matthew are two idealistic, determined people who have supported each other through the challenges and exhaustion of combining school, family, and careers. Their life-style was completely unprecedented in either of their families.

Matthew's relatives, mainly Irish, all lived nearby. Although several of them had been to college, Matthew was the first one to become a professional. Linda's origins are Mexican, and her relatives all live in Arizona. No one in her family had been to college.

Matthew and Linda shared a clear vision about their academic and career plans. Neither went to law school to get rich quick, but rather to gain power in dealing with the civil rights issues to which they were committed. Linda had done well in high school and wanted very much to continue her education. Her mother could not afford to send her to their state university. Shortly after her high school graduation, an aunt advised her to move to a state where the university system was less expensive. Her aunt suggested that once Linda had established residency, she could combine school with working, reducing her costs still further.

The couple married in 1965 and had two children within the next few years. While finishing up his undergraduate studies in 1965, Matthew must have been one of the few antiwar demonstrators who combined his protest activities with a job as a policeman.

While he was in law school, Matthew worked days as a fireman and attended school at night. For several years, Linda combined motherhood with working as a stenographer, bookkeeper, or department store clerk. She never lost sight of her goal: to get an education.

At age 25, with two toddlers and a law-student husband, Linda started taking a few night classes at a nearby university. Once she proved to herself that she could do it, she decided to enroll as a full-time student.

She encountered her first roadblock when she asked about financial aid. "I had already spent two semesters at night and gotten straight A's. [The administrator] told me I could wait to go to school until my husband got out of law school." Linda feels she was turned down for aid because she was a woman.

"I got so mad that I became involved with organizing a child-care center on campus. I got the parents involved and got the center going. It was a great sacrifice of time and effort."

Linda got her bachelor's degree without financial aid by bringing her children to the campus child-care center she helped to create. The confrontation with what she saw as sex discrimination and her resulting desire to organize helped persuade her to pursue a law degree.

Linda's decision was honed further during her junior year. She was selected to attend a three-week symposium in Washington, D.C., on racism and its impact on U.S. foreign policy. "My colleagues were all graduate students, and I was the only minority member and the only mom," she explains. "It greatly expanded my horizons."

Matthew got his law degree in 1971 and went to work as a lawyer for a large labor union. Linda graduated summa cum laude in 1974 with a bachelor's degree in social science. She entered law school in 1976 and was through by 1978.

During the couple's academic years, juggling their obligations to their son and daughter wasn't easy. "Life was a lot less complicated for their friends than it was for our children," Linda explained. "It was always more comfortable to have a mom who went to PTA meetings. I tried very hard to meet the demands most of the time. If the kids needed something, if they needed to talk to me and I had something else to do, I usually shelved what I had to do so I could be available to them.

"I always crammed my classes into as few hours as possible, so that I could be home as early as possible. It was important to me not to take extra time away from my family, and I'm satisfied that I didn't. When I was in law school, I never started studying before 9:30 p.m."

Linda estimates that she averaged about 3 hours of studying a day. She was exhausted most of the time. "But it was so important to me," she commented, "to be available and to try to maintain some normalcy about the schedule at home. Sometimes, you can only do that at great cost to yourself, but it's much easier to maintain your relationships if you at least give them the time."

Linda's and Matthew's children are both college students now. Although they had less time with their mother than most of their peers, some of the interests they developed stem from experiences they had during their childhood.

"They are probably much more progressive in their thinking than most kids their age," Linda said. "They have marched in an antiwar demonstration with 500,000 people. They have marched with farm workers. They picketed Safeway. They have met mayors, supervisors, and governors. They are used to traveling in many circles. We have tried to teach them not to be cowed by anyone's position. They are growing up with a great deal of poise and self-confidence."

By the time Linda started law school, Matthew had already been through it. He explained the importance of setting and sticking to priorities. "When I went to college," she said, "I had almost a straight-A average. It wasn't hard to do. When I entered law school, Matthew warned me, 'You're going to be competing with people who have a lot more time than you do, and they are either your intellectual equals or superiors.'

"He told me to be satisfied with doing a fairly decent job. Otherwise, he said, I would drive myself crazy. That's the only thing that got me through. I had to learn that I couldn't do everything, and I couldn't be the best at everything."

Linda graduated from law school and immediately found a wonderful position as a civil rights official for a federal antipoverty program. She headed a civil rights compliance unit that dealt with discrimination complaints made by people working for organizations receiving federal funding. She researched, wrote, drafted decisions, and trained workers in affirmative action and civil rights compliance throughout the West.

Life was busy but smooth and productive for about three years. However, 1981 was a year of enormous change for both Linda and Matthew. Within a matter of months, the federal government cut off funding for the agency where Linda worked, and Matthew decided to leave his job with the union.

The couple had been generating an impressive income, and in 1978 they had bought a home outside the city where they worked. However, the commute was proving too difficult. They realized they needed to move back into the city at a time when housing prices were sky-high. "Suddenly, our income went down to practically zero," Linda remembers. "We almost lost our home."

She and Matthew had always wanted to establish a law practice together, and they tried it briefly that year. They were overwhelmed by the sheer mechanics of making the practice into a business that would generate a profit. "Neither one of us was prepared for that," explained Linda.

"We didn't know what it took to run a private office. We couldn't go through all the years of uncertainty about income. One or the other of us was going to have to get a job with a steady salary. So I did it."

From 1982 through 1984, Linda worked in the public defender's office. She had never imagined herself as a courtroom lawyer, and suddenly here she was, arguing child abuse and neglect cases in juvenile court, then adult criminal cases in front of a jury. She found the cases difficult and upsetting. When she moved into the adult division, the pressure became too much. "I really don't have the emotional makeup to be part of a system that sentences people to jail or to death."

By the end of 1984, Matthew's labor law practice was stabilizing. Linda was 39 years old and realized that whatever she chose to do next was probably what she would be doing until retirement. She too wanted to establish a law practice.

Today the pace of Linda's law practice is frenetic. In order to take home any money, she needs to generate $3,000 to $4,000 per month in revenue. When the practice was three years old, she estimated it would take at least another two years to make a profit. She felt a tremendous pressure to catch up.

"We're at least ten years behind the people who have had privilege, who were able to go to college directly after high school," she said. "This is the only chance anybody in our family has had to establish something. I've got to give it everything I've got. If my children want to become lawyers, they are not going to have to go through what we did."

A gift from Matthew to Linda in 1985 reflected his concern about the possibility of burnout. He bought her Jane Fonda's *Women Coming of Age,* written for women over 40. Linda said, "I looked at the book, and I said: 'This is nice of you, but where do you get the idea that Jane Fonda's life-style has anything to do with mine?' I shelved the book and didn't touch it again for about nine months.

"I don't know what made me pick up the book again, but I started leafing through it, and I found it very inspiring and informative. She advises older women to get some exercise to lift their spirits. It doesn't have to be anything like her morning workout." Fonda said that even walking briskly several times a week has distinct benefits.

In 1986 Linda started an exercise program of walking and jogging around her neighborhood. "I haven't lost a lot of weight, but I look much better and I feel much better, and that's very important. You really do need to take care of yourself when you reach our age," she said.

Linda is contemplating a change in life-style: "I've struggled enough. I'd like more money. Most of the people I know who are my age have traveled to Europe, take trips to Mexico, wear nice clothes, and drive new cars. We have been lucky enough to live pretty well, but in the high-income-and-high-outgo bracket. I want some of the luxuries.

"I want to make absolutely certain I can help my children. If they want to go on in school, I want to be able to provide them with that opportunity. It's going to take a little more time to get there." She would also like to register for a few classes—just for stimulation and self-improvement. Courses in literature and acting head the list.

Linda has the stamina to accomplish the goals she has set for herself and her family. "I also have the wonderful advantage," she commented, "of being married for twenty-two years to a man who has seen me through all of this."

Not long ago she and her associates moved into the same building where Matthew has his practice. "It's really good to have him here," she said then. "He's more experienced than I am, and it's very helpful to me. Everybody's wondering how long it will be until we get tired of seeing each other every day, but we're past that stage!"

In fact, as this book goes to press, Linda has joined her husband's labor law practice. The eleven attorneys represent unions and individual employees involved in disputes with their employers. Linda was also recently appointed to a state commission and has been conducting seminars for other lawyers.

Matthew comments: "Not bad for a Mexican kid whose family didn't have the bucks to get her a college education, and who was told by her high school counselor not to try because the odds were too long."

CHANGES/TRANSITIONS

CHAPTER 11
DROPOUTS, STOP-OUTS, AND DROP-INS

Jackie's pursuit of a master's degree fell by the wayside when she became the primary care provider for both her parents. Cindy left school when her husband was offered a job that required relocation. Joan, trying to juggle a preschooler, a strained marital relationship, a full-time job, and a degree program, wound up quitting school.

The six women in this chapter all dropped out of school before completing their planned degree program. Yet, none of them feels the time they spent as reentry students was wasted.

Jackie, Joan, and Cindy actually intend to enroll in degree programs within the next few years. In the meantime, Jackie has taken courses to get a real estate license, and Joan obtained extensive training in crisis intervention counseling.

Everyone in this chapter continues to take classes for the sheer pleasure of learning. Dorothy reflects their general attitude: "Any study is worth it in terms of growth and development. . . . Not everyone has to be a pragmatist."

Needs and interests are ever changing. Daphne decided not to become a practicing psychologist just as she was completing her master's degree. Joan's focus evolved away from her major, management, and toward counseling. Claire stayed in an M.B.A. program just long enough to get a working knowledge of investing. She and another M.B.A. dropout then went into business together.

If you are contemplating a return to school, early educational/career counseling might save you a considerable amount of time and effort. Claire now realizes she could have gotten the knowledge she wanted by taking a few undergraduate courses instead of enrolling in an M.B.A. program. Joan now believes she should have chosen her major based on interest rather than on what was available.

There are no prescriptions to be offered for how to approach school in such a way that completing your degree program is guar-

Degrees of Success

anteed. One essential ingredient, however, according to many of the women in this book, is emotional and moral support from family and friends.

Tension at home can be the deciding factor when the going gets rough. When someone is a worker/wife/mother/friend/student/person, sometimes the role that gets dropped is student.

Timing is often a consideration when it comes to introducing a major commitment into your life. Joan, a single parent, is reluctant to finance her own education just as her daughter is finishing high school and thinking about college. Cindy and her husband agreed that she should be a full-time homemaker during their children's preschool years. A master's degree in accounting became completely irrelevant to Jackie after her parents became ill.

The term "dropout" conjures up a static state. The stories in this chapter belie some of the stereotypes associated with this term. Each woman here was able to gain something positive from her encounter with academia. And in varying degrees they are all going back for more.

GETTING JOB CONTACTS AND A SENSE OF SELF-WORTH

In 1980, Joan was working full-time as assistant to the director of a local college's continuing education program. She was also enrolled in the college's weekend bachelor's degree program. Her marriage was strained, and she wanted to spend more time with her 8-year-old daughter.

It was simply too much to handle, so she dropped out of school. Shortly thereafter, she divorced, tried to cope as a single parent, and did her best to keep the household afloat financially.

Joan has gotten a great deal out of her education, even though she has not to date completed her degree. She established contacts through school and, in fact, found out about a recent job from a woman with whom she had gone to class. Even though the Midwestern city in which she lives is large, Joan is always running into women who went to college with her or who know about the weekend degree program.

"At the time I entered school," she said, "I was getting some very negative feedback from the people around me, especially my husband. Being in school helped me to see myself in a different light, more as a person of worth. I'm not trying to blame everything on my husband, but I needed validation that I was a worthwhile person, and going to school gave me that.

"Going to school helped me to grow and move on. Even though I left, I think I became a better person for having been there for two years. It was worth it, even though I quit, even though I don't have the degree."

Joan's return to school was definitely a solo flight, not part of a team effort. She said in 1978, "My husband's attitude was 'If you want to do it, do it, but don't bug me.' I could do anything that I wanted, as long as everything else got done." At that time, both Joan and Kevin were working full-time. He was a biochemist, while she worked at the college. Even though they were both working, she wound up with much more than half of the housework and child-care duties.

Joan was getting very mixed messages from Kevin. "He never complained if dinner wasn't on the table, but he never helped make dinner either. I was under a lot of pressure and he wasn't helping. Yet, he was always saying he was willing to help. It was frustrating."

Believing that actions speak louder than words, Joan concluded that Kevin simply didn't care about her pursuit of a degree. She said in 1978, "It bothered me that he didn't care. The way I solved that was looking at myself not as his wife, but as an individual, and saying, 'I'm not doing this so that he'll think I'm great. I'm doing this so that I can help myself.' His attitude isn't important to me anymore."

Joan started the degree program, at age 31, by taking an English class two mornings a week. The next semester, she took a course in psychology and worked in the admissions office as a student aide. At the beginning, she wasn't as interested in the degree as she was in doing something interesting, "something to just bring some life back and make me feel more like a person in my own right," she said.

Soon she was working full-time as a secretary and receptionist in the admissions office. Once she got the job, much of the financial pressure that school had been creating was diffused: tuition was free for full-time employees. She decided on a dual major in management and communication—because they were the only majors offered at that time!

In June 1979, Joan was hired as office manager in the college's office of continuing education. She was quickly promoted to assistant to the director. In this capacity she was responsible for organizing, monitoring, and moderating the continuing education women's programs. She was also involved with counseling women who were thinking about returning to school.

Joan was concerned about spending less time with her daughter, Teal, who was still in elementary school. "When I'm spending time with her, it's usually on things that have to be done," she said. "Before, we would take a day off and be together, doing our own thing. Now, there's no time for that. We're shopping for something that has to be bought, or we're at the grocery store."

Although a weekend degree program fits nicely with people's work schedules, it can naturally wreak havoc on a family's weekend time. When Joan was in school full-time, she was on campus all day Saturday and Sunday every other week. She would study on weeknights and usually on both days of the weekend she was not in school.

It was at this point that Joan dropped out of school. Talking about her decision seven years later, she wished she had finished the degree. "I think I was looked at, at the time, as a person with so much potential. Now, years later, where am I? I'm still struggling with the questions of who I am and where I'm going."

Joan left her job at the college to work as a medical secretary in a hospital. She was promoted to executive secretary within the psychiatry department. She greatly enjoyed her work environment—the contact with patients, faculty, and staff. She now realizes that she gets a great deal of satisfaction from working with people in a counseling setting.

One reason Joan left the bachelor's degree program was her discovery that she was not nearly as interested in management as she had once thought. Yet, in her position at the hospital, she was able to handle many managerial responsibilities well. She enjoyed combining her managerial talents with her interest in counseling. Thus, although she did not have her degree, she believes that completing two years of college helped her move ahead in a satisfying work environment.

Joan has enjoyed her work settings but not the role she has played in them: "I am always on the border between professional and clerical. The thing that keeps holding me back from crossing that border is the lack of a degree. It's not just the piece of paper I lack; it's the knowledge."

Joan did not feel as if she belonged with either the professionals or the clerical staff in the department of psychiatry. "Daily I came in contact with patients and people with problems," she said. "I associated more with doctors and professionals than with clerical staff. Still, I was not part of either group."

In retrospect, Joan can see that she's always been motivated to make a decent living, especially after she and Kevin separated in 1981. She had thought that studying management would enable her to earn a good living.

She now concludes: "Even back then, I should have found some way to continue in a service-oriented degree program such as psychology or social work. But because I was thinking so hard about survival and money, I opted for management. This was totally wrong for me; it's not what I wanted or what I ever would have been happy doing. I don't think being in management, even at a high salary, would ever make me happy.

"Sometimes I think I use Teal as an excuse for not accomplishing more," she said. "Other times I think of the choices I have made. I have tried to be a good mother and role model for my daughter. To me, this means spending time with her and being there when she needs me."

After six years at the hospital, Joan quit in the fall of 1986 over what she calls political issues. She thought she was going to a better position as an office administrator at a construction company. The salary was decent, but she hated the job and quit after ten weeks.

"This was an extremely hard period in my life," she said. "I had wanted to find a people-oriented job." She returned to the hospital as an administrative assistant with a weight management program. It meant a downgrade in pay, but she was relieved to be back in a counseling setting. "I'm part of a multidisciplinary team, even though what I do is essentially clerical."

Through the recent shifting around, Joan has clarified her interest in counseling. She is volunteering with the women's crisis hotline and has become a member of its board of directors. She is reassessing her career and educational goals.

The same doubts she had ten years ago still plague her—except now she is in her 40s, and Teal is almost ready to begin college. If Joan had it to do over again, she would have found a way to go to school full-time. She would also have chosen her major based on her strongest interests, not on what was available close at hand.

"I'm still fighting the questions 'Where do I go from here?' and 'What do I really want?' What's important to me? Do I have what it takes to get what I value? Are my needs as important as Teal's?"

Joan is thinking about returning to school for a bachelor's degree in psychology. She wants to make sure she needs a degree in order to work in the field. Then she wants to investigate ways to get the degree without overloading her life. At this writing, she has an interview for an administrative assistant position at a nearby university. If she gets the job, she can take 6 units tuition-free each semester.

She says, "I hope that sometime in the next few months I can be back in school finishing my degree. I wasn't sure this day would ever come, and I know I have a long way to go. Yet I am feeling very optimistic."

A DEGREE OF SPUNK, ABILITY, AND INTEREST

In 1987, Daphne at age 59 was teaching at an international school in the Middle East following three years of living in Crete and a two-year teaching stint in Brazil. Daphne believes that "spunk, ability, and driving interest" help you chart your career path—with or without going through the academic mill.

Her opinions on the value of college degrees are unique among the women in this book. To comprehend why she would complete a master's degree thesis in psychology (at age 51) and then not turn it in, one needs to review her life story.

Daphne married in 1950, during her second year of college, then dropped out of school when she and her husband were offered teaching jobs in Alaska. Alaska was an adventure. By 1953, the couple was back in the States, established in a suburban southern California life-style. The year 1957 found Daphne a full-time homemaker with three children under the age of 5. She describes the slow-simmering crisis that precipitated her return to school.

"Three preschool-age children made me want to get away from the house, be with adults, and think about something besides the house and kids and family. I wanted to meet people besides housewives who would only talk about babies, diapers, and child development on a 'cutesy' level."

Early childhood education had been her major seven years earlier, and she chose to take a class in kindergarten methods that met Saturday mornings. The course was less than inspiring, and with her husband's encouragement she decided to pursue classes she was more interested in. "I took a course in American literature and got hooked," she said.

As Daphne negotiated her way through the first few semesters, she began to realize that her relationship with her husband was deteriorating. This made her focus on school even more intensely. "I felt going to school was the only way I could get a divorce and be self-supporting." She became an English major and headed toward a career in teaching.

"During the last year I had to take methods courses, in which I learned two useful things: not to discuss what I was doing in the classroom with any other faculty members and to be good friends with the principal's secretary.

"The rest of the stuff was very ticky-tacky, and only student teaching offered relevant experience. The pressure of grades, getting a good recommendation, and pleasing the master teacher kept me from experimenting fully and taking risks, something I regretted; I would have liked to work in schools with more flexibility and trust in the child's abilities as well as the teacher's integrity. Taking risks in one's training is the best experience."

During her last semester of student teaching, Daphne and her husband separated. The couple was the first on either side of the family to divorce. Daphne found herself with very little money and three children in elementary school. Neighbors and friends helped out with child care, and somehow she was able to care for her family and finish school.

Daphne enjoyed teaching high school students, although she didn't like dealing with "the structure that school administrators represented." Then, remarried and with five and a half years of teaching under her belt, she quit her job in order to immerse herself in studying ceramics. Once again, she found her way to a college campus and enrolled in as many art classes as she could fit into her schedule.

When her second marriage ended in 1969, Daphne decided to make a total change in life-style. She bought land in a rural part of northern California. When the children were 14, 16, and 17, the family moved north.

Forty-one years old when she relocated, Daphne explained what it was like to charge off into the unknown. "It was terrifying to trust that my desire to live in that beautiful place was more important than anything else in my life." All her funds went into building materials; she and her children built their own home.

Daphne was unable to find a buyer for their former home in southern California, and her financial picture was bleak. The family was on welfare for a year. Daphne managed to trade and sell some of her ceramics to keep afloat. Then, in 1971, she found a full-time job as a family planner.

In 1972, when she sold the house in southern California, she suddenly had a little extra money and no children living at home. She spent the next year traveling around Europe and working in Greece.

"When I came back," she recalled, "I realized I was, for the first time in my life, coming back to an empty house and no job. I had used up all my resources. It was terrifying."

In 1974 Daphne discovered a lump in her breast. It turned out to be malignant, and she had a mastectomy. While she was still reeling from the experience, she learned about a program in humanistic psychology not far from where she lived. She did a three-month residency there. "I learned a lot about my cancer and my own life's process," she said. "A process was started there and then; it continues to sustain me, and I am ever grateful."

Daphne decided to undertake a master's degree in psychology. The decision necessitated another major change. She would have to move back to a metropolitan area. When she entered graduate school in 1977 Daphne was 50.

"Since I had been an English major, it was easy for me to write, read, organize, and express myself," Daphne said. "I did very well in school, especially in my experiential work because of all the workshops I had done in psychology. It was the easiest time I ever had."

Daphne packed a two-year program into less than a year. She managed to complete her thesis before the end of her first academic year. She was at a crossroads.

"I didn't submit my thesis for its final acceptance for a number of reasons. Part of it had to do with lack of respect for the program and personnel. Also, after working for two years in institutions like halfway houses and a ranch for disturbed children, I realized I didn't like working in an institutional setting."

Daphne decided against setting up a private practice in the rural area where she had built her home. Because of the population size and economic conditions there, she knew it would be many years before she could establish a clientele that would sustain her economically. "It would be difficult to separate my economic needs from the client's progress. The temptation would be there to create a dependency in order to overcome the fear of losing that income," she said.

Daphne also did not want to "jump through the set of hoops," as she put it, that getting licensed required. She abandoned the idea of becoming a practicing psychologist and went back to ceramics. "I joined the masses of voluntary poor until it got too tiresome and the pressure to produce pots to sell was surpassing my desire to spend time making pots that pleased me."

At that point, Daphne drew on old skills and old passions: teaching and travel. She saw an advertisement for a teaching job at an international school in Brazil and applied successfully.

"I suddenly realized that there was a career in international schools; I was on the circuit, and I was loving it. I have not always gone to the place of my choice, but I have sometimes gone to fascinating places I never would have chosen."

Regarding going back to school in order to find a career or a job, Daphne said, "It is self-evident that the tickets, the degree, are valued. Society values them, and sometimes more than the accomplishment on the job or the capabilities of an experienced person.

"I think there are many other ways to get into a job or career, and I am not sure that the degree mill is the best way for anyone with a 'degree' of spunk and ability and interest.

"I sometimes feel I have sold out to the establishment by earning a degree instead of going for the experience and the performance on the job. Let my life and the way I live be proof of my merit, if proof is indeed necessary.

"Career goals and degree programs don't satisfy a real need for me, though I went through the motions in order to achieve economic stability. I wish I could have gone to school as one of the leisure class, to simply learn for the sheer joy of learning, at whatever pace and by whatever means that suited me."

Although Daphne is not a staunch believer in the standard merits of degrees, she sees educational institutions as community resources. "I will return to school sometime," she explains, "as the university offers good facilities for anything I may be interested in following up. School is a tool for the community, and I expect I will use it that way."

Concerning her future, Daphne commented from the Middle East in 1987: "While I am fast approaching 60, I do not see retirement ahead. I cherish a desire to go to China to work there for a few years. Then, there are the Slovak countries, and oh so much more. My only fear is that I will be judged by my birth date and not my worth when I apply to work."

A DEGREE BECAME IRRELEVANT

Claire dropped out of an M.B.A. program in 1979, after three years and 30 units. She says she never wanted the degree. She was interested primarily in gathering skills and knowledge in accounting. When it came to the classes on organizational behavior and management, she decided to call it quits.

Claire got her "money's worth" from her M.B.A. days —in a totally unexpected way. A course she took in securities led her to dabble in the stock market on a purely theoretical basis. "I like numbers," she recalled, "and I used to play with the stock market at the kitchen table. I would chart it. I never had a penny in it. I never intended to."

A friend from the M.B.A. program, Sonya, also not interested in completing the degree, suggested that the two of them pool their resources and invest in the stock market by working out of a securities office. Because of the class, they had both learned the terminology of investing. They now had the mathematics background, and they understood inventory turnover.

The two friends walked into a securities office and told a securities analyst they wanted to "conduct business." They were soon escorted into a room in which desks, phones, and computers were available to the public. Claire said, "No, we can't work in a public place. We need our own thing." It was a large office, and it looked as if there was plenty of room in the back. Much to Claire's and Sonya's amazement, the securities analyst said she would see if the two could share a desk.

So, before Claire and Sonya had invested a single cent, they had their own desk, phone, and computer. Soon, they realized that they would do better with option trading, so Claire took a class on "puts and calls." "That's what we're doing to this day, and we're doing very well," Claire commented recently.

She and her husband, Norman, have friends who are licensed stockbrokers or are otherwise involved in Wall Street activities. Claire said, "If I want to tease the men, I tell them how I got my desk. They all had to work so hard for theirs, and I just walked in and asked for it—as if I had it coming to me."

The securities company eventually remodeled, and the Claire/Sonya desk went by the wayside. But by then the ticker tape was available on cable television and they had found a broker they trusted—a former geologist.

Claire and Sonya got a great deal out of the M.B.A. program, even though they didn't graduate. "Going back to school," Claire commented, "got me somewhere I'm happy to be, with the stock market and securities. My goals changed."

Initially, Claire went back to school at age 41 in order to gather skills for employment. She already had a bachelor's degree with a major in education. She had taught for three years before she married and had her two children. She had no interest, however, in pursuing a teaching career.

Claire can pinpoint the moment when she became uncomfortable about not working—an incident that occurred about three years before she started taking classes. She and Norman, an executive in the clothing industry, had traveled from New York to Chicago on a business trip. They attended a dinner party at which most of the guests were couples where both husband and wife worked.

"They were all busy talking about their work. When someone asked, 'By the way, Claire, what do you do?' I had to say, 'Nothing.' It was reinforced wherever I looked. I did nothing."

Claire decided to enroll at a nearby university in 1976. She settled on accounting because she thought it would offer a flexible work schedule. Perhaps she could work just during tax season—or two or three days a week.

While she was in school, Claire got a job in the accounting department of a bank. All went well for the first six months. However, Norman's three-week vacation is preassigned to March each year, and Claire went to the head of the department to request time off.

"I told him I had to take off," Claire explains. "He said, 'Sure. How many days?' So I said three weeks. He said, 'Three weeks? Before taxes? This is our busiest time.' He told me he would have to find someone to take my place, and to call when I came back to see if they had an opening. When I came back, I realized that I could never do anything at tax time because that's when Norman's business has him take vacations. It wouldn't be fair to anybody."

Claire was not overly upset about leaving her job at the bank. She said recently that the work was quite boring. "I think I was committed more to becoming an accountant than working as an accountant," she said.

She wanted to go on taking classes. But she didn't like the idea of being a student without a goal in mind, and so she chose to focus on accounting. In 1978, several years into the program, she still did not believe she needed the degree.

"I'm staying with it," she said at the time. "But I don't feel driven to get a diploma at the end. As long as I enjoy it, I'll continue. When I stop enjoying it, I'll quit. I would miss school. I think I'll always take courses."

What Claire wanted was a challenge in her life. Her son was going off to college, and her daughter was busy with many high school activities. The family had just come through a very rough year in which Norman's and Claire's parents had all died. A brother that Claire was very close to was moving to Florida.

"I felt isolated," Claire explained. "School was something I knew I would enjoy: the discipline of it, the homework, and the things I learned that were so far afield from what I had taken when I studied education. It made me feel very good about myself. I bit off more than I could chew, and I ended up swallowing it and not choking. To undertake something difficult, to handle it, and to do well was so satisfying."

Claire's husband and children were very encouraging. "They were excited. I even got a pencil case and gifts!" In 1978 Claire observed, "Norman's in awe; to him accounting is such a remote field. He's impressed that I can do it."

Although Norman was proud of Claire, he didn't take her student role entirely seriously. She said his attitude reflected her own. In 1978 she explained, "It's not a serious, meaningful thing to me, so it isn't to him, either. If he knew that it was very important to me or if we needed it financially, he would be completely supportive."

Claire had an unforgettable first day at school. "When I went to my first class I was really nervous. I couldn't understand what they were talking about. It didn't make any sense at all. 'This is a beginning class in accounting?' I asked the professor. It turned out I was an hour and a half early. I was in the wrong class!"

Claire demonstrated to herself that she could meet the challenge of school. When she was in college thirty years ago, a B was cause for celebration. This time around, she was a straight-A student. "My kids thought it was hysterical," she said. "I was a real nerd—the Goody Two-Shoes who did the homework right away, as soon as she came home from school. Well, I liked doing it that way. It made me feel good."

There was another benefit from returning to school for both Claire and Norman. Norman had never been particularly enthusiastic about keeping the basic accounts that every family needs. After Claire became an expert, he was relieved to turn all of it over to her.

"I pay all the bills. I organize everything for our taxes. Norman took care of most of this before I went back to school, and he kept most of the records at work. He was very dependent on the accountant there. Now it all comes home. I wanted to do it. I'm much more efficient and neater than Norman is, and I'm better organized with numbers."

When it comes to investments, Norman's and Claire's roles have changed dramatically since her return to school. She said, "If Norman had opened up a money market account, I would have had to say, 'Where's the money market account? I want to take out some money.' Now he has no idea whether or not we have a money market account, where it is, or how much money is in it."

The couple's children also respect Claire's expertise in financial matters. "My son would always talk with Norman about money. Now he talks to me. It's no longer just: 'Mom, I'm not feeling good.' I've become a more complete person in his and my daughter's eyes."

FEAR OF SUCCESS

Twelve years after dropping out of a Ph.D. program in classics at Boston University, Dorothy said fear of success played a critical role in her life.

"I pulled out at the last minute," she explained. "There were 24 credits required plus the thesis. I was taking the last courses and had an A+ average. I couldn't write the last term paper. Inside of me the emotional resistance to succeeding, to finishing that heavy course load, was so great I was unable to write my last paper for a course in which I was doing so well. I think I was threatened by the possibility of success.

"Eventually, the time limit ran out. I didn't get credit for that course, so I had my master's degree plus 21 credits toward my doctorate. That's how close I came."

Dorothy was depressed during her three years in graduate school. The depression got worse as she got closer to completing her degree. Two years after she left the Ph.D. program, she said, "I didn't lack confidence in my intellectual ability, but I couldn't produce work under pressure to meet requirements set by third parties. I can produce beautiful work when it's for myself. When it's required of me, I crumble."

In 1956, at the traditional age for college, it never dawned on Dorothy not to go to college. It was the thing to do, especially in her family; both her parents were Ph.D.'s. "I was still a child, and going to college was what my parents and parent surrogates told me to do," she said. "I didn't have an idea what I wanted to do in life. I just fell into college through parental pressure and certain natural abilities that I took for granted."

When Dorothy returned to school at age 32, she believed she had very clear goals. She wanted to teach at the college level. Furthermore, she wanted to become a classicist and historian.

However, the strain was great. Dorothy was a single parent and had been working part-time as a social worker ever since her son, Dean, was 6 months old. She was in poor health, she says, due to stress and exhaustion from her job and taking care of an infant. She had thought that the life-style of a classics professor would give her "the easiest life," but she came to see she was fooling herself.

"In order to be tops in my field, and that's what I wanted to be, I would have to put in an 80-hour week. There was so much else in life that interested me. I just wasn't willing to do that."

There were other significant factors involved with Dorothy's decision to drop out of the doctoral program. Dean was 2 years old when she went back to school, and she was very unhappy about having him in day care on a full-time basis.

"I thought it was a very good school," she said. "It was stimulating and supportive; it had a large number of teachers in relation to the number of children. But I think I put him into too much day care. It would have been better for him to go three mornings a week rather than full-time. It would have been better if I had had enough money or time to go to graduate school part-time. He was angry at my not being home. I was tired, crabby, and distracted. I didn't have the patience for him."

Another problem Dorothy confronted was an upheaval in her long-term relationship. "I was in a very bad relationship that had lasted quite a while and depressed me deeply. It was quite an obstacle, affecting my self-confidence and my scholastic ability."

To make matters even more complex, Dorothy's interest in classics was shifting. She wanted to change schools, which would mean an additional two years of studies.

"It took me a year to make the decision to leave the doctoral program," Dorothy explained. "During the last year, I was hesitant, and that caused me a lot of agony. But I eased myself out, and now I'm at peace with my decision."

Dorothy believes she benefited from her graduate studies even though she didn't finish. "Any study is worth it in terms of growth and development. I learned a lot while I was in graduate school. Not everyone has to be a pragmatist."

Dorothy has focused on her personal growth in recent years. She went into therapy, which she said is the most important thing to have happened to her in the past ten years. She converted to Judaism and joined a synagogue. She enrolled recently in Hebrew and Spanish classes.

Her relationship with her son continues to be very important to her, and she has put great effort into helping him get scholarships to good private schools. Raising him well is one of her two primary goals. The other goal relates to many of the same interests and skills that sent her to graduate school: she wants to become a successful translator. She has been doing free-lance translating for several years now. "I have a literary agent in New York who tries to match my work with a publishing company. I'd like to translate one literary work after another," she said. "I hope it will take off as a career. My higher education is, as always, an unending source of pleasure for me in terms of books, television, movies, conversation, travel, and friendships. But it did not lead to work in which I felt happy and fulfilled. I feel I succeeded because I value my education and love my work."

Dorothy has been a farm and nursery assistant for five years and plans to hoe beans and translate until she is at least 65.

EIGHT YEARS OF FAMILY CRISIS

Jackie received a bachelor's degree in history in 1970 and a certificate to teach high school. Although she did substitute teaching for three years, she was unable to find a permanent teaching position. She decided to become a CPA after a thorough investigation of the field. Job opportunities looked very good.

Jackie started the master's degree program in accounting in 1976 at age 27. She expected to graduate in January 1979. She had had her fill of clerical work. "I want to be a professional," she said while in school. "I've gotten a taste of degrading work."

At the time, Jackie was free of obligations. Her passion was figure skating, so she combined school with as much time on the ice as possible. Her parents, neither of whom was college educated, were very proud of her goal to become a CPA. They were happy to support her financially throughout the academic program and to have her live at home with them.

In 1978, when Jackie was asked if she had to give up anything in order to go back to school, she replied: "No. I'm very flexible. I have nothing else I have to do."

Sadly, her life suddenly changed. "My dad became sick. My mother had a stroke," she said. "Little by little, everything in my life fell away until there was nothing left. It was easier to drop the master's degree; there was too much stress. Stress over a long period of time weakens you. No matter how much you try, you weaken. I dropped school—just like that."

When Jackie dropped out she had three courses and a thesis to complete. There was really no conscious decision to leave school. Her studies simply did not fit into her life-style as the primary caregiver for her parents.

Jackie's father died in 1982 after being very ill for several years. Soon her mother required 24-hour care. Jackie hired a live-in housekeeper and went to work as the office manager for a large scrap metal business. She describes her job as boring. "There's nothing there for me, nothing that makes me want to get out of bed in the morning," she said.

However, the job had some distinct advantages while she was coping with her mother's condition. "The reason I ended up at the job was that the people there knew me. I was under no pressure. If for some reason I couldn't get to work, it wasn't going to matter. And the pay was always going to be there at the end of the week. The security was there."

Jackie has two brothers, who were not involved with caring for their parents, but who provided the finances needed. "They would tell me, 'Whatever you need, get,'" Jackie said.

Despite this, tension between Jackie and her siblings reached the boiling point a number of times. Both brothers were married. "One sister-in-law told me, 'It's your mother and you're the daughter, so she's your responsibility.' And I ended up not talking to my other brother for six months. He and his wife felt that they were doing too much for my mother."

The responsibilities involved with caring for her mother were enormous. There were trips to the doctor, grocery shopping for the house, managing around the housekeeper's time off, and grappling with rehabilitation and physical therapy. "You never knew what was going to happen. My mother had a pacemaker. When she was still walking, with a cane, there was always the fear that she might lose her balance, that she might break her hip," Jackie said.

The option of putting her mother in a nursing home was always there, but Jackie did not see it as the best course of action. Although her mother was physically debilitated, her mind was functional. Jackie was convinced that if her mother went into a nursing home, senility would set in.

Jackie's mother died in 1985, and Jackie panicked. She was nearly 40 and she hadn't finished her degree. She was a certified teacher, but she hadn't taught for many years. She had a job, but she didn't like it. Should she go back to school? How should she find another job?

As Jackie saw it, she was starting over in almost every aspect of her life. "I sit back and look at all this. I've come out of these eight years. I don't have a family. I don't have a satisfying job. I'm starting my social life all over again. I'm starting from zero."

By 1987, Jackie felt she was emerging from an excruciating chapter of her life. She was picking up the pieces and discovering several options for pursuing meaningful employment.

In January of 1987 Jackie got a license to sell real estate. However, she is not enthusiastic about real estate as a career and is reconsidering teaching. Although she would ultimately need to finish her master's degree, Jackie was recertified in 1986 because she already had credits toward a master's degree. She recognizes that the teaching field is opening up again, and she has begun looking at job possibilities.

She has also resumed ice-skating. "That's where I'm happiest. I could spend all day on the ice," she said. If Jackie became a high school teacher, she would have her summers available for skating. She could also arrange specific times for skating after work during the school year. Jackie mentions one other job possibility: teaching figure skating. She has achieved a high level of skill as a figure skater—she has a bronze medal in dance and is working toward a silver medal.

Jackie is hesitant about committing herself to teach ice-skating. "Before I go out and teach someone, I want to be sure I can give these kids enough. When they're paying you $35 an hour, these kids have got to achieve, they've got to produce. Sometimes, when they don't, it's because the teachers don't have enough to offer."

Hope and optimism shine through at the end of Jackie's interview, and she asks, "Are you going to write another book ten years from now? Maybe I'll have something good to say then."

PLACING FAMILY NEEDS FIRST

Cindy and Larry liked their life-style in the mid-1970s. Each was pursuing a master's degree and working, Cindy as a first-grade teacher and Larry as a physical education instructor and football coach. Each had the long-range goal of earning a doctorate in administration. They had no children.

"We understood what the other person was working toward," Cindy said, "the kinds of problems that came up and the kinds of stress involved, because we were both going through the same thing."

Early in their marriage Cindy and Larry decided that his education would be given top priority. This meant that when there wasn't enough money for both to begin their master's degrees, she held off going for a year. It meant that if they were short of funds, she might take 3 credits instead of 6.

Cindy's pursuit of the master's degree in reading supervision got stalled when Larry finished his degree and found a job as an assistant professor in another state. Accepting the job meant moving. Cindy was only about 12 credits shy of completing her degree, but the college would be too far away for her to commute from their new home.

In addition, Cindy was already pregnant with their first child, and she was taking a two-semester maternity leave from teaching and her master's program. Larry was planning to work on his doctorate. Funding two degrees and a growing family would have created a financial hardship.

By 1987 Cindy and Larry had two children, ages 4 and 8. Cindy's goals at age 35 were the same as they had been nine years earlier. "My last child will be entering kindergarten in September, and I hope to be able to go back to teaching again. My goal will once again be to finish a master's degree," she said.

Cindy's decision had been a conscious one. She had weighed her options and decided to stay home with the children while they were preschoolers. "I have been faced with the dilemma that almost every woman faces: career or family and home. There are no right decisions, no wrong decisions. There are a lot of gray areas, and no matter which decision you make, there are going to be days when you feel you have made the wrong decision and days when you feel you made the right decision.

"I decided not to put my children in day care. I did not bring them into the world to be raised by someone else. Putting my career goals on the back burner and not finishing the degree that I coveted caused me a lot of pain personally.

"The decision has also given me a lot of joy because I have been with my children. We are very close. They are gifted, artistic, and creative. I think a lot of that has to do with the nurturing aspect that a mother brings to a situation, a mother or a significant person in the child's life."

Cindy described what she calls the woman's dilemma: "For a man, it's very simple—go out, get a job, go back to school, pursue a degree. He does not become pregnant. He does not have to stay home to nurture a small child.

"For a woman, it is difficult to balance all the different roles we are forced into by society. I heard a saying once that went something like this: We have found something that does the work of five men: a woman. I know exactly what that means."

Cindy has been battling major health problems these past nine years. She has been diagnosed as having a form of rheumatoid arthritis called ankylosing spondylitis, a degenerative bone disease that causes great pain and crippling. The disease produces cysts and tumors. By 1987 she was fighting an orbital tumor behind her left eye and trying to avoid radiation therapy.

Cindy firmly believes that mental attitude affects physical well-being. Because of her love for teaching, she planned to resume it, part-time, once she sent her youngest off to school, and then continue her education.

"I want to continue with what makes me happiest—teaching, going to school, finishing that degree," she said. "I think that would influence my health. Your mental outlook is very important when you're fighting something as devastating as what I'm fighting right now. Personal frustrations can have a bad effect on one's health, and I want to do as much as I can now."

Cindy wishes she had finished her degree before she and Larry started a family. She said, "It would have been so much easier. But we can't live on ifs. This is the real world we have to cope with."

Many of the units Cindy accumulated will not transfer to programs near her home. "I may have to start from scratch, but I would do it." Both Larry and Cindy think there will be difficulties associated with her return to school—the financial strain, coordinating their needs with the children's, transferring credits—but they are open with each other about their concerns.

In 1987 Larry said, "I regret that she didn't have the opportunity to finish her master's degree. She had to stop when I moved into this job. Also, we had young children, and she devoted her life to the children. Now I'm looking forward to her going back to school and getting the degree."

Cindy enjoys being a student. In fact, back in 1977 she was surprised when she received a salary increase in her teaching position as a result of her master's degree credits. "I was so pleased and happy about being in school; it had not even occurred to me that I was going to be monetarily rewarded. Being paid was the icing on the cake. I love to learn. Once you stop learning, you stop living," she said.

Cindy has other plans too. "I would like to illustrate and write a children's book. Even though I have been at home for nine years with small children, my mind has not turned to oatmeal; I have been working on a lot of creative projects."

The latest correspondence from Cindy indicates that she is now teaching kindergarten and loves her job. Although the pain from her disease is ever present, her health has stabilized. Looking into the future, she said, "Perhaps my sons and I will be in college at the same time, with them pursuing bachelor's degrees and me working on a doctorate. That would be great."

CHAPTER 12
BACK TO SCHOOL FOR ANOTHER DEGREE

The women in this chapter all achieved their original academic goals. They were motivated, years later, to pursue an additional degree due to changing circumstances and a combination of ambition and frustration.

Martha, Roberta, Sylvia, and Cybil are retooling at a point in their lives when most people are thinking about slowing their career pace. In their 40s and 50s, they feel at their intellectual prime.

These women continue to identify and pursue long-range goals. As Cybil put it: "If you don't have a dream or goal to shoot for in your life, then there's no purpose at all."

Cybil, in her 40s, is taking a year away from her job as a third-grade teacher in order to finish her master's degree. She will then combine teaching with pursuing a Ph.D. part-time. Her new career goal: to teach education at the college level.

In Roberta's case, teaching English as a second language on a part-time basis was comfortable for many years. Because of her husband's high salary, there was little financial pressure. Now in her 50s and divorced, she cannot find full-time work in her field and needs to be able to count on earning more money. She is back in school pursuing a master's degree in order to qualify herself for a career as a clinical psychologist.

The master's degree in art history that Sylvia earned in 1970 got her exactly what she wanted at the time: a museum job and then her own art gallery. Her current enrollment in a Ph.D. program in creative writing is not career motivated. Now divorced, she says the Ph.D. will provide "self-esteem, prestige, and enrichment." In addition, the classes offer her an opportunity to interact with people who have similar interests.

Martha certainly thought that she would be able to find a job teaching high school German when she entered a master's degree program in German at age 35. The job opportunities were not there when she graduated in 1976, so she settled for a job teaching fourth grade. Several years into teaching, she developed a new goal: to become an educational administrator. She should complete the program in her early 50s.

These women followed a familiar pattern: each slowed down in her 20s to accommodate family responsibilities. Each grappled with establishing a fragile blend between traditional family life-style and career ambition. Cybil, for example, quit college her senior year, when her first child was born. She didn't resume her education until six years later, and even then, her husband objected because their second child was still a preschooler. Sylvia found a coveted position as a museum curator shortly after her graduation. She turned it down, however, because her husband was adamant that she work only part-time.

By the time Cybil has her Ph.D., she will be at least 45. Roberta will be nearly 60 when she breaks into the competitive field of clinical psychology. Martha, now 50, is talking about becoming headmistress of a school in Europe as part of her five-year plan.

Why take on the rigors of academia at this point in life? These four women feel at home in an academic setting. They have demonstrated success in both the working world and the classroom. They see an academic environment as one in which they can gather new skills for their long-range plans.

TRYING AGAIN: GETTING ANOTHER MASTER'S

When Martha entered a master's degree program at a state university in 1972, her goal was to teach German at the secondary school level. After graduating in 1976, she found a job teaching high school German for one semester. Martha believes she would have gotten this temporary position just as easily without the master's degree. However, when the temporary job ended and she couldn't find a permanent job in her field, she accepted a position as a fourth-grade teacher.

After several years of teaching, Martha decided she would pursue a degree in educational administration. At last report, she was already 30 units (out of a total of 36 units) into her second master's degree and had received certification as an educational administrator. She was combining evening school with elementary teaching during the day. Her career goal is to become an elementary or high school principal.

However, Martha is not overly optimistic about her chances for quick success in this field. In 1987 she discussed the job situation near her home. "All the principals are male; all the superintendents and assistant superintendents are male. I'm not banking on finding an administrative position soon, because I'm female and because I'm almost 50. Most of the superintendents who are hiring are men, and they will probably hire men."

Martha is convinced that sex discrimination also played an important role in thwarting her attempts to find a job as a high school German teacher ten years earlier. "I had better qualifications than some of the candidates vying for the same jobs. In three instances the job was given to a male teacher less qualified than I was," she said.

In addition, she and her husband, Warren, also a high school teacher, believe that elementary and secondary school teaching is frustrating because the opportunities for promotion are minimal. In fact, the couple actively discouraged their daughter, now a civil engineer, from becoming a teacher.

Martha feels the pressure of time. She wishes she had pursued the master's in educational administration back in 1972 rather than taking the time to get a master's degree in German, a degree she hasn't been able to use.

"I set my goals too close to what I thought I could achieve in the immediate future. I didn't think of administration then; I should have gone straight for the administration degree. That was my mistake. I'm 49, and I think I'm too old to get hired easily."

She acknowledges that the master's degree was not a complete waste of time. She wanted a teaching job—at the time—and the degree helped her land in the right ballpark. Also, even though she would have been eligible for her current job without a master's degree, she was able to begin at a higher salary because she had an advanced degree.

Although Martha is discouraged about her chances of finding a job in educational administration, she is determined to press on. She has already benefited from working on the second master's degree; she got an internship for her School District Administration certification last year, and it led to a part-time position as director of continuing education. The $7,000 extra in annual income is welcome, but the money is not as rewarding as the opportunity to be an administrator.

"It's in a district that's about ten times the size of the one that I teach in, so I am in circles now that I would not have been in as a teacher from my district. It's given another dimension to my life. I have some say. If I had not gone back for my degree in administration, I don't think I would have gotten the job." Martha's boss in the part-time position has been very supportive of her work in his office. Perhaps the experience and connections will help pave the way for full-time employment as an educational administrator.

There are many positive changes in Martha's life as a result of her student role. "I've met more people. I'm much better rounded, in my opinion. I've expanded goals rather than worrying about day-to-day things. I read more. I've had the opportunity to interact with people much younger than I am, and this made me realize I was a little old-fashioned in my thinking. My attitude has improved. My husband thinks it has helped a lot in improving my self-image," she said.

Martha's husband and children have backed her all the way. Having parents in school was the norm in this household. Warren was earning a master's degree just after the youngest child was born. The oldest of the three children was in third grade when Martha began her first master's degree.

Martha believes that she has been a good role model for her children. "They could see the value of studying. They could see that I had to spend time on writing and editing papers. I would ask the older ones to critique some of my papers. We've always put a lot of emphasis on education, whether it got us someplace or not. Getting someplace wasn't the point. Improving the mind by being challenged was. We have always talked about it, not in terms of money, but in terms of improving self-worth," she said.

Earning a great deal of money is not nearly as important to Martha as finding a position in which she will have the power to make decisions. Five years from now, when the last of their children is out of college, she might consider becoming headmistress of a school in Europe. She is bilingual and thinks this type of job could be an ideal way to stay in the field and see the world.

GATHERING LUCRATIVE SKILLS

Roberta's divorce in 1986 created dramatic changes in her financial situation. Consequently, she is back in school to get a master's degree in clinical psychology, hoping that this degree will lead to more lucrative employment than the one she earned in 1976 (a master's in teaching English as a foreign language).

When Roberta resumed her studies the first time, in 1975, she was 44, married, and the mother of children aged 8, 10, and 15. She taught French and Latin at a high school near her home. Her husband, a realtor, brought in over 80 percent of the family income.

Her first return to school was prompted by the news that the high school was going to close. After taking one semester of a master's degree program in French, Roberta decided instead on a master's in teaching English as a foreign language.

Roberta's schedule was grueling. For most of her reentry days, she continued to teach full-time, and she took 9 units of master's degree credit each semester. She would work until 3 p.m., then take evening classes. Correcting papers and writing papers kept her busy on the weekends as well. "I was working weekends and every evening. At times, the children got fed up with it. They wanted me to help them with their homework. I felt pressured and irritable."

Roberta described her mother/wife/worker/student juggling act. "I worked in tight little cubes of time. I'd get up at 6:45 a.m. From then until 8 was family time. From 8:30 until 3 p.m., I was teaching. I'd try to get everything done within that time. At 3 or 4, I'd become a student. Then I'd come home and do family things. Weekends were divided between doing the barest minimum of mothering and housework and writing papers or studying.

"I didn't really have any trouble dividing my time; I was motivated. I probably overworked. I was overprepared in many ways. I suppose that's a form of lack of self-confidence."

Roberta and her husband were separated when she was pursuing the degree, although she described the relationship as "on-again, off-again" for many years. He would come over once a week to stay with the children when Roberta had to attend a 3-hour evening class.

Roberta was willing to undertake the challenging schedule because she knew she wouldn't have to keep it up forever. And school was familiar turf, since she had spent so many years as a teacher. In two years she completed the program with a 4.0 GPA.

Success in terms of finding a job came early. Roberta held a part-time teaching job while she was still in graduate school. Shortly after her graduation, she was the successful candidate for a community college position. She has been working there ever since and earns $29 an hour. Unfortunately, the position is only part-time.

Full-time jobs in Roberta's field are almost impossible to find in her area. Because of her age and because she is now single, she wants to earn more money and have the security of a retirement plan.

"I can't make enough money at part-time teaching. I don't want two part-time jobs. I need a full-time job now, and I can't get one in this field. Also, I'm a little bit bored with teaching, and I'd like to do something else," she said.

Back in 1975, if she had known what her needs were going to be now, Roberta would not have chosen the career path she did. "I would have gone into clinical psychology," she said. Her interest in pursuing a career as a clinical psychologist is an outgrowth of her own therapy after she separated from her husband.

Roberta enrolled in a clinical psychology master's degree program in 1985, and expects to graduate soon. Then she will need to put in 3,000 hours of practical experience as an intern, in a paid position if all goes well. Her goal is to develop a private practice.

Roberta commented recently about her hopes for the future: "I would like to be working for myself in the field of clinical psychology. I would like to be able to arrange my time so that I have sufficient leisure for interests, like ceramics, reading, and sports. I'd like to be able to socialize more and do some traveling."

CHANGING CIRCUMSTANCES: SCHOOL SERVES A NEW FUNCTION

Sylvia has gone back to school three times since she received a bachelor's degree in history at the traditional age in 1963. Each experience with school has been accompanied by dramatically different sets of circumstances and expectations.

With her husband's support and encouragement Sylvia first pursued a master's degree in art history. In 1970 she graduated three months before the birth of their first child. The degree, she reasoned, would help her get the type of job she wanted.

Ten years later, Sylvia, then the mother of three, went back to school just to take a few writing courses. She did not have a career or degree in mind but soon discovered that she was extremely interested in fiction writing. This time her husband, Dennis, was unsupportive and seemed to her to be threatened by her growing commitment to writing. In fact, Sylvia feels her writing may have precipitated their 1984 divorce.

The year 1987 found Sylvia taking courses leading to a Ph.D. in English. She expected this degree to give her "self-esteem, prestige, and enrichment."

Sylvia's various returns to school fulfilled different needs as her circumstances changed. After receiving her bachelor's degree in 1963, she held a series of jobs she enjoyed. She worked as an executive trainee at a major department store, as an assistant stylist for an advertising firm, and as a stylist for a fashion photographer.

In 1967 she went abroad to marry Dennis, who was in the Peace Corps. For the next year and a half, Sylvia taught art history and wrote travel pamphlets for a tourist organization.

When they returned to the United States, Dennis accepted an executive position with a manufacturing company in a small Midwestern town. The move was a significant one for Sylvia, who had spent most of her life in major metropolitan surroundings. She decided to return to school.

"I was going to be moving to a small town, and I wanted a major interest to occupy my time. I also wanted to retrain myself for a different field. I had been trained in fashion, and I wanted to get into art history. My ideal was to find a job in a museum."

When asked in 1978 who had given her the most support for her student role, Sylvia replied that Dennis had. In fact, the idea for her return to school was initially his.

Sylvia was able to realize her career goal almost immediately. In 1971 she took a part-time position as assistant public relations director for an art museum. Soon she was offered several coveted full-time positions, but she turned them down. "I could have been a curator, but my husband wouldn't let me work full-time. So in a sense the degree was successful, but the relationship was not."

After a year and a half with the museum, at Dennis's suggestion, Sylvia opened an art gallery. The gallery was open only part-time so Sylvia could balance her personal and professional life as Dennis wished.

During the seven years Sylvia owned and operated the gallery, she was completely immersed in the art world. She was on the painting and sculpture selection committee at the museum where she had worked, and she served on advisory boards for a gallery associated with an art school and the Arts Commission for her state. In addition, she was judging art shows and lecturing.

In 1979 the family decided to move to a city about 5 hours away from the company at which Dennis worked. Sylvia was delighted to be back in a metropolitan area. She began writing about art and published reviews and articles in national and regional publications.

In 1981 Sylvia opened a new gallery focusing on contemporary art and major graphic artists. She hired a full-time assistant, which gave her the flexibility to get away for "children's doctors' appointments, first-grade puppet shows, fourth-grade presentations on the presidents, and sixth-grade band concerts.

"I was out of a small town and into a big city where I could take courses and go to the symphony and theater. I had some freedom, and I had a chance to be myself for the first time in a long while." Dennis was home only on weekends.

"Dennis was living the life of a small-town bachelor, in a sense, and I was living the life of a big-city parent. I was taking courses and absorbing culture, becoming more independent, capable, and aware."

A turning point in Sylvia's life and in her marriage centered on a writing course that she took at that point. The teacher gave Sylvia tremendous encouragement. "She said my writing had improved 400 percent, and she encouraged me to take the advanced course. It was thrilling," Sylvia commented.

"Even though I was starting the art gallery, I took the advanced course. I had to get up at 5 a.m. to write the papers. I was running an art gallery. I was a single parent all week. But the only support I was getting was from the course."

In 1983 Sylvia attended a writers' conference. Although Dennis was completely involved with Sylvia in setting up the art galleries, he was extremely upset by her growing enthusiasm about writing. "Going to the writers' conference was probably the downfall of my marriage," Sylvia explained. "My husband was pretending to be supportive. He drove me out there, but after I got back, when I was asked at a party how the conference was, my husband walked away and left the party.

"When I wrote at home, I hid it from him. The writing revealed things I think he didn't want to see. He didn't see the writing as a way of communicating."

The writers' conference was a high point in Sylvia's life, but it was a crossroads as well. "It involved a crumbling of my marriage, but the marriage was crumbling anyway. This just called attention to it. I had lived a very isolated life, and I started to realize I did not have to be a victim. I had a voice. I could make choices. I was entitled to a life of my own.

"That's positive and negative. Such a realization can throw you into a crisis with your spouse. I felt that I had sacrificed my rights as a person to stay in the marriage. I had a right to have a life that was rewarding."

When Sylvia started taking writing classes, she said that she did it "to find something that was just for me." When she enrolled in the Ph.D. program in 1986—her third academic reentry—she did it because she wanted the status of the degree. She was secure financially. "I want a Ph.D.," she explained, "not because I think I can get a job with it, but because I want the status, the prestige."

She has other reasons. Sylvia is writing a book about an artist, and she believes the Ph.D. will give her credibility as an author. Also, now that she is divorced, she finds it difficult to maintain an active social life. "At least going to class helps you meet people who are intelligent and interested in what you are interested in. The Ph.D. will lead to social interaction with the types of people I enjoy spending time with. A degree is often a key to a lot of different doors. I feel that a Ph.D. will add tremendously to my confidence."

Sylvia has her oldest and youngest children—both still teenagers—living with her. She is going to school part-time and does not think that it takes time away from them. "They are proud of my going to school, especially my daughter. She sees me studying, and I think I set a good example when I'm reading, doing homework, and turning in assignments on time. I think it's a very positive influence," she said.

Her school role gets mixed reviews from her youngest son, Melvin: "He wants more of my time; he wants to know I'm available if he needs me. His major technique for showing anger is to hide the paper I'm currently working on! One time I had to go to his school to find out where he had put my paper, due that day, for which I had stayed up all night."

Sylvia had one false start in choosing her Ph.D. program. The curriculum focused specifically on English literature and literary theory, areas with which she did not have much familiarity. After trying to read 10 hours a day for three months, Sylvia realized it was not the right program for her. She switched to the creative writing program and is very comfortable once again.

EDUCATION CHANGED HER FOCUS

In 1970, when Cybil, an elementary education major, was a senior in college, she left school to be with her newborn. Both she and her husband, Greg, felt that she should be home with their son.

Cybil and Greg had spent the first few years of their marriage as college students. The year 1970 was a milestone for them. Greg graduated with a bachelor's degree in chemistry and immediately found a job as a research chemist. The new position meant a major relocation from the South to the Midwest.

Cybil felt extremely frustrated about her incomplete education. "I felt like less of a person in 1970 when I didn't finish my degree and my husband did. That was something only I felt—that a little piece of paper hanging on the wall made him a better or more complete person. But that's the way I felt at age 22," she said.

Greg felt Cybil should not go back to school, even part-time, until their daughter, born in 1972, was in first grade. The couple had many arguments and discussions, and finally Cybil resumed her studies one year before Sheri started kindergarten.

"By waiting so many years I was fooling myself that I would enjoy my family and then go back to school. I was unhappy. I felt unfulfilled. It was something I had not finished; I should have finished. I think my fears grew as the years went by. Would I be able to finish that degree?"

If Cybil had it to do over again, she would not have waited to finish

Back to School for Another Degree

her degree. She would have gone to school when her son, Todd, was 6 months old. If she had gone this route, she would have been finished when he was 15 months old. "Then I would have had the option of staying home with him or working immediately and finding some day care for him."

Cybil does not recommend mixing a student role with mothering preschoolers. "It's awfully hard to juggle the guilt feelings and the scheduling and other pressures of family life while going to school in the best of situations. But if you compound it by having children between the ages of 2 and 5 who need you to watch them, see them develop, and so forth—you may feel very guilty when you leave them.

"Once they start school, you can take courses, be away from home, and do research without interfering with their schedules. If I were to do it over again, I would have gone when my children were very young, so that when I left them with their grandmother or a neighbor for the afternoon, they wouldn't have known I was gone. Or I would have waited until they started school to go back and finish my degree."

Cybil's year and a half of part-time studying was a rough period for her family. Sheri and Todd were 5 and 7 when their mother graduated. "I know they missed having Mom bake cookies. They would ask, 'Why don't you bake us cookies anymore?' My husband would lose his temper with me occasionally because I felt I couldn't handle it anymore. He would say, 'Just forget the degree; your responsibilities are with your children.' I would be a liar if I said there was no hitch in going back to school. There were many nights I cried about trying to handle the family, the pressures, the papers—wanting to be perfect."

During her senior year, Cybil did no studying from the time the children came home from school until after they went to bed. She would study from 9 to 11 p.m. On Saturdays she would finish up, whether it took her 2 hours or 10. In 1978 she said, "I try not to be supermom, superwife, superstudent. I try to erase the super and just be mom, wife, and student."

In retrospect, Cybil wouldn't recommend her reentry life-style to anyone. "I would have set up times in the evenings when I would be away from my family. My children were very young, and they were in bed by 7:30 p.m. I could have left the house from 7:30 to 11 every night, and they would not have known I was gone. If my husband had not wanted me to leave every night, I could have gone two or three nights a week instead. I could have had total quiet at the public library or the school library. I think I was fooling myself to think that I was studying at home with the TV on and all the interruptions."

During her senior year, Cybil commented on her husband's attitude: "He encourages me. In a way, he feels that I should be at home, but, in another way, he knows I have to do this for myself. He knows I'm doing it for the family, too. I think our relationship will improve 100 percent because I will have the confidence that comes from doing what I want to do.

"Right now, the relationship is suffering because I ask him to take care of the children. He folds clothes while he's watching television. We don't go out. Generally, on Saturday I'm gone the whole day. But we both can see the end, and that helps."

Greg was definitely ambivalent. When the going got rough at school, he would advise Cybil to give up. "This made me into a fighter," she said. "It would make me so angry I would work twice as hard."

Greg was asked if he had any advice for husbands of reentry students. He said, "Be patient! Try to picture what it's going to be like when it's done. Keep the goal in mind."

Greg mentioned many benefits to their family from Cybil's return to school: added income, his wife's growing self-confidence, better time management. "One of the big benefits to me is that the B.S. degree is an insurance policy. If something happens to me, Cybil can make it on her own."

After her graduation in 1978, Cybil was immediately hired as an elementary school teacher. She worked there until Greg was transferred to the South in 1984. The move required a tremendous adjustment for the entire family. The children, who were then 12 and 15, left old friends behind them. Greg had the pressures of a new job. Cybil had to prove herself all over again as a teacher.

"After teaching six years I had to take a national test. I questioned whether I could pass. It was a very emotional time for me. I had an excellent teaching record for six years, had graduated from a good university, and now had to prove myself again."

Cybil quickly got a job as a third-grade teacher and has since received the maximum incentive pay awards several times. She was one of three in her county to apply for the NASA Teacher in Space Program. She was not selected, she believed, because she had been working in the county for only six months. She was very disappointed and the space shuttle's tragic end affected her deeply.

Shortly after the family's move, Cybil decided to pursue a master's degree in education on a part-time basis. "I want to be the best in my field. I want to keep abreast of all the new techniques and methodologies of teaching children, and I want to know what's out there," she said.

Cybil believes there is a delicate balance between aggressive and assertive behavior. "I have to be careful," she commented, "because sometimes I can overstep the boundary, especially at home.

"I am the queen bee in the classroom. I'm the boss. At home, I'm not the boss. I may be the partner in the relationship, but my husband has told me many times that he is not one of my third graders and to please not talk to him as if he were."

When she went back to school the first time, Cybil felt that the time away from her children was very difficult for them. The second time, however, she believes they actually benefited. "They seem to be more independent. I am fully confident they will be able to function on their own when they leave home. If I had stayed home and not gotten a degree, they might not have developed as fully."

Cybil brings in only 25 percent of the family's income, but she and

Greg believe that her salary alleviates financial pressure. Vacations, furniture, and lots of extras are affordable because she works.

The children understand the benefits, too. When she was 15, Sheri said, "I have gotten nicer things because my mother has a job. I think my mom feels bad because she didn't spend much time with me when I was little, but it really never bothered me. In the long run, I became more independent. My mother always manages to come to all of my activities, and she supports me in all I do."

Last year, Cybil enjoyed speaking to an education class at the university she attends. The professor asked her if she had ever thought about teaching at the college level. "A light bulb went on, and I thought: 'Maybe this is what I want to do.'"

Cybil is formulating new goals. She would like to finish her master's degree by next year, when she will be 41. Toward that end, she was devoting the 1988–89 academic year to full-time studies. Next she wants to enroll in a Ph.D. program as a part-time student. By age 45 she hopes to have her Ph.D. and be a college teacher. "It's still in the dream stage, but if you don't have a dream or a goal to shoot for in your life, then there is no purpose at all."

CHAPTER 13
RIPENING GOALS

In the United States, people change jobs on an average of once every three and a half years. Moreover, a study published by Future Directions for a Learning Society indicates that in any given year more than 40 million Americans are in some stage of career transition. People who earn academic degrees as adults are often part of the group confronting changing objectives.

The goals of the six women discussed here have not undergone dramatic transformation; rather, they have evolved and ripened. These women are all in the human services field, where the potential for burnout is high. All have been involved with providing direct services to specific groups. The women who are happiest with the evolution of their careers are those who have added administrative responsibilities to their jobs. It is interesting to note that all of them are still involved with jobs that are directly related to their reentry training.

Debbie was happy to work as a counselor in an academic setting for seven years. However, outside of work, she was always torn as to which social service agencies she wanted to give her time and money to. Today, she is the director of a fund-raising federation of fourteen social action and service organizations. In this capacity, she makes it possible for other social service workers to effect change.

Norma, a learning disabilities specialist by training, now heads a staff of twenty as clinical administrator of a county medical center's child development department. She was recruited from her former position by the head of the center. She finds the new post tremendously fulfilling.

Sandra has also gotten more involved with administration. She has focused on a different clientele and a different type of work environment. A social worker by training, she is now a mental health consultant and project coordinator involved with serving children, parents, and teachers in day-care centers.

Ida, a learning disabilities specialist who works with a tutorial program, wishes she had studied to be a lawyer instead. However, at age 50, she has decided to stay put. She was promoted when the coordinator of the tutorial program left. Instead of switching fields, she feels comfortable combining her administrative work with a growing private practice.

In 1987 Catherine was suffering from complete burnout after working nine years for the same county child protective services agency as a social worker and administrator. She was ready to bow out of the human services field altogether. But she found a position in which she serves a completely different population—the elderly. She is delighted to have a different clientele and to be focused on mental health rather than social work.

Martine is at an impasse. She finds the work for which she was trained, first teaching and then nursing, to be low-paying and unenjoyable. However, her top priority is to have her work schedule mesh with her children's schedules; in that sense her position as a school nurse is ideal. Perhaps as the children get older, she will search for a more interesting and lucrative nursing job.

As interests and circumstances develop, so do opportunities. The refocusing and reshaping of goals is part of a natural growth process. Before any major job change, it makes sense to ask yourself exactly what it is about a particular job that makes you want to change it. Is it the actual work? the setting? the people encountered? the limits imposed on productivity or creativity? the methods used to get to the end result? Does the need for change have to do with truly disliking the work or with disliking the particular role you play within the organization?

The women in this chapter saw options within their field of expertise and chose to stay there rather than set out on an entirely new path. From the point of view of time and expense saved, their career moves seem particularly cost-effective. The message: it's possible to alter one or two "ingredients" without throwing away the whole pie.

PAVING THE WAY FOR SOCIAL CHANGE

In 1970, Debbie was depressed and reclusive. She chain-smoked cigarettes, had a lifetime habit of biting her nails down to the quick, and was terrified of learning to drive due to her space-perception disability. She described her relationship with her husband as mediocre.

Today, Debbie is a whirlwind of activity. She is the director of a fund-raising federation of fourteen social action and service organizations. She and her 17-year-old daughter, Esther, are active in an inner-city theater group. Debbie has even actualized a lifelong fantasy: to be a torch singer. Her husband of twenty-one years, William, encouraged her to step into the world of music, and together they have made a name for themselves as musicians.

A severe case of postpartum depression after Esther's birth resulted in Debbie's spending little time outside her home for almost two years. As luck would have it, Wendy, a counselor who moved into Debbie's and William's downstairs apartment, dragged Debbie "kicking and screaming" into her consciousness-raising group.

"Wendy was with me every step of the way," Debbie said. "She was the one who got me driving. We had driving lessons where I was clutching the wheel, my knuckles white, and she would just say, 'OK, put your foot on the brake and start breathing.' She was the one who told me about the social work program and made school seem like something I could do—as if it were just down the street and available to me."

Shortly after Debbie became friends with Wendy, she and several other parents decided to start a cooperative day-care center. "There were about 400 things involved with putting it together and running it," Debbie recalled. This flurry of activity, however, helped bring her out of her depression and into contact with a new social circle.

"I had been home for two years, and I socialized only with other housewives. When our family joined day care, we got involved with a very busy and energized group of people, most of whom either were students or were working. They were terrific role models of women who could have babies and still be people."

Debbie applied for a clerical job at one of the first abortion clinics in the country. She was offered a counseling position there instead. Her response was, "What am I going to do?" She returned to school in order to learn how to do her job.

Although terrified by the most basic questions of where to park and how to register, Debbie was astounded by how quickly she found her niche on campus. Through persistence and stamina, she surmounted the hardships of being a slow reader, graduating with a 3.6 GPA.

"My entire life changed. I felt like a different person. I regained the self-confidence to do new things. I instituted a lot of personal changes, such as giving up an eighteen-year smoking habit. I quit biting my nails. I began doing brave things like teaching classes and workshops.

"Before I went back to school, I just got up and grumbled my way through the day—without goals, without anything. I didn't acknowledge that I had any choices. I began to make decisions about the kind of life I wanted."

During her student days, Debbie had her eye on the counselor position in the social work department at her alma mater. She was the successful applicant and stayed with the job for seven years, providing direct services such as academic advising, career counseling, and placement.

According to Debbie, the period before she returned to school was filled with tension between herself and her husband. "We started out with a good relationship and lost sight of it during the roughest years.

"At a time in a relationship when so many couples split up, part of the reason why we didn't was that we were too chicken. We thought about it and talked about it, but we were too complacent. Later, we realized how glad we were that we didn't. We have so much together;

it was just covered up for a while. We were able to salvage the relationship and fall back in love with each other."

With Debbie as a role model, William decided to finish his bachelor's degree in chemistry in 1977. He had worked as a chemist at a major corporation for many years and was recently promoted to vice president and technical director.

Debbie had been attracted to William initially because he was a successful musician. Music took a back seat, however, when he decided to earn his living as a chemist. Several years after Debbie got the university counseling position, the couple started playing music together. Their musical partnership was a turning point in their marriage.

One thing led to another. By 1980 William and Debbie had joined an early music group that has become well known in their area. Debbie—following a childhood fantasy—found an accompanist, and, with William on the flute, she became a torch singer at age 35.

Today Debbie and her daughter, Esther, are often leads in the same theatrical productions. On any given evening, friends and colleagues show up at their home to run through scripts or to play music.

In 1983 Debbie had to confront a major emotional challenge: her mother was diagnosed as having Alzheimer's disease. Debbie's work as a social services professional served her well while she was finding good programs and care for her mother. "I had access to gerontology specialists," she explained, "and I could pump them for information. I knew how to use the system."

Debbie was her mother's primary caregiver for several years, shuttling back and forth between home and her mother's apartment. She located an excellent adult day-care center, and eventually her mother became a resident in the affiliated nursing home.

"When I wasn't busy crying, being trained in the social work field helped me see to it that the whole thing got taken care of as well as it could be. When we went to the nursing home, I knew what questions to ask and what to look for."

After Debbie had joined the family support group, the director of the nursing home hired her as a free-lancer. Her duties consisted of editing a manual and serving as script consultant for a video designed to train paraprofessionals working with Alzheimer's patients.

As Debbie's confidence and self-esteem grew, so did her vision about ways in which she could have an impact in the field of social services. She felt that many people were providing direct services, but few could see the larger picture.

As a result, Debbie has changed jobs. She is now the executive director of a federation of social action agencies. This alternative-style fund-raising organization is focused on issues such as women's rights, housing, unemployment, senior citizens' rights, and the nuclear freeze. "There are so many good causes and organizations," said Debbie, "and in this position I'm working for fourteen of them. That feels wonderful."

As director of the federation, Debbie is primarily responsible for expanding its fund-raising capabilities, especially through employee payroll deductions. Debbie is the only paid employee. Although a degree is not necessary for her job, she feels it was important because it put her on the path to improved self-esteem. "I wouldn't have dreamed of attempting this job before," she said. "There's no way I could have done it."

The next major transition in Debbie's life will come when Esther leaves for college next year. "She is our only child and we are peers much of the time," she commented. "Her leaving will make a gaping hole. It's been great to have a girlfriend to giggle with in the house. At the same time, I'm really excited about the adventure she is about to embark on, and I'm kind of anticipating the new freedom and privacy William and I will have."

IF SHE HAD IT TO DO OVER AGAIN, SHE'D BECOME A LAWYER

Ida, a specialist in reading and learning disabilities, is the coordinator of a tutorial program. She also has a private practice as a psychoeducational therapist in a New York suburb. If she had it to do over again, she would pick a different profession—law.

In 1969, when she enrolled at the C. W. Post Center of Long Island University at age 32, she and her husband had 3-year-old twins at home plus two boys ages 5 and 9. Ida's aim was to study something that would fit into the life-style of a couple with a house full of children. Elementary school teaching seemed ideal.

"I never wanted to be a teacher," she recalled, "but I didn't know what else would make sense in terms of time and space. Instead of working from 9 to 5, I would get a job from 9 to 3 and be home when my kids got home."

Herb, Ida's husband, was very enthusiastic about her pursuing an education and a career. The couple had always shared in the daily responsibilities of the household. "If I was cleaning up the kitchen, Herb was bathing the twins." Ida's parents also pitched in, happily taking care of the children so that Ida and Herb could spend evenings out.

Late-afternoon classes did not prove to be a stumbling block. Herb, an electrician, arranged his hours so he could be home. The couple was also delighted to discover that his electrical union would pay her tuition.

Ida's career goal evolved while she was in school, and she decided to become a reading specialist. The master's degree she earned in 1973 was in elementary education. Her first few years of work convinced her that she should study childhood learning disabilities as well. This led to certification in reading in 1975.

She immediately found a position as a volunteer tutor at one of the best centers for reading and learning disabilities in the area. Two years later, she was hired there as a learning disabilities specialist. As her expertise in the field of learning disabilities grew, she developed a private practice as a psychoeducational therapist.

In 1978, at age 41, Ida had begun to believe she had chosen the wrong profession. "Had I known then what I know now," she said, "I probably would have gone into law.

"Law always interested me; but, as broad-minded as I've been, it never occurred to me to become a lawyer. I thought law was for men. In 1969, if somebody had said to me, 'Why don't you become a lawyer?' I certainly would have thought about it. But it just never occurred to me."

By 1987 Ida had concluded she should have been less concerned about selecting a field that fit into her family's schedule. As it turned out, most of her tutoring had to be done after school, when she had hoped to be home.

Given the amount of time she spent on her education, she wished she had chosen a field that engaged her imagination more. With hindsight she realized that if you are happy with your work, all family members benefit.

Charting out a new career path at a late date didn't appeal to her. "At this stage, I don't have the energy to go back to school and become a lawyer," she said. Also, she and Herb were beginning to slow down the pace of their life-style. They had only one son still living at home. Although there were still the expenses of three children in college to contend with, the twins were graduating that year. Thus at age 50, Ida was focusing less on career and more on travel and leisure activities.

In recent years, Ida has been able to balance various aspects of her work in ways that make it more challenging and stimulating. In 1985 the coordinator of the volunteer tutorial program retired, and Ida moved into the position. Now she is responsible for as many as fourteen tutors. She also works with physicians, psychologists, social workers, educators, parents, and hospital administrators. The position is half-time, which Ida likes.

Her job gives her a degree of prestige and status, and her private practice has blossomed. "I enjoy the administrative aspects, but private practice is more lucrative. It's a very good combination," she said. "What I learn here in the tutorial program I use in my private practice, and what I learn in my private practice I use here." Her son is building her an office at home.

The niche Ida has carved is not her ideal, but it is satisfying in many ways. Her two jobs give her the opportunity to help people, assume a role of responsibility, earn money, and work with pleasant colleagues. "I would have preferred to be in a more exciting profession, like law, but having taken this road and doing what I'm doing, I'm satisfied. My life is very full," she said.

JOB DISSATISFACTION AS A CATALYST FOR CHANGE

Catherine says she is ready for a complete career change. After nine years of working as a social worker and then supervisor for a county child protective services agency, she wants to leave the human services field. She wants to devote more energy to her personal life.

In high school Catherine thought she would like to be a psychologist. As she continued her education, she sharpened her focus. She received a master's degree in psychology in 1977 and got her M.F.C.C. (Marriage, Family, Child Counseling credential) in 1985.

Earning her master's degree at age 34 brought closure on many levels. She ended her marriage. After accepting a new job, she moved hundreds of miles away with her two young children. She viewed relocating, away from family and friends, as a plus. "It turned me into an independent and self-sufficient adult," Catherine said.

Dependency had always been a major issue for Catherine, she says now. "This is the first 'adult' job I've ever had. In fact, these past nine years are the first adult years I've lived. Prior to that, I was with Francis, and that didn't count because I never made any independent decisions. I love having my own house, making all decisions no matter how bad, having my own money, trying to figure out which plumber to call, having the whole house to myself when the kids are out, and deciding whether to nap, watch television, or call a friend. It's wonderful!"

Earlier Catherine had been ambivalent about taking steps toward independence. In 1974, she was just short of getting her master's degree in psychology when her husband was offered a position 200 miles away. Had Catherine stayed on just a few months, she would have been able to get the degree and find a job.

"That would have been OK with my husband," Catherine said. "Instead, I transferred a handful of credits and started all over again. School was fun, I got out of the house, I didn't have to hold down a job, and I preferred school to anything else.

"Francis claims now that he suggested the option of staying there, but I didn't hear it. I blamed him because I didn't finish; it was my own fear of graduation. I didn't know what to do if I was out of school."

While in school for two additional years, Catherine realized she was miserable in her marriage. She believes that her divorce was a direct result of her being in school. "I probably would not have divorced Francis, or at least not with the confidence with which I did, had I not graduated from school and had successful academic and personal relationships while in school. There was a direct correlation between school and divorce."

According to Catherine, Francis also believes that school played an important part in the breakup of their marriage. "From his perspective, it wasn't the education, but my hanging out with what he called 'militant lesbians.'"

According to Catherine, "militant lesbians" was an extreme description of her friends. She says the women's movement was thriving, and she was able to develop friendships with other women who were confronting some of the same issues.

"There were a lot of women students my age, and instructors, too. It was a time of burgeoning women's rights and talk about role differences and androgyny. I focused more on my marriage and my need to get out of it. I've never been so miserable as I was with Francis those last couple of years."

For the past nine years, Catherine has concentrated almost exclusively on her professional life. She describes her relationship with her children as one of "benign neglect." She also comments that, until 1986, she had only a few meaningful relationships with men.

"I've spent a great deal of energy on my work, and, except for recently, I've loved it," she said. "It's been exciting, and I've been successful. I got promoted quickly and over the years have been given a lot of authority and special projects."

Recently, the administration at the agency changed, and Catherine was transferred. Although it was a lateral transfer, it felt more like a demotion. Her dissatisfaction with the new position served as a catalyst for a complete reevaluation of her professional life.

"I don't like my new job, and I don't like the new administration," she said. "I'm burned out on people lately and no longer care about working in this job. I need to figure out what to do. I've only been miserable for the past four or five months, so I guess I'm hoping it will go away."

Catherine felt trapped in her position. She had a good income, and commented, "I'm really stuck in a way. Any new job would demand a large pay cut. I didn't realize how easily one gets sucked in after a few years on the job. The pay raises, retirement plan, and health benefits are very seductive. A change of jobs because you're unhappy with the present one can mean a major financial setback."

At the same time, Catherine believed she would much prefer to use her energy to improve her personal life.

She had met someone, Victor, who was causing her to rethink her goals. In a major switch in focus from the professional to the personal, she said, "I want to marry and try that old institution again. I want more financial security. I need to develop more interests. I'm struggling with golf and bridge. I need to build up my health. I want to be slimmer. I want two bathrooms and a gourmet kitchen. I want to talk with my kids. And I want a job either teaching at a junior college or consulting," she said.

A letter from Catherine as this book goes to press reports that she has been able to change her job focus without changing fields and is very happy. She is now a geriatric mental health program supervisor working for the local Area Agency on Aging. In this position, she is responsible for supervising clinical staff who provide outreach and mental health intervention to senior citizens in their homes and in residential care facilities. She is also "on loan" as a therapist to two offices of the Mental Health Department and has started a small private practice.

"I'm really glad for the employment change," she said. "It's fun to learn new material, work with a different—and grateful—clientele, and meet new people. I'm glad to move into the mental health field and away from social work, although the two are very closely aligned."

She finds the balance between her personal and professional life shifting once again. "I'm distancing again from Victor. I think I lack balance," she said. "When work is falling apart, I look to the personal to meet my emotional needs; when the personal is falling apart, I do the opposite. Or, when work is going well, I don't need the personal stuff so much. How do other women keep a balance in their lives?"

FROM MAKING COFFEE AT PTA MEETINGS TO RUNNING A CLINIC

For many years Norma felt like a subordinate, even in her own family. Fearful of assuming a leadership role, her first outside involvement was with the PTA as the person who made the coffee. Now, at age 51, she is a clinical administrator of a medical center's child development department, responsible for a staff of twenty.

A learning disabilities specialist by training, Norma was not even seeking the administrative position. She was working at the facility as an educational diagnostician and therapist when the head of the center told her they wanted her to fill the post.

"It never occurred to me that I would go beyond teaching and a private practice, which I enjoy tremendously," Norma explained in 1987. "I have a long history of being the follower. I was the backup for my husband, for someone who had something important to do in this world." Fifteen years ago, Norma passed up the presidency of the elementary school PTA because she didn't think she would be effective.

Norma's style as an administrator reflects the sensitivities of someone who knows what it is like to feel subordinate. When asked if all twenty people answered directly to her, she replied: "No. I don't want it that way. They don't answer to me. We work together for the good of the children. I'm a facilitator.

"I suggest to the chief where the problems are and how they might be improved, changed, or corrected. I speak to each of the individuals involved and ask for feedback. I find solutions from the input of the people involved."

Norma already had a master's degree in early childhood education in 1974, when, at age 38, she enrolled at a nearby university in a master's degree program in special education and learning disabilities. She had worked as a kindergarten and first-grade teacher before she married Arthur, a psychiatrist.

Initially, Norma was certain that she did not want to resume a teaching career. Fifteen years earlier, when she was in the classroom, she felt frustrated by her inability to reach the children with learning difficulties. In 1974 the career counselor at a women's center pointed out that all of Norma's interests and skills still added up to a teaching-related career. "It hit me. It was the kids whom I couldn't teach that fascinated me. So I went for a master's in the kids I couldn't teach."

There was a personal crisis brewing at the time Norma decided to return to school. "I started therapy about six months before I went back to school. It was a necessity. I was so disturbed and distraught and upset with myself and my role in this world."

Norma mentioned that she had a long history of being unable to defend herself, to speak up when she had been offended. "I would just sit there and feel bad." School helped her to feel better about herself.

In 1978 she said, "I'm not just happy. I'm high, full of joy. Even when something isn't going right, I feel something good will come out of it. Before I made the decision to go back to school, I was often tired, depressed, annoyed at minor problems, and just generally feeling very dull. I began looking at my expectations for myself. I did not need to be all things to all people. I could be me, and that was enough, more than enough."

Norma hinted in 1978 that the increase in her self-confidence and assertiveness tipped her family's balance. When asked if there had been any negative changes as a result of returning to school, she laughed and replied, "It depends on whom you ask. Because I'm taking less garbage from people, they are sometimes shocked by the change in me. That applies to friends, children, husband, and relatives. My new priorities are very different, so people have to get used to a somewhat different Norma."

Norma said that her children—ages 9, 11, and 13 when she started school—were initially very put out by having a mother who was no longer as readily available to them. They had to assume many more chores at home, and they were forced to become more independent.

"The kids were old enough to understand that Mommy goes into the office, closes the door, and needs silence to study because this is heavy stuff. Give her half an hour. No interruptions. Whatever it is, you can handle it." She continued, however, to take great interest in her children's activities—the practicing, the concerts, the special programs. Felicia, the oldest child, had been the least interested in academics. Norma hoped, during her reentry days, to provide a good role model for her. She said, "Felicia is very proud of me. She has plans for herself that are way beyond what they might have been. As she sees me becoming more confident, daring, successful, I think it affects her."

Norma is now in charge of far more than her work life. She and her husband, Arthur, separated in 1986. Commenting on their relationship, she said, "I took care of him the way his mother used to take care of him. When I began to ask for more than he was willing to give, he couldn't bend."

Norma credits school with giving her a tremendous amount of experience in confronting frightening situations. She found that if she plunged in, she could be successful. Throughout her marriage, she had been terrified by the prospect of someday finding herself alone. The last few years have proved, in her words, "that what scared me to death was really not so horrible.

"While we were still married, the idea of being alone frightened me—to take care of myself, to be without a man. Not that he was so terrific, but at least he was here. I discovered that that's not right."

No longer timid, Norma is protecting her interests as she and Arthur go ahead with a divorce. "I'm not the lady Arthur thought he married. I'm protecting myself. I'm setting the guidelines and taking charge of the situation as much as possible. I've learned how to defend myself and not be manipulated by guilt or sensitivity to someone else's feelings when it's a detriment to me. Some of the words that fall out of my mouth amaze me."

Much to her surprise, Norma has found she is able to create a pleasant social life for herself as a single woman. She has met a number of interesting people and has been seeing one man, who is a caring, supportive person.

"It's been a painful road, but it was worth everything to feel self-reliant, competent, and accepted by people I admire as equals," Norma commented. "I may not do everything well enough, but I do quite a few things well. As long as I believe that, no one can hurt my self-concept or assurance."

Feeling confident and good about herself has affected all aspects of her life. Her interest in helping the PTA was replaced by volunteer work with a nonprofit organization that supports multiple community enterprises.

Even though she feels that a Ph.D. would not make a significant difference careerwise, Norma is considering entering a doctoral program in cognitive functioning and learning. She said, "I will never be finished learning, with or without a degree."

FED UP WITH TEACHING AND NURSING

In 1975 Martine, at 31, wanted to pursue a master's degree in nursing. She was interested in the field and felt she would be highly employable. She was caring for two preschoolers. A career with flexible hours was a high priority.

The commute to a school where she could get a master's degree turned out to be prohibitive. Consequently, Martine enrolled in a registered nurse program in 1977. The nursing school was a half-hour drive from her New England hometown.

The pressure of trying to balance family and school was enormous. Martine's husband had just received his Ph.D., and his jobs for the next few years would be one-year contracts with various universities. Martine knew she might not be able to continue with school.

Another pressure point was that child care was practically nonexistent in their area. Martine was forced to schedule classes around her child-care schedule.

"It's difficult to have two careers in the family," Martine commented in 1978. "Something has to give. It's usually the wife. Having ambitions of my own puts incredible strain on the marriage. I might have to give up.

"I feel guilty about my plans," she continued then. "I feel OK as long as I know the kids are happy, that the sitter or the program is a good one. But if there's any problem with the children's schooling, schedule, or sitters, I can't handle the worry. It's impossible to study once I get home. There's a constant feeling of guilt."

Martine had worked as an elementary school teacher and she knew she could drop nursing and return to teaching. However, jobs were hard to come by and teaching wasn't what she really wanted to do.

Having graduated in 1979, Martine is currently working as a nurse and teacher in an inner-city high school. She runs a miniclinic at the school and performs pregnancy tests, strep tests, lab work, physicals, and more.

Martine doesn't feel particularly positive about teaching or nursing right now. "My schedule matches the children's," she said. "My problem right now is not what job I have but the fact that no matter what I do there is not enough time to manage the house and kids and have a little time for myself. Some of it has to do with the ages of the children. They are all involved with activities now. We live in a suburban area, which means driving everywhere."

There have been major changes in Martine's personal life. She divorced, remarried, moved to a different town, and, in 1981, had a third child. Being available to her children is her top priority right now. Because of this, she will continue to work as a teacher and school nurse, even though she no longer really enjoys either.

The main sore point for her about opportunities in either field is the low pay. She and her second husband, a statistician, are coping with the financial pressures of three children as well as a home in an area where the cost of living is high. The family needs to be able to count on Martine bringing in a decent monthly income.

Martine feels very pessimistic about any woman's ability to cope with a family and career successfully. She believes she should have worked for the degree she wanted initially—a master's degree in nursing instead of an RN. It would have taken the same amount of time but would have opened up her job options considerably. She has considered getting an M.B.A., but the academic program and subsequent work schedule would not jibe with the family-centered life-style she has chosen.

Ending on a slightly more optimistic note than her previous comments, Martine says she is not actually sorry she became an RN. As her children get older and require less of her time, she believes she will be able to find more satisfying work.

CHANGING FOCUS, MAINTAINING BALANCE

Sandra is someone who carefully planned her life-style to balance family with work. Trained as a social worker, she is now working three-fifths time as a mental health consultant and project coordinator for early childhood programs.

Sandra's original goal was to be a social worker serving women and families. She has worked in special needs adoption and has been a family therapist. "My goals haven't changed; they have ripened," she explained. "I've modified my view of how I can contribute. My goal is the same: to find a population that isn't being served, to use all of my work energy and enthusiasm toward solving some of the problems, and to not get into my career so deeply that I neglect my family commitments."

When she and her second husband and two children moved from the Midwest to New England in 1980, Sandra discovered that there were plenty of family therapists to go around. "I was in a swamped field," she concluded.

She was able to find a job using her expertise with a group she has always enjoyed—preschoolers. "It will be a long time before we swamp the field of early childhood education!" she said. As part of a preschool enrichment team funded by the Department of Public Health, she provides services to day-care centers and nursery schools. The team has the capability of serving children, teachers, parents, and the programs. In addition to providing services, Sandra is also the project's coordinator.

Sandra has been involved with balancing the care of her children, school, and work since her undergraduate reentry days sixteen years ago. Her oldest child, Noah, was an infant, and Sandra arranged her classes at the University of California at Berkeley and Mills College around his nursing schedule. Later, while she was in graduate school in the Midwest and separated from her first husband, she was coparenting and juggling Noah's day-care schedule. Several years later, after she had remarried, Jonah, born in 1978, was added into the balancing act.

Sandra believes that most men's attitudes about working mothers fall into one of two categories. Some men are supportive but don't understand wives wanting to take time off to be with the children during their early years. Others want to be "king of the mountain," spending all their energy on earning a living; they resent their wives deviating from full-time motherhood.

Sandra's husband and her ex-husband are very flexible people. While she was in graduate school pursuing a master's degree in social work and still married to her first husband, Stuart, she and her son moved closer to the school, commuting home on weekends. Stuart, a social worker, supported her decision and willingly took on additional child-care responsibilities.

Jeremy, Sandra's second husband, a family therapist, encouraged her to take a few years off from working after Jonah was born, though the decision involved some financial hardship. Teamwork is a high priority to Sandra, Jeremy, and Stuart—professionally as well as personally.

When Jeremy and Sandra decided to move to New England, Stuart and his wife relocated from the Midwest to the East in order to make it easier for Noah to spend time with both his families. The couples live near each other. Jeremy works part-time as a family therapist so that he, too, can be more available to the family.

Sandra doesn't think graduate school placed a strain on her first marriage or caused its demise. "The divorce was a result of the marriage," she explained. "I had been a very passive person. I was not unhappy. It was a family, and it worked. Going to school marked the beginning of decision making for me. I was an adult for the first time. My readiness to divorce was precipitated by the decision to go to school."

Sandra explained recently that it is a constant battle to maintain a balance between work and her home life. "When I flew out of the office today there were people who wished I hadn't left, even though I had put in more than my time. But working part-time helps keep you from getting washed away. When I'm there more, the work becomes more compelling, and then I get swept away."

Women today, Sandra feels, are often pressured to define themselves by what they "do" at a time in their lives when career decisions could be inappropriate. She is glad no one pressured her to go on to graduate school earlier than she did.

"Graduate school would have been much harder with a 2-year-old than with a 4-year-old," she said. "If more people had been staring at me asking, 'Who are you?' earlier, I think I would have gone back to school sooner, and it would have cost me a lot emotionally."

Creating boundaries around her work or studies is an essential ingredient for Sandra's successful balancing act. At one point, she chose not to join a study group that met too close to the family's dinnertime. Though it was a painful decision, Sandra felt good about it.

"I know what it costs not to be available to your kids, not to have food ready when they need it, not to be there when they need you. I remember feeling put upon at the beginning because I was in school with people who did not have little kids. But, once we have families, we cannot be obsessive students. Women who are willing to make practical compromises—not ethical compromises—end up feeling much more relaxed."

As her interests focus on early childhood and the coordination of programs, Sandra is moving away from social work. She is contemplating returning to school when Jonah is older, and she is thinking about a Ph.D. in some aspect of human development.

Sandra would like the stimulation of a research project. "This is something I didn't know about myself while I was in graduate school. I haven't done a formal research project yet, but I want to soon. That's one reason I changed jobs. I needed to manipulate variables, and I needed more freedom to find out what to hypothesize. I would like the satisfaction of using my thoughts and experiences to teach myself something."

Sandra remains adamant about refusing to become driven. "The truth is," she remarked, "that with Jeremy's and my social work degrees, we can achieve enough comfort with a job and a half."

CHAPTER 14
SPECIAL FAMILY CIRCUMSTANCES

Life is usually unencumbered for students going to college at the traditional age. They attend their classes and maybe have a part-time job, but there's plenty of time left over for getting social life and personal relationships in order. They are usually the center of their own universe.

There are very few "islands" in this book. Of the ninety women in the survey, fewer than a handful were responsible for no one but themselves. Almost all of these students served as important pivotal points in other people's lives. In addition to their studies, they were juggling responsibilities to children, a husband, parents, companions, and jobs.

The stories in *Degrees of Success* are filled with other people's turning points and transitions, as well as those of our participants. Husbands, for example, make career changes that necessitate relocations for the family. Retirement of a spouse means adjustment by the partner.

Children are born, and new mothers struggle to find a balance between career and family. Likewise, children grow up and leave home; suddenly, mothering—once a full-time job—becomes sporadic. Divorce can bring circumstances and variables no one ever imagined when they said, "I do."

Older parents need more care and attention. With a median birth year of 1940, many of the women featured in *Degrees of Success* are already coping with the illness and death of husbands and parents. Others are finding that their own physical limitations affect what they can do.

"Take charge of your life" sounds like good advice. More good advice: "Try to remain in sync with your family." In many cases, these two pieces of advice are mutually exclusive.

Being in sync can mean having to surrender a certain amount of ambition. For example, Andrea's husband is nine years older than she is. When she graduated with a master's degree in museum education at age 45, her husband was already thinking about slowing down at work. His retirement, and a heart attack, made long weekends at a house near the beach sound good to both Stanley and Andrea. But Andrea can't combine these extended weekends with working for a museum. She is enjoying her life-style, but it wasn't what she planned when she decided to go back to school.

Connie's ideas about going to work changed three times because of switches in her husband's work tempo. When Russell became completely immersed in starting his own business, she decided to return to school to prepare for employment. When he sold his business, she resigned from her position as a hospice nurse. Now Russell continues to work for the business, and Connie has decided to return to her work.

Several women in this book have been confronted by the death of their spouse. Jocelyn's husband died at age 42. She entered an M.B.A. program when sons Laurence and Henry were just 10 and 8. In 1987, degree in hand, Jocelyn realized she would have a lot less trouble finding a job if she relocated from the town where her sons had spent their entire lives. However, staying put is a top priority for this family. Their living situation is a reassuring constant that helps them come to grips with their loss.

The need to relocate because of a husband's job can wreak havoc on one's academic and career plans. Marissa dropped out of a master's degree program when her husband got a job in another state. Several years later she was divorced. Her former husband's second move precipitated a court battle over the custody of their son. Several years after that, she left her satisfying position as a psychiatric social worker when her current husband needed to relocate in order to get a master's degree in architecture. Each move, initiated by someone else, has required major adjustments by Marissa.

The stereotypical view of the reentry woman involves small children. However, many have changed academic and career plans because of aging or sick parents. Lorraine was involved with two sets of parents in addition to her nine children. She always sought to maintain an unusually delicate balance between family, school, and career.

Brenda was a well-established weaver. She has been offered visiting professorships at universities nationwide. However, her debilitating back problems are aggravated by her creative efforts. For several years, she devoted a tremendous amount of energy to learning how to live—and create art—with her physical disability.

It is remarkable that there is so little bitterness expressed by the women who have had to change their plans because of circumstances beyond their control. These seem to be highly adaptable people.

Adaptability is, in fact, part of the reentry package. You quickly learn that the only constant is change. Combining an academic program with a full life prepares you to confront change in a positive way. Learning to confront change is a skill shared by the women in this book.

PROVIDING CONSTANTS TO COMBAT GRIEF

In 1978 Jocelyn, at 33, was working three-fifths time as a high school history teacher. She was contemplating returning to school for a master's degree in social work with a primary focus on gerontology. At that point, she and her husband, Marshall, had two preschoolers. The couple's major concerns were finances and finding additional child care.

The family depended on two incomes. Jocelyn figured that she could attend school part-time for the first two years and full-time for a third year. By going to school part-time, Jocelyn could continue teaching and generating income.

However, because she was still unsure about exactly which career to pursue, Jocelyn taught full-time while making up her mind. She was able to arrange the extra child-care hours at home. Over the next several years, her focus began to shift from social work toward business or law.

A family tragedy was responsible for the sense of urgency Jocelyn ultimately felt about identifying a new career goal and pursuing it. Marshall, a research scientist, was diagnosed in 1982 as having cancer. He died in April 1984 at age 42. Laurence and Henry were just 10 and 8 years old at that time.

Providing constants for her sons became a top priority. The family had lived in their home since 1975. They were attached to the neighborhood, the area, and the network of friends there. Although Jocelyn was contemplating a career change, she wanted to alter her family's living situation as little as possible.

"My husband's illness and death colored the kind of time I want to spend with my children," Jocelyn explained in 1987, "and to some extent the goals I have set for them. I really like this environment as a place to bring up children in. I will sacrifice some of the things I may want to do, or career goals that I have, because I think the environment is so important to the boys."

Jocelyn entered an M.B.A. program in September 1984 at age 39. She said, "I had hemmed and hawed between going into the business program and going to law school. When my husband became ill, it became even more important to me to get started. After he died, I decided to go to school full-time, to jump into it right away. The courses in human resource development simply looked more interesting than law school, and that's why I finally decided on the M.B.A. program."

Teaching high school full-time had been very demanding. Laurence and Henry were therefore used to their mother having a commitment to school.

Although graduate school required a great deal of her energy, Jocelyn planned carefully for plenty of family time. She continued to take the summers off, and, as a student, she actually had more vacation at Christmas. The threesome took up downhill skiing shortly after her return to school and spent as much time as they could on the slopes. They played tennis together. In 1986, to celebrate her graduation, the family spent the summer traveling in England and Scotland.

Jocelyn believes her relationship with her sons actually improved when she became a student. "They had a new kind of role model—a student mother in addition to a teacher mother. They were almost pleased to see me struggling with some of my courses, so that I could be more sympathetic about their struggles in school."

Jocelyn reported a great deal of personal growth during her M.B.A. days. "Overcoming the many challenges made me feel good about myself and reminded me that I was, in fact, a strong person and could carry on," she said.

As Jocelyn wended her way through the two-year program, she realized she would like to use her human resource development training by working in the public sector. "I would like to have a responsible job where I feel I'm not just pushing papers," she said, "but somehow making life better for people." Her home is within commuting distance of the state capital.

By January 1987, Jocelyn had received her M.B.A. degree and spent six months looking for a job. Although she went to a number of job interviews, she did not find an appropriate position and was beginning to worry.

"I'm finding that if I want to stay here, I'm going to have to start in an entry-level position. In some companies, to get a human resources position, you have to start as a personnel clerk. So I would be competing with 18-year-olds being paid $10,000 to $12,000 a year. This is not what I had in mind! If something does not come through with the state government, then I may have to relocate."

Luckily, that did not have to happen. In the fall, Jocelyn found a job in which to use her M.B.A., her human resources expertise, her teaching, and her general organizational skills: she was hired by the state to design and coordinate programming for workers who will be involved with new automation techniques.

"Many of these people have had highly specialized jobs for twelve to fifteen years," she explained, "and are very anxious about job security. I am pleased that upper management sees the need for good training programs and I'm excited about the challenges."

Jocelyn's position could lead to a number of activities she thinks she would enjoy: video production, editing a quarterly newsletter, writing magazine articles, and presenting statewide training programs. She will also be training and directing a staff.

Jocelyn said, "It's a dynamic situation and unlike anything in my previous experience. I am glad I stayed and found it!"

ACKNOWLEDGING PHYSICAL LIMITATIONS

Brenda pursued a master's degree in fine arts to ensure that she would be in the running for highly competitive college teaching jobs.

The ideal, she felt, would be to combine part-time teaching with her own artwork. The M.F.A. degree helped Brenda actualize her career expectations. What she had not counted on, however, was any kind of physical disability.

In 1987, at age 43, Brenda was no longer able to ignore three very painful cervical disks. The work most precious to her, weaving, is the very physical activity that causes her great pain. Consequently, she has had to change her entire work pattern during the past few years. She has to take better care of her body.

"I never thought anything would happen to my body that would keep me from doing what I wanted to do," she said. "The degree gave me the freedom to do what I wanted, but now, regardless of what degree I have, I have to pay attention to something else."

Brenda has been spending a great deal of time and money rehabilitating her back. The experience has made her see that there are physical limits to what she can do. She has had to alter the tempo with which she always approached her work. The changes, as Brenda sees it, are in intensity.

"I'm having to calm down a little bit. I was too enthusiastic about what I was doing, and now I have severe health problems because of it. It's always been that what I do, I do intensely. It's the kind of personality I have."

Her spine is a major priority right now. Brenda has been getting physical therapy, does special exercises to strengthen her back, and even attended a special course for people with back problems. She has forced herself to weave fewer hours each day.

"Back-breaking" schedules have always been a part of Brenda's life. Being a full-time student in the M.F.A. program in 1975 meant commuting a total of 90 miles each day on the freeway. In addition to attending school, Brenda was teaching art at a nearby university. "I was overdoing it," she said. "That was part of the way I did things, thinking that anything is possible."

In retrospect, Brenda believes she should have figured out a way to save up enough money to attend school without working. "I was always split," she commented. "I had to teach to pay for schooling. I had to get the degree as quickly as possible because I knew the teaching job wouldn't last forever. It was very rough."

The pressures that Brenda felt were grounded in reality. To get a college teaching position in art without a terminal degree was unusual. There were the occasional jobs offered on the basis of reputation, but it was almost impossible to command a decent salary without the degree. In addition, Brenda's marriage to an art professor had ended shortly before she went back to school. She wanted to get the degree and relocate.

Brenda received both her M.F.A. and her divorce decree in summer 1977 at age 34. She was able to relocate after finding a temporary teaching job in California. From there, she accepted a position as a visiting artist in Arizona.

Living in the Southwest and becoming involved in the work of a papermaking facility there had a profound influence on her artwork.

She said, "My art developed in a way that wouldn't have happened had I gone someplace else." Unfortunately, using the papermaking equipment put her under tremendous physical strain.

At the end of the three-semester visiting professorship, Brenda returned to California to teach part-time in the Bay Area. Recently, that job ended, and Brenda was looking for more work.

"I'm not willing to relocate at this point. I like living here, and not having a job hasn't held me back so far. I'm a little worried, but I think something will come along." She considers being an artist a full-time job in itself—as long as the savings hold out.

Recently, Brenda was awarded a grant from the National Endowment for the Arts. This confirms her confidence in her skills, her credentials, and her reputation. She has developed a good balance between her work style and her physical needs and limitations. In the future, she expects to find a part-time teaching job that will also allow her plenty of time in her studio.

KEEPING PACE WITH A SPOUSE

One factor that motivated Connie to return to school in 1977 was that her husband was busy with a business he had started. At age 35, she wanted to have her own interests as well and decided to pursue an RN credential at Metropolitan State College in Denver.

Clearly, Connie had gone to school to nurture personal growth. "I'm not promising anyone that I'm going to finish this program," she said then. "It just feels as if I'm doing something constructive with my time, and it's purely for me. It's made life complicated, but it feels great."

Connie believes that being in school benefited her entire family. She was a lot happier. "If I hadn't gone back to school, I would have been miserable to have been just a housewife and volunteer worker.

"This way, I was able to grow and develop new skills, make choices, and pave new directions for myself. Without that, I'm sure my marriage would not have been as interesting, and I would not have been an example for my children."

After an initial adjustment period in which the couple argued about who was going to do what in terms of household chores, Connie and Russell felt their relationship improved. "He's much more interested in me as *me* now, not just as his wife," she commented while in school. "And I think he's beginning to see that I work really hard all day, too."

Russell, who holds an M.B.A. degree, added, "The fact that she can relate to other people outside the household and has different experiences to bring home makes her more interesting. I don't see any negative effects for us as a couple. It's fantastic! She's excited and energetic. Everything doesn't get done the way it used to, but she's the one that feels bad about that."

Connie reported she used to feel guilty when Priscilla and Michelle at ages 10 and 8 complained about spending less time with her. Priscilla reported at the time: "She's never here. She goes all fast and gets mad. I'd like her to stay home and do errands. I don't like Dad sending us off to school. He makes bad peanut butter and jelly sandwiches."

However, both Connie and Russell felt she was setting a good example for the girls. Connie said, "We are much more interested in each other and have much more respect for each other since I started school. They're taking on more responsibility and making better decisions."

Connie completed her degree in 1979 and got a job as a medical-surgical nurse working part-time in a community hospital. She loved the work. The hitch was she had to work every other weekend. "With teenagers and a busy husband," she explained, "the only time the family ever got together was on weekends. Working on weekends made it difficult for us to do things as a family."

She left the hospital after four years and got a position as a hospice nurse where she could arrange her own hours. The whole family felt that the type of work she was doing had special meaning. "My involvement with hospice is very good for my kids," said Connie. "It has taught all of us about a different aspect of life."

However, because of the very nature of the work, Connie realized she would not be able to do it indefinitely. "One cannot take care of the dying forever. After four years of some very difficult cases, I put my hands up and said, 'OK. That's enough.' I'll miss it, but it's time for a change."

Thus, in 1987, after eight years of rewarding work, Connie was without a job and facing a crossroads. Russell had sold his business, and the two children were away at school. She found herself torn between wanting to work on a project and wanting to do more things with Russell. Connie had enjoyed the balance that was created when she and Russell were both completely busy with their work. His expected change in tempo prompted Connie to reevaluate her own. She knew what she didn't want to do but wasn't sure what she did want. "I'm in my mid-40s, and I'm finding I'm going through a sort of adjustment or crisis," she commented at the time.

She wasn't sure what kind of time commitment Russell would have to make to his job. His responsibilities were reduced, but he continued to work for the company as part of the purchase agreement.

"Russell's in a period of change," Connie said in 1987, "and I find that I am, too. I'm not interested in working 8 hours a day, even though my kids are gone. I want to be flexible. Russell will be traveling, and I'd like to go with him. It's very strange not to be working."

Her need to be involved outside her home crystallized about six months after she quit her job and found herself at a fashion show. "I looked around thinking, 'What am I doing here?' It was not interesting; it was not something I wanted to be doing. It made me realize I needed to get myself going. Having the leisure to go to fashion shows in the middle of the day is not for me!"

Connie immediately began doing volunteer work, working as a victim's advocate with the sheriff's department and as a nurse at a clinic for low-income families. Also, she was asked to help set up a residential home for elderly people who want to remain independent.

"I had some skills that were useful in each of these areas," Connie says. "So even though I was not getting paid, I was able to do interesting work. It gave me a chance to take a breather and decide what to do next.

"By having gone through the nursing program, I am much more helpful to my family and friends. I now have credibility in the community as well as with my own family."

By last year, Connie found she really missed her involvement with nursing. Russell, as it turned out, was just as busy at work as he had been before he sold his business. Consequently, Connie decided to return to her work with hospice.

She says, "I enjoy being part of an organization again. I'll still have the flexibility to travel and be a mother when needed."

The time away from paid employment was constructive. Connie used it to reassess her direction at age 45. It gave her an opportunity to take better care of herself and even design a good exercise program to incorporate into her daily schedule.

THREE MOVES IN TEN YEARS

Marissa's academic and career decisions have been profoundly affected by the career and academic plans of her former husband and her current husband. Their three major moves between 1973 and 1983 created dramatic changes in her life: disruption of a master's degree program, a custody battle that resulted in personal crisis, loss of a good position as a psychiatric social worker, and a new career focus.

When Marissa's and Raymond's son, Bart, was 2, in 1971, Marissa entered a master's degree program in psychology. Raymond was about to get his Ph.D. The couple was living primarily on student loans in a small East Coast college town.

Marissa's motivations for pursuing the advanced degree were complex. She had a bachelor's degree and certification to teach art. Although she was still interested in working with children, her focus was shifting from education to counseling or therapy. Also, she wanted to do more than parenting.

"My goal was probably to just get out of the house and to have some kind of life of my own. I was feeling diminished in my self-esteem by being a stay-at-home mom. The women's movement was having a big influence on me," she said.

Raymond was giving Marissa mixed messages about her decision to return to school. "He felt it would be too much of a burden on my time. He would say, 'Bart needs his mother. I need you at home. We can't have both of us so burdened. There has to be some give somewhere.' I was pretty willing to go along with that because I was somewhat scared about school.

"But he also didn't like the idea of being married to someone who was just a housewife. I was his reflection. Staying at home, being a mother, and taking care of the house were things he wouldn't want to do. Therefore, he couldn't understand why anyone would want to do them.

"In some ways, I was responding to his pressures to go out. I didn't know which were his pressures and which were mine. It confused me. He was giving me lots of double messages: Go out there, but don't really be out there."

When Marissa applied to graduate school as a part-time student, she was not accepted. The next year she reapplied as a full-time student and was admitted.

By 1973 Marissa had completed all the course work for the degree and was preparing to begin her thesis. Raymond was offered a job as an associate professor and consultant halfway across the country.

"I just didn't have what it took to complete the degree long distance," she said. Her goals were becoming clearer; she knew she wanted to do clinical work and needed supervised training. There was a master's degree program in social work administration at the school where Raymond would be teaching. It involved extensive opportunities for internships.

"I had been vacillating for years about the conflict in my marriage," Marissa said, "about whether to stay in it or leave it. A lot of my indecision, conflict, and paralysis stemmed from fear that I wouldn't be able to support myself. When I applied to go to graduate school again, I was still married. But I had a pretty good sense my marriage wasn't going to last and that school was a vehicle out."

Marissa and Raymond separated in 1976, just before she started work on the master's degree. Although tuition was waived because Raymond taught at the university, there was still the financial difficulty of running two households. Marissa found a house with three roommates within walking distance of the campus. The rent was reasonable, and the couple decided Bart would live primarily with Raymond during the week and spend his weekends with Marissa.

Thinking back about her first year in the social work program, Marissa said, "It was a very stressful time. I was dealing with the loss of my mate, the loss of financial security, fear of the unknown, being a single parent, and the demands of schoolwork."

After graduating in 1978 with nearly a 4.0 GPA, Marissa found a job she liked. She was a counselor with a feminist counseling referral service. The agency focused on advocacy for women who were struggling with the economics of divorce.

It was a happy period for Marissa, one of settling in. She and Raymond were doing well in their coparenting roles. Bart was now dividing his time equally between the two households. And Marissa's relationship with a former housemate, Philip, had evolved from friendship into a long-term commitment. They married in 1979.

The stability Marissa had worked to create was short-lived. Toward the end of 1978, Raymond accepted a job in the South, effective the following June. He was also planning to remarry shortly after the move.

The coparenting balance was irrevocably jarred when Raymond proposed Bart move with him. A bitter custody battle ensued. When it was over, Marissa and Raymond had agreed that when Bart entered junior high school in 1981 he would live with Raymond.

Marissa believes that if she had not decided to go to school and place such an emphasis on her own professional development, things might have turned out differently. "Raymond made a lot of assumptions at the time that I was a 'women's libber' and wouldn't care about where my child lived, or something to that effect. After all, he thought, I was in school, and after that I was working, so therefore I wasn't just a mom."

Six years later, discussion of the custody battle and her subsequent separation from Bart is still tremendously painful. "I feel like I went through a civil war, like I lost a husband and a son in a war that ripped up my family. It was a war for liberation, and it was extremely costly." Marissa and Philip knew that Bart would be leaving in two years and did their best to create a close-knit family until then.

During that time, Marissa also changed jobs. She liked her new position as a psychiatric social worker at a private hospital. She worked as part of a team of social workers who did family, group, couple, and individual counseling. The social workers also worked with psychiatrists and occupational therapists to create treatment plans. "I received decent pay and a fair amount of respect and felt happy about what I was doing," she commented.

More change was in the air, however. Philip was thinking about getting a master's degree in architecture. He had been working for ten years with an organization that used a humanistic approach to design; the degree seemed a logical next step.

The best school for what Philip wanted to do was in the Southwest. He applied and was accepted while Marissa and he were still reeling from Bart's departure. They decided that Marissa would follow him shortly, but they both expected to return as soon as he got his degree.

It was very painful for Marissa to contemplate leaving a job that was essentially ideal. However, the idea of a separation from Philip after coping with Bart's leaving was unthinkable. In fact, the hospital was very encouraging about the prospect of Marissa's being rehired when they returned.

The two and a half years that Marissa spent in the Southwest were very productive in terms of reevaluating her personal and professional goals. In September 1983, she took a temporary job at a preschool. Soon she realized she loved working with children. The couple also decided that when Philip was finished with school, they would move back to the East Coast in order to live nearer both sets of parents. (Marissa's mother's story is in Chapter 4.)

Within a month of moving back East in 1985, Philip found a position with an architecture firm, and Marissa was hired as head teacher by a preschool.

"It seems like it's a totally different discipline. Yet many of the kinds of things I do and many of the skills are similar. I see a lot in common between therapists and educators. Both can create a positive environment for learning, growth, and change.

"The counseling situation emphasizes problems, pathology, and dysfunction and tries to correct negative occurrences. In the educational setting, a lot of what you do is preventive in nature. You're trying to set up initial situations that will foster attitudes, behaviors, and feelings so that people don't have as many problems later in life. I had wanted to work with families, and a lot of the work I do is with families, in terms of parent conferences and day-to-day exchanges."

Today, Marissa and Philip are both enjoying their work and their proximity to their parents. Bart spends many school vacations and large chunks of his summers with them. Both of his families put energy into working out ways to get together.

Marissa hopes to continue with early childhood teaching and to branch out into teacher training. She and Philip want to put down roots. They are trying to save enough money to buy a home.

KEEPING PACE WITH RETIREMENT

Andrea entered a master's degree program in museum education at age 43 in 1975. Because her husband, Stanley, is nine years older than she, she realized she might just be starting to feel comfortable professionally at the point where her husband would be considering retirement. During their middle-age years, this difference in age has put them out of sync professionally. Andrea commented recently: "It makes me feel ten years older than I really am because I have to choose between what I might be doing at my age or what I might be doing if I were his age."

She chose to pursue the master's degree anyway. When Andrea made the decision, their daughter, Naomi, was in college, and Neil, their son, was a senior in high school. Andrea had been taking stock of her life for several years.

"What have I done? What do I want to do? What will I be doing in ten years, in twenty years?" These were the kinds of questions haunting her. "Twenty years from now, how will I feel about myself if I keep doing what I'm doing this year? A little bit of this and a little bit of that fit together to keep me busy, but was I satisfied?

"I had clay up to my elbows, and I was always in sloppy old clothes. I had had enough of that. The part of me that wanted to be with people, be involved with education, be involved with art but not with my fingers in the clay turned me toward the museum. The museum education program seemed to pull together all my interests. That was very exciting.

"I knew I was a creative, talented, energetic, productive person. The question was: Would I feel better about myself if I put it all in one direction, into one focus? It was a crisis, trying to think it through. I realized that I would be disappointed twenty years from now if I didn't try, if I didn't go back to school. I wanted to see if I couldn't go in a career direction that united my skills and interests. I needed to try; otherwise, I was going to be miserable."

Andrea had worked as an elementary school teacher and as director of a nursery school. However, aside from three years with the nursery school, she had been out of the work force since Naomi and Neil were born. Since their birth she had combined parenting with volunteering and her own artwork.

Stanley's and Andrea's marriage was quite traditional. She was responsible for the home, and he, a financial manager and budget officer almost all of his adult life, was the source of income.

Stanley was deeply concerned about Andrea's malaise. If school and a new focus would help alleviate this, he wanted to be completely supportive. He said in 1987, "Raising children had been an isolating experience for her. Going back to school was a break from being progeny oriented. It put her into the mainstream.

"I felt good that she was doing it. Here was a person who had guts and was willing to explore new endeavors. I felt proud of her. I think, too, that it made her happier, which would, of course, make the spouse happier." He quickly and willingly assumed many household tasks.

The master's degree program was extremely intense, competitive, and demanding. "I was in an altered state then," Andrea explained. "I was under a lot of strain.

"My priority was to do the program, and to do it A+++. I was quite out of tune with anything that was going on in the family. I was going to survive the program, and I needed to marshal all of my energies to do it. I was a nervous wreck. I was unapproachable emotionally, and not an easy person to live with."

The family had established a relationship with a therapist several years earlier. Andrea commented in 1987 that the family was able to use the same therapist as a resource to deal with some of the problems that arose from her student role.

Andrea does not remember Neil, her son, acting resentful of her student role during his last year at home. She said, "I was so determined and so goal oriented I probably wouldn't have noticed burning bushes at my fingertips at that point!" However, once Neil was living away from home, he did in fact complain on several occasions: Why hadn't his mother waited until he was out of the house before she went back to school?

Both Andrea and Stanley now believe they should have spent more time talking with Neil ahead of time and throughout his last year at home. A more thorough explanation of Andrea's needs and goals and why she had chosen that particular time and program might have helped. Actively soliciting Neil's reactions might have served to alleviate his resentment in the long run.

When Andrea entered the master's degree program in 1975, her goal was to get a full-time job as soon as possible after she graduated two years later. After graduation, she gradually worked into a consulting position at a museum. She loved the work and the ambiance.

However, because she wasn't on the payroll, she had to constantly "hustle" projects. After several years, she was growing weary of the ever-present challenge of drumming up more work. In addition, she began to feel frustrated when ideas she proposed went unrecognized.

So once again, her malaise grew. Then, in 1981, Stanley had a heart attack—shortly before his planned retirement. Fortunately, his recovery went very smoothly. If Stanley's heart attack and retirement were not the reason for Andrea's growing disinterest in a career, they certainly served as a very important catalyst.

"His heart attack and the fact that he's retired," explained Andrea, "had a tremendous impact on the choices I've made. We've bought a second house, near the ocean. It's much more important to him than it is to me. The flexibility of going there and spending Thursday through Monday doesn't dovetail with a job."

Stanley is not putting any conscious pressure on Andrea to spend such long weekends at their second home. He demonstrated, while she was in school and later when she was working, that he was quite happy to accommodate her schedule.

Andrea appears comfortable with the couple's life-style right now. She enjoys frequent visits out of town to her daughter's family, and the freedom to take other trips whenever they like. Besides, she had been growing frustrated with the kind of consulting she was doing and did not want to make the effort necessary for advancement in her field.

Andrea says she does not want to work. On the other hand, if someone were to offer her a part-time museum job in which she had some decision-making power, she says she would take it. Meanwhile, she enjoys being a museum docent, a position she has held since 1978.

Andrea feels she got a good return from all the energy she spent in school. In years past, she had felt she was much too dependent on Stanley. Acquiring new skills in a challenging setting has made her feel more distinctly her own person.

"More than anything," she said, "what I got from the program was the feeling that I can probably do anything if I set my mind to it. That was really more important than the degree itself. I survived something that tested me to the limit. I feel very good about it. It's contributed to a very positive development in my personality."

WIFE, MOTHER, AND DAUGHTER FIRST

Lorraine was president of her high school class and student senate leader in 1946. Shortly after graduation, she married her high school sweetheart and put college on the back burner. Twenty-six years later, with her husband's encouragement, she decided to pursue a college education. She and Nick had nine children ranging in age from 6 to 22.

Thinking back to her student days, Lorraine said, "The family should always come first. Everything else is secondary. I always reminded myself that it was wife first, then mother, then student. And I had the roles of daughter and daughter-in-law. Our mothers were both in their early 80s. I did all the shopping for my mother, took her to the doctor, and spent time on the phone. My father-in-law lived with us while he was sick."

Lorraine has endless reserves of energy. This petite woman, buoyed by her family's encouragement, carved an impressive academic and career niche for herself in spite of her many obligations.

Lorraine had always wanted a college education but felt that she would not be able to handle going to college and raising preschoolers at the same time. The catalyst for her academic reentry at age 44 was her inability to advance at the antipoverty agency where she worked part-time in the early '70s. She wasn't promoted because she lacked a college degree.

"I was working with a community organizer who was a college graduate," Lorraine said. "He was leaving the position and suggested that I apply for his job. He told me I was as good as he was, if not better. I applied and went before the board, but the man they hired was a college graduate. He knew nothing about the job. I had to take him around and show him all the things I knew, and he was getting over twice as much money as I was. I felt crushed when I didn't get that position."

Although Lorraine was eager to begin college right away, she waited until her youngest son, Andrew, was in kindergarten before resuming her education in 1971. She took two courses at a satellite of the state college in Rhode Island. The night classes were tuition-free and were what she described as "wet my feet" courses. Nick stayed home with the children. When Andrew entered first grade, Lorraine transferred to the Community College of Rhode Island as a full-time student.

Nick encouraged Lorraine to pursue a degree. In fact, he had been attending school part-time for several years, pursuing a bachelor's degree in business administration from Bryant College while working in industrial management. He was enjoying his classes and knew that Lorraine would too. "Going to school was a suitable outlet for her brilliant mind," he said.

Nick wasn't worried that Lorraine's student role might mean additional responsibilities around the house for him. "It seemed like the house ran more smoothly," she said. "Everyone rallied around me. They were all so proud. Nick's and my relationship blossomed. He would take over a lot of things around the house just to give me a chance to study. The children all pitched in too."

Lorraine was careful, however, to maintain what she felt was the appropriate balance between her home life and school. For example, she was always there when the children came home from school. Similarly, she always made dinner. She felt it was important to be available in the evenings to help out with homework.

The balance tipped during the academic year 1973–74. Nick's father became seriously ill, and Lorraine took the year off from school. She moved her father-in-law into their home during his convalescence.

When Lorraine received her associate degree with high honors in

1975, the entire family watched her march down the aisle to receive her diploma. The two oldest children already had their bachelor's degree, and another two were college students at the time.

To get to that point in her education, Lorraine had given up many things: tennis lessons, television, movies, telephone calls, sleep, and most social activities. "The only exercise I get now," she said in 1975, "is dancing at weddings."

Nevertheless, Lorraine remained active in her community. She was elected director-at-large on the executive board of the state association for retarded citizens. She served on an advisory committee at her children's elementary school, headed a neighborhood improvement committee, and taught Christian doctrine classes at her church.

Through a "resumed education" program Lorraine was accepted at Brown University. She and her son Louis were the first mother and son to take a class together in the Ivy League school's 200-year history!

Lorraine remembers the two years when she was a full-time student as frenetic but happy. "It was a wonderful time. In Rhode Island, to go to Brown University is considered the ultimate. Nick was bursting with pride."

Tuition at Brown was steep. Fortunately, Lorraine qualified for financial aid and student loans because her husband and five of their children either were in college also or had just graduated.

During her years at Brown, Lorraine decided that she wanted to pursue a master's degree in social work. "I wanted to be able to make some changes in the world," she explained, "and in my own community."

As part of her work-study package, Lorraine requested internship placement at the headquarters of the state association for retarded citizens. The state did not, at that time, have a social services program for the mildly retarded, so Lorraine introduced and developed the concept of providing services for this underserved group, and she sought grant money to launch a pilot project.

The delicate balance between family life, school, and career shifted again during her last semester in college. Her mother suffered a heart attack during midterm exams. Lorraine and Nick decided to have her mother move in with the family. Lorraine assumed responsibility for her mother's care. In order to complete her degree, she got a home health-care aide to be with her mother during school hours.

When Lorraine received her bachelor's degree in sociology in June 1977, at age 48, she was the fifth family member to do so. Nick had graduated two weeks earlier. The two oldest boys were pursuing M.B.A. degrees, and Louis, Lorraine's classmate at Brown, had graduated in 1976. Two other children were already following in the family footsteps. Once again, all nine children applauded as their mom received her diploma.

Lorraine continued to work with the statewide agency for retarded people on a part-time basis as a social worker. When funding ran out, she was hired by another agency to coordinate senior direct-service aides and a home meal program for the elderly. "They were looking for someone with a degree," she stated. "Going to Brown made a big difference."

"It was my first full-time job since I had been married," Lorraine said. "I'm sure I got it because of the college degree. There was a lot of competition. I had to go before the board, just like the other time I was interviewed."

Even before she started to work for the agency after her graduation, Lorraine knew her career would be short-lived. "Family has got to be number one on the priority list. If it isn't, then everything else is just a farce. Our family problems were becoming too pressing," she explained. "My mother-in-law needed me. So did my mother. I didn't have a career per se. I just wanted to do whatever I could for the people who needed me."

In 1978, Lorraine pulled back from major work commitments. For the next four and a half years, she was an interviewer with the U.S. Bureau of the Census. The part-time work and flexible hours allowed her to help care for both mothers. Much of the work was done on the telephone at home.

Lorraine's mother celebrated her ninety-fifth birthday in 1987. The year was punctuated by medical crises: a bout of pneumonia, complications from a reaction to medication, and a fractured pelvis and collarbone. Constant supervision is now a necessity.

Lorraine remains active outside her home. She is involved with her church and a prayer community of which she is the scribe. Through the prayer community, she has become a social activist.

Lorraine has been the spokesperson for her church after a series of ecumenical seminars and workshops. "I get up in front of a large group," she said, "and speak about whatever subject I have selected for the evening. I'm able to do it because of the confidence and poise I've acquired since I've been back to college. I don't think I would have had the self-confidence before." In 1986 she had the pleasure of chairing her fortieth high school class reunion.

Lorraine's school days may not be over. She hopes to pursue a master's degree in either family counseling or theology. Even though she is nearly 60, there is no air of urgency about her desire for more education.

There were still many family graduations to attend. In 1987 Nick received his M.B.A., and Gina, second youngest, got her B.A. The youngest of the nine children, Andrew, completed his bachelor's degree in 1988.

Recently, Nick has been taking a more active role in coordinating the care of his mother-in-law. His schedule is much more flexible now because he teaches part-time at a community college and substitute teaches at a Catholic elementary school. Lorraine is now working part-time as a medical assistant.

"Nick feels strongly that it is good for me to be away from the house and doing something interesting," Lorraine said. And her mother enjoys the company of a home health aide and her senior companion. Also, the youngest daughter, Gina, is back home and helping out.

Nick and Lorraine believe their own focus on education served as motivation for their children. Marie, age 29 and number six in the family, is a registered dietitian. She said, "My mother was a very good role model for all of us. She did well in school. She showed that it could be done, even with so many children and so many years behind her. She did it, and she did a great job."

"I loved every minute of school," Lorraine said. "It's all happy memories. The ramifications have all been good. I just thank the Lord that my return to school happened before the two mothers became ill and needed me. School was just sandwiched right in there. If I hadn't done it then, I would never have been able to do it."

EPILOGUE

"Guess which one I am," she said, walking toward me with open arms. I hadn't a clue, even though we had been in touch with each other for more than ten years.

In August 1988, I had lunch in a New Haven, Connecticut, restaurant with a number of the women whose stories appear in *Degrees of Success*. It was the most unusual reunion I have ever attended: almost all of those "reunioning" had never met.

The most frequent means of communication between these women and me over the course of more than a decade was by cassette tape: they responded to a set of questions, and I listened. Suddenly, here we were: face to face, having actual dialogues. The "cast of characters," related through their involvement with the book, were conversing, having a marvelous time.

"How did *you* wind up in Pam's book?" was the question most often repeated. While exploring the various choreographies that led to initial interviews, some of the women even discovered connections between themselves.

Ellen (Chapter 5) turned out to be Anne's (Chapter 10) children's teacher during their junior high school years. "We thought she had been *born* a scientist," Anne commented when she discovered that Ellen had been a reentry student. Anne and Tracy (Chapter 1) were surprised to learn they had attended the same law school. In fact, Anne's husband and daughter were in law school at the same time as Tracy.

There was a great deal of discussion about life-style tempos and the continual effort that was needed to maintain balance. Elaine (Chapter 2) was finding her position as a junior planner tremendously satisfying. The hard part, she explained, is juggling a full-time job and a family of five.

Vivian (Chapter 10), Lorraine (Chapter 14), Ellen, and April (Chapter 8) discussed recent adjustments in the balance between their personal and professional lives. Vivian, for example, when last interviewed, talked about wanting to be more available to her husband, her mother-in-law, and the families of her *fifteen* children.

She had just resigned from her job as assistant personnel director at a nursing home.

It wasn't long, however, before she decided to actualize a lifelong dream: to study acting. So, at age 60, Vivian is enrolled in acting school and loving every minute of it. I have to agree with what one of her children was quoted as saying about her: "I wish I had one third of her energy." How many grandchildren? Twenty-eight at last count.

Vivian and Lorraine, the person who greeted me with open arms, had a great time talking with each other. It isn't often that Lorraine encounters anyone who has raised more children than her nine! She, too, has added a major time commitment to her already full life. An enthusiastic supporter of her alma mater, Brown University, she was recently elected president of her county's Brown Alumni Club. The club raises money for academically oriented causes, with special emphasis on those that relate to women.

April has cut her work week back from 60 to 45 hours in an effort to create more time for her personal life. She is spending 30 hours a week as operations manager for her community center and the remaining hours working as a masseuse. A major recent change is her separation from her husband. She explained that she would like to have the time to simply "enjoy life more fully." She is also concerned about her mother's health and wants to be able to visit with her more often.

Ellen and her husband have rented out their family home and taken an apartment in town. When last interviewed, she was debating whether or not to resign from teaching in order to devote herself full-time to directing the school's computer program. She has, we learned, opted to resign from teaching. Although she will miss the classroom contact with the children, she is looking forward to the leisure time that materializes when there are no papers and tests to grade.

Tracy, Louise (Chapter 3), and Marissa (Chapter 14)—like Ellen—have made major changes in where they are living. Tracy, in 1987, stated that a prime goal was to own her own home. Less than a month before our luncheon, she moved from her rental into a house she had just purchased. She had progressed from being a junior college student to becoming a corporate lawyer in less than ten years, and now she had achieved her next goal as well.

Louise mentioned that she and Clarence had just moved to a smaller house around the corner from their family home of twenty-seven years. Visits back and forth are made nearly daily, however: her daughter and family bought the homestead.

Marissa and her husband were continuing to work toward the purchase of their own home. To cut down on expenses, they were spending six months living with her parents. Marissa, still the head teacher at a nursery school, has become involved with a day-care task force that provides aid to a city in Nicaragua. In July, she and several coworkers went there to distribute materials and help organize a new day-care center.

Anne and Stephen had just returned from a special family occasion, the marriage of their son. Anne reported that her law practice is growing, and she finds it very stimulating.

Ruth (Chapter 4) continues to be actively involved with volunteer work. She is treasurer of the local National Organization for Women (NOW) chapter. She and her husband, Joe, take full advantage of the many educational opportunities offered by nearby universities.

After lunch, we decided to take a short walk through the Yale University campus and ventured out of the air-conditioned restaurant into the blazing heat and humidity. The writer in me couldn't help but step back to observe the scene: a group of women out strolling on a scorcher of a day, lots of bravado and laughter, nonstop conversation. The shared experience of having chosen to pursue an education as an adult made for instant familiarity. Varying degrees of struggle and triumph formed the bond. The ivy-covered walls provided the perfect setting. As we parted, former strangers now hugged each other good-bye, saying: "See you in the book."

APPENDIX
SUGGESTIONS FOR SUCCESS

Family, friends, faculty, and college staff are all likely candidates to provide the returning student with a key ingredient: moral support. The women featured in *Degrees of Success* also want to offer *their* encouragement to readers who have just started out on a reentry route or are considering doing so. Know, as you wend your way along whatever academic path you choose, that we all wish you well!

CHAPTER 1

"Realize that you are probably as capable as the next person. If you plan major changes in your life, do not expect it all to fall into place right away. It may take a while for you and everyone else to adjust to the changes, to get used to the sacrifices. Expect inconveniences and struggle. Remind yourself frequently of *why* you are doing what you are doing."

Tracy

"Don't be afraid to ask for help. If you don't know how to fill out a form, ask someone to help you. The forms are constantly changing and so are the policies. College personnel are being paid to help you, so use them! There's all kinds of money out there. You just have to connect with it. Make the financial aid counselors work for you. If you're still having difficulty, talk to someone else. Find reentry students who have been on campus for a while. Ask one of your teachers. All kinds of people are willing to help. When I was a student, I was never turned down when I asked for help."

Tamara

"If you are afraid, go slowly. Why not take an adult education course or one night class at a college or university? See how it feels. The older you are, the more life experiences you've had—it all helps

Degrees of Success

you do better in any course you're taking. The older you are, the easier it is to return to school and get good grades. If you are an older person, a giant goal at the end of a tunnel may be very frightening and overwhelming. This might prevent you from going back onto a college campus and filling out that application. What you might want to do is just go back and take one or two courses. See how you like it. Take it little by little before setting a major goal."

Cathy

Note: HOME (Helping Ourselves Means Employment with Education) is a nonprofit nationwide organization dedicated to providing support and information to people on public assistance or with low incomes who are interested in attaining further education and employment opportunities. The *HOME Door*, a quarterly newsletter, is a marvelous networking channel. For further information, write to HOME, 867 High Street, Suite C, Worthington, OH 43085.

CHAPTER 2

"You have to tell people this is important to you, even if you're taking only one course. Your family needs to understand that you need a specific time to study. Work it out with your husband: every Wednesday night or every Saturday morning will be *your* time, without interruptions. Take one course and see how you like it. You'll realize you're not as dumb as you may think. You kind of have to force yourself to have the confidence that you can do it."

Elaine

"You need some alone time, whether it's a retreat for the weekend or going for a solo hike. Tutoring can be helpful. Why not hire a high school student to do the dishes or the cleaning? Hire somebody to type. It's been important for me to realize I don't have to do it all. Do what you can to make your work load easier."

Christine

"Going back, without a career in mind, is a wonderful way to enrich your life. In every course I've found something to enjoy. It enhances your life so much. I laugh when people say, 'So what are you going to do with the degree?' What can I say to them? It is its own reward."

Judith

"To anyone who's thinking about it, go! If you don't have any career goals, just take a course. I don't think you need to have a career goal in order to go back to school. Do not go to a four-year university straight off. Begin at a two-year school where they welcome returning women students. If I had gone straight to the university, I might not have gone beyond the first semester. The community college welcomed me with open arms. It made all the difference in the world."

Susan

"I hope nobody does what I did. I took a student job on campus to help pay for my education. My salary came to something like $4 an hour. On days I didn't have classes I would commute (3 hours) to go to my campus job. A loan makes a lot more sense. Education at a state college will cost you a lot less than at a private college. You won't have a big loan to pay off. In the long run, going to school full-time is less expensive. Also, when you're going full-time you get caught up in what you're studying, and that's better. It's best to go to school full-time and not work."

Julia

CHAPTER 3

"You need to schedule time with each child individually and time when you nurture your husband-wife relationship. You also need to schedule time for yourself—time to do nothing. You need to sit back and recoup your emotional and mental resources. Appointments you make with yourself should be as unbreakable as an appointment with a doctor to have a suspicious lump checked. Attention to exercise and nutrition is also vitally important."

Jill

"A person's need to grow must be put first. Anything you hold onto ahead of that would lose its value if it were in the way of your growth and your evolution as a person. I don't understand how it is that some marriages withstand that, but I guess I believe that those are the marriages that are worth holding onto."

Lydia

"When you've been out of school for a while, it's a good idea to take a couple of courses rather than to pick up a full load. You have to get your confidence back."

Louise

CHAPTER 4

"Don't be afraid to ask questions. I felt very shy about asking how to do things and where to go. I wish I had been a little more gutsy. If you are feeling uncertain about what you want to do, get counseling. Test things out before you get involved with a degree that might not be taking you where you want to go. I've seen too much of this—someone specializes in something too soon or before having had a chance to test it out. Do volunteer work in your area of interest, or get involved with the college work-study program. That's a wonderful way to get a feel for something. Talk with people who work in the field and find out exactly what they do. Do some reading."

Gloria

"You need something positive in every hour—even if only for 5 minutes—something just for you. Get a cup of coffee. Go for a run around the block. Do something fun. Plan something special for yourself every day—and something every week or two. Look through the television schedule, and plan your study time before a program you want to watch. You won't be able to watch everything you want, so pick the one you want the most, and make it your reward for having studied.

"Don't go back to school without conferring with your family and making it a family decision. Even if it is your decision, it's important to include your family in it. When you need to study or need time to yourself, you're more likely to get it if they've had an opportunity to negotiate with you about your going back to school. Get counseling ahead of time so that you can be clearer about your age difference and your role differences before you start school. It was hard for me to budget my time. It was hard for me to develop study skills. It might even be a good idea to take a course in study skills if there's been a lot of time between the last time you went to school and this time."

Lee

"Don't become too grimly earnest about being in college. Just try to enjoy it. Going back to school is a big adventure. Even if nothing comes of it, it's worthwhile. Start with courses in subjects you're good at. I started to take statistics and discovered I had forgotten how to do fractions, so I dropped the class. I didn't take statistics again until I took a remedial class.

"If you have a good relationship with your children, going back to school can only give you something more in common with them. I tend to be terrible with spelling and grammar, but my kids were great proofreaders. I think you should use your children in these ways as much as possible. It gives them a feeling that they are part of it all."

Abigail

"So often women's lives are defined by the needs of others, and they really don't develop their own potential. Going to school is one way to become independent, to grow, to develop confidence. I liked the idea that I could provide for myself financially. School was a step in that direction. Moving toward economic independence is really very important. Women have to be serious about a career. A career is the path toward becoming an independent person."

Ruth

"Accept the fact that it's OK to fail. Actually, there is no such thing

Suggestions for Success

as failure if we realize there's a lesson to learn—and learn it. There's a proverb: The pessimist sees difficulty in every opportunity; the optimist sees opportunity in every difficulty. It takes a lot more energy to be negative than it does to be positive. If you have the germ of wanting to go back to school, take the risk because it will open a whole new life to you.

"You need to know that you are number one; you cannot be there for anyone with whom you are intimately connected unless you are number one for yourself. You have to be able to take care of your needs in order to be able to take care of your family, friends, or others. Open communication is of the utmost importance. Be willing and able to be vulnerable; say what you need, what it is you want, what it is you are not getting. If you stay home to be there when your husband gets home from the office every day, have meals on the table, sit with him while he eats, *but* you feel tremendous hostility, it won't work. It will disrupt your relationship, not help it."

Diana

CHAPTER 5

"Eat well, keep healthy, exercise a lot, and be sure your priorities are straight."

Eleanor

"Anticipate some depression and perhaps a lot of frustration. Things will take longer at first. It will get much better when you relearn the skills you had when you were younger. There are so many positive things that will happen—when a grand idea strikes, when a paper writes itself, when you get the spark, when you ask the right questions. Watch for these positives. If you have a family, they need to be as committed as you are for four years or however long it takes."

Savannah

"To figure out who you are and what you want out of life, use your intuition, get all the advice that you can, and get a lot of life experience. You need a support system, especially if you have kids. You need to believe in yourself, trust yourself, trust your intuition about what's right for you even though it seems stupid to someone else. It's never too late to do something new or different. What's important is to keep going. If you maintain your curiosity and sense of aliveness, the sky's the limit."

Elizabeth

"If you find you don't love what you're doing, you might be in for a lot of frustration. It's not like choosing a major when you're 20 and free of relationships and responsibilities. There's a lot more riding on your decision now.

"You can get lost in the forest of the files in the admissions office. I

225

Degrees of Success

did. I entered a semester later because someone simply lost my file. You have to go to bat for yourself. You have to hand-deliver documents."

Maureen

CHAPTER 6

"Sacrifices your family team puts up with are made bearable by your sense of direction, your work toward something, and their feeling they are helping you. To know what you're doing, to know how long it's going to take, to know there's an end in sight for everyone is helpful. That sense of knowing where you are going is what can pull you through a lot of difficulties. You have to have faith that it's worth making that first step, that it's worth the hassles and the difficulties."

Laura

"Talk to a lot of people. Find out what they do and how they got there. Don't assume that the obstacles are going to be really big, because they may not be."

Allison

"Get career counseling and testing. Evaluate the results before deciding what you are going to do. You need to spend a lot of time and effort setting career goals. If you have a chance to get some experience in the field while you're in school, I think that's helpful."

Pat

"You have to really want to do it. I don't believe in doing anything unless you're psyched up to do it. If going to school is what you want, don't stop going, even if you have to take just one course a term. Stay with it; once you stop, you form the habit of 'Oh, I can't go back.' Going to college is a very fulfilling experience. Try it and see how it works out."

Natalie

"Let people know what it is that you want to do and elicit their support. Don't try to do it all yourself. People can get into a really strange mode of trying to cope with things entirely by themselves. Try to get a lot of support. I struggled because I wouldn't tell people what I was doing or what I needed."

Sheila

CHAPTER 7

"If you want something badly enough, you can get it. It helps to have an understanding husband. I was lucky. I had the ambition and a helpful, understanding husband. Even taking one course a semester for years and years will get you where you want to go eventually."

Alice

"Talk to other people in a similar situation. I don't remember having that, but I think it would have been nice to have lunch with another woman who had a family and was working on her Ph.D. We could have shared notes and experiences and consoled each other."

Lucy

"Don't wait for people to explain everything to you. Ask questions."

Kay

CHAPTER 8

"Make sure you have mentors in graduate school, people who are going to give you support and push you along. Don't bite off more than you can chew. If you have a job that takes 80 percent of your strength, then don't put more than 20 percent into anything else."

Mary

"The busier you are, the easier it is to budget your time. You accomplish more when you have six things to do than when you have nothing to do. Suddenly every minute becomes precious. The things you give up will be very low priority items. You'll always be a little behind, but you'll have time to accomplish everything that's important."

April

"Don't take on more than you can handle. Start slowly and build with it. Even if you're only going for a two-year degree, don't worry about getting it done in two years. Try to make changes as gradually as possible. It's extremely difficult to manage everything. Take just one course if that's all you have time for. Don't let school overwhelm you."

Sarah

"Pamper yourself. Treat yourself well. If you're by yourself on the weekends, don't heat up leftovers. Make yourself a nice dinner. Do things that will help keep you human."

Donna

"Anybody who decides to go back to school should investigate what kinds of jobs actually exist and what kind of training is needed to get them. That's the only way to actualize a goal. Find out what people want and prepare yourself to fit a particular job description."

Florence

Degrees of Success

"Don't be afraid to change your goals while you're in school. If you've gone into a program and find halfway through (or a quarter of the way through or even three quarters of the way through) that it's the wrong program for you, then get out of it. You can find other schools better suited to your needs and goals. I'm sorry I didn't switch programs."

Carolyn

CHAPTER 9

"Let the student role be just one of your roles within the family. Leave plenty of time for the kids.

"If you have doubts about your capabilities, start slow. I started by auditing a class, because I was so frightened of failure. Then I took a class for credit. I took only one. When I began to see I could do it, I was ready to go all the way with it."

Marilyn

"Some women feel they've been on leave from life. Returning to a formal education situation is a perfect way to begin a mental process again. I would encourage that. If someone is unsure of a career, college is a stimulating situation that will offer choices and ideas."

Terry

"If it's at all possible, begin as a part-time student with one or two courses. Don't have unrealistic expectations for yourself. Remember that you are only human, and no one can do everything at once. Remember all the other things you have achieved in your life, and know that you can do well at this one too, if it's geared to your needs. Five years is going to go by anyway, so do your very best with those five years. Give it a good shot."

Annette

"If I had enrolled in a lot of the programs I looked at, I never would have finished. One program required two years of languages, and I don't have an ear for languages. Evaluate each and every program and decide which one is best for you. I didn't take a full semester's worth of courses. I took one or two courses each semester. It takes the pressure off if you are trying to continue a normal life. Don't overload yourself, because that can create problems."

Rachel

"You should sit down and discuss your reentry plans with your family. How do they feel? Why are they feeling the way they do? Why are you feeling the way you do? Their support is very important. Some of the women I met going through school found the process difficult because they didn't get help or support from their family."

Libby

Suggestions for Success

CHAPTER 10

"Set a goal and learn what will be required to achieve it. Set out on a track that will make it become a reality. Be studious, persistent, and patient. Make a special effort to include your family. Rely on them to give you moral support and encouragement."

Carla

"Go back to school, and you'll enjoy it. Your life will be enriched. If you're interested in art, take art courses; if you're interested in history, take history courses."

Vivian

"Before making any decision about going back to school, a woman needs to outline her goals and the ways they will affect her family, in terms of financial gain and time. Any sacrifices that the family (as a whole and as individuals) will have to make should be understood clearly. The mother will need help around the house, which means additional help from every member of the family. The benefits should also be discussed: what it will mean to each member of the family if the mother succeeds in attaining her goal."

Lois

"Go for it. But I don't believe women have to be superwomen. If you're going to take on the role of student, you have to let go a little in other areas. Get your family to help with the chores. Change, education, and growth are what keep life interesting. My education changed my life."

Kate

"It's basically between you and the books. You're going to be able to succeed if you do the work. There's no magic about it: if you do the work, you're going to get by. The person who talks the most in class and sounds the most intelligent isn't necessarily the brightest.

"Establish your priorities. You need to know why you're in school. Then you have to take a good look at the impact it's going to have on your life and how you're going to deal with that."

Linda

CHAPTER 11

"If you have a good relationship with someone to begin with, entering school and making a better person of yourself is only going to enhance that relationship. If the relationship is on rocky ground, then changing your role in the family, changing your role in society, and changing your image of yourself may or may not have negative effects on the family. The student can share her education with her family so the new things she learns become incorporated into the family life-style. We all like to be part of something, and if you have a

Degrees of Success

good family relationship, then sharing information and knowledge can only make that better."

Joan

"Let go of all the flak about the inability to study or learn after a certain age. Each entering student is also part of the education. If you value yourself and your life experiences and recognize your own humanity and that of others, then school is a place to share that. Each person is as important to the process as the professor, the system, and the goal of degree-getting. The degree-getting as a goal is a hollow victory unless the process of getting it enriches your life."

Daphne

"Don't feel guilty. There are certain things you're entitled to, and if you think going back to school will be fulfilling, go ahead. I don't think there's anything wrong with changing your goals as you go along.

"It's very helpful to get friendly with other students. Having friends to look forward to meeting on Monday mornings at 8:30 makes it a lot easier."

Claire

"The best possible arrangement for a reentry student is to have a warm, supportive family—her mother or sister living nearby so that the children can be in their own tribe. Taking children off every morning, leaving them with strangers, and picking them up late in the day when you're tired is destructive to the mother-child relationship.

"Make sure you want the degree and that you're not using it as an escape from something else. If you've had emotional problems before, you will have them in school. They will be more severe because of the difficulties encountered in trying to juggle many things."

Dorothy

"I encourage anybody to go back to school. Don't be disappointed if you don't get what you want when you want it. Anything you gain, you never lose. You can always build on it at some point in your life. You never know when you might use it. I don't think that any time you put into school is ever wasted. Here I am—reevaluating everything I've done and where I'm going again. But at this point, I have by no means given up. I'm just starting over again."

Jackie

"Try to get your spouse and children involved in college life. There are so many opportunities that a college can offer a family: dance companies, symphonies, plays, lectures, sports, art galleries, physical fitness courses. Many activities on a college campus are free. We go to the college library many Sunday afternoons, and we're involved in a college physical fitness course as a family. Once a week we swim in the college pool. If a student draws her own family into the college family, then they will understand what college life is all about. Perhaps they will not resent her going back because they will see what is beneficial to them as individuals and as a family. I think it's important to let the family know that this can be an enrichment of the entire home environment.

"It's important to have a support network of other older students, because they know what you're going through. They can give you support and sympathy and show you the ropes. College, like any other aspect of life, has its ups and downs and quirks. If you know the ropes, it will make your life a lot easier."

Cindy

CHAPTER 12

"Make sure that there are job openings in the career you have selected, that there are plenty to apply for. Don't do something exotic like German languages!

"Don't wait until your children are a 'good' age. Go ahead and go to school even if you take only one course at a time. The courses add up. It took me four years for my first master's degree, it has taken me three years now for the second master's degree, and I'm not done yet. Don't wait until you can go back full-time—it's an excuse—you might never do it."

Martha

"I think you have to keep in mind how financially independent you want to be and how financially independent you might need to be at some later date. I wasn't sufficiently aware of that."

Roberta

"When you make a change in your life, it changes everything around you. If you're married, be sure that your spouse has some inkling of what's involved and that he'll give you support. If he's not supportive, and you do it anyway, you need to be prepared for the fact that it may ruin your marriage. However, maybe your marriage is already ruined, and this is just the final blow.

"I think the children survive pretty well as long as you have time for the things that are important to them. You simply have to take time for them. If you have a big exam the next day and you feel grouchy, children sense it. They want to know that they are as important as that exam. You've got to resolve things with your children before you can get back to your studying. You may have to go without sleep sometimes. That's just the way it is. You need to be very motivated and determined.

"I would say take as light a course load as you possibly can your first semester. Take one course to see what kinds of demands are expected at that level. Get some idea of what kind of involvement and commitment it requires. Start off slowly. Don't lose your perspective and do nothing but study. For three months one summer, I studied

10 hours a day. Fortunately, my children were gone a lot of the time. Reading 10 hours a day is stupid. You've got to live your life. I'm not sorry I did it, but if I had it to do over again I'd realize that if it took that kind of effort, then maybe it wasn't the right program for me."

Sylvia

"It's awfully hard to juggle the guilt feelings and the scheduling and other pressures of family life while going to school in the best of situations. But if you compound it by having children between the ages of 2 and 5 who need you to watch them, see them develop, and so forth—you may feel very guilty when you leave them. Once they start school, you can take courses, be away from home, and do research without interfering with their schedules. If I were to do it over again, I would go back to finish my degree when my children were very young, so that when I left them with their grandmother or a neighbor for the afternoon, they wouldn't know I was gone. Or I would wait until they started school.

"Make one or two days each week 'children's time.' Do what they want to do. Go to the zoo or the park. Bake cookies. Set aside Tuesday and Thursday afternoons from 2 o'clock to 4 to do exactly what they want to do —a movie, a walk, playing with dolls, whatever they want. That might really help. Even though they are young, they would know that this was their time. It might help them to understand about your needing your time."

Cybil

CHAPTER 13

"I got it into my head that I had to take four courses every quarter in order to graduate by the time I was 30. I ended up losing a quarter and graduating late anyway. You don't have to be so hard on yourself. There are choices. Maybe you can take three courses each quarter and graduate one quarter later. Usually, taking it a little slower is not going to make that much difference, except to make your life easier."

Debbie

"The years go by quickly. Make good use of your time in school. Change if you're not doing what you want to do. Make sure, when you're through with school, that you've gotten out of it what you wanted."

Ida

"Get a housekeeper. Demand that your husband and children help out. Believe that you deserve the time."

Catherine

"The family's attitude is affected by how you feel about yourself

Suggestions for Success

and what you feel you're entitled to. You have to have the confidence, self-understanding, and assurance that you're right to do what you're doing. When you approach your family with the thought that this is the way you do it, and you say it with confidence, then they accept it. When you show the least bit of uncertainty about what you are saying, then they become uncertain.

"Accept the possibility that the student role you are taking on may or may not be appropriate. Be open to any suggestions for alteration of your route. In other words, keep your antennae up, and see what's around. Perhaps you've gone through the academic program and come out with a degree, finding it really doesn't suit you. See if there's a modification of this field that would suit you better. You have to know yourself and be open to learning more about yourself."

Norma

"My current advice, which may be different from advice I would have given ten years ago, is pay attention to the timing of your choices. It sounds like such a little thing, but I think many women have put themselves through undue stress because of time pressure. People are afraid they are going to get off track and then never be able to get back on. But once we have families we cannot be obsessive students. Women who are willing to make practical compromises—not ethical compromises—end up feeling much more relaxed."

Sandra

CHAPTER 14

"I did not stop and look at whether people with my skills were needed in this area. If you don't want to relocate, you've got to consider that very carefully before you go through all the difficulties of going to school.

"Nobody can do everything well. You may have to change your standards—whether it's how neat you keep your house or how often you bake cakes or how well you expect to do in your courses. Even though you try very hard, you may not do something very well. This was brought home to me in my math courses. I tried very hard and simply could not understand what was going on. That doesn't mean I am a failure; there are so many other things I can do well, and those are the things that help keep me going."

Jocelyn

"Make sure you know there will be jobs available. The romantic notion of going back to school to get a degree and then finding out later that you're underqualified or overqualified or a job doesn't exist is a heartbreak."

Brenda

Degrees of Success

"It's helpful to set goals, to have some direction to work toward. It gives you a sense of purpose. You bring interesting things to talk about into the family situation. It's worth it in the end for everybody involved."

Connie

"It would be helpful to talk to at least one person who is actually in the field you are thinking about. Try to be very practical about how your education will apply to the specific kind of work you want to do."

Marissa

"Include your family members—all of them—in one way or another, not necessarily at the same time. Let them know what you're thinking about. Keep them posted along the way. Structure your conversation to include their reactions, their concerns, and their anxieties so that you get their feedback. Then you can respond to that. Stay open. Women returning to school should be aware of the kind of strain they are going to be bringing into their lives."

Andrea

"Wait until the children are old enough so that you can leave them without hassling the family's setup. Don't rush into it. Take one course at a time for a while. That way the house doesn't get into such a turmoil with the mother gone all day. Plan your classes so they don't conflict with your husband's needs and your children's needs, because they are your first priority."

Lorraine